VOLUME

12

The New York Times

CROSSWORD PUZZLE OMNIBUS

200 Puzzles from the Pages of
The New York Times

Edited by
Will Shortz

ST. MARTIN'S GRIFFIN ✖ NEW YORK

THE NEW YORK TIMES CROSSWORD PUZZLE OMNIBUS, VOLUME 12.
Copyright © 2002 by The New York Times Company. All rights reserved.
Printed in the United States of America. No part of this book
may be used or reproduced in any manner whatsoever without
written permission except in the case of brief quotations embodied
in critical articles or reviews. For information, address
St. Martin's Press, 175 Fifth Avenue, New York, N.Y. 10010.

www.stmartins.com

All of the puzzles that appear in this work were
originally published in the *New York Times* daily editions,
from November 22, 1993, through September 26, 1994.
Copyright © 1993, 1994 by The New York Times Company.
All rights reserved. Reprinted by permission.

ISBN 0-312-30511-7

First Edition: September 2002

10 9 8 7 6 5 4 3 2 1

VOLUME

12

The New York Times

CROSSWORD PUZZLE OMNIBUS

1 *by Fred Piscop*

ACROSS
1 Understood
4 Some tracks
9 __ Rizzo ('69 Hoffman role)
14 Santa __ winds
15 Actress Anouk
16 Significant person?
17 Kauai keepsake
18 Small person
20 Legit
22 Caroline Schlossberg, to Ted Kennedy
23 Type style: Abbr.
24 Big Mama
25 Church part
29 Rummy variety
32 The mark on the C in Čapek
33 Calendar period, to Kirk
37 Caustic substance
38 Traditional tune
40 Pub quaff
42 Logical newsman?
43 Long-lasting curls
45 Depicts
49 Health-food store staple
50 Jerry Herman composition
53 Dash
54 Michelangelo masterpiece
56 Journalist Greeley
58 Used booster cables
62 Tina's ex
63 Correspond, grammatically
64 Regarded favorably
65 Pince-__
66 Former Justice Byron
67 Air-show maneuvers
68 Palindrome center

DOWN
1 French
2 __ time (singly)
3 Taipei's land
4 Honolulu locale
5 Fat fiddle
6 Fuse word
7 First name in hotels
8 Big rigs
9 Campus mil. grp.
10 Daughter of Zeus
11 Calendar abbr.
12 Theology sch.
13 Eye
19 __-man (flunky)
21 Hooch container
24 Magna __
26 Rights grp.
27 "Oy __!"
28 __ out (supplement)
30 Hoosegows
31 Footrace terminus
32 Stage actress Hayes
34 MS follower?
35 Love, Italian style
36 Newcastle-upon-__, England
38 Esne
39 Judge's exhortation
40 Prone
41 Name of 13 popes
44 Oscar the Grouch, for one
46 Julia Louis-Dreyfus on "Seinfeld"
47 Pool-ball gatherer
48 Common cause for blessing
50 Strawberry, once
51 "Any Time __" (Beatles tune)
52 Auto-racer Andretti
55 Words of comprehension
56 "David Copperfield" character
57 Ten to one, e.g.
58 Gossip
59 "That's disgusting!"
60 High-tech med. diagnostic
61 Foreman stat

2 *by Norma Steinberg*

ACROSS

1 "Shane" star
5 Late actor Phoenix
10 "Dark Lady" singer, 1975
14 "__ in a manger . . ."
15 Author Zola
16 "__, from New York . . ."
17 Haircuts?
19 Kathleen Battle offering
20 "__ we having fun yet?"
21 Glowing
22 Kuwaiti structure
24 Opening word
26 Broadway show based on a comic strip
27 Dubuque native
29 Imperturbable
33 Become frayed
36 Former spouses
38 Conceited smile
39 Hawkeye portrayer
40 Recording auditions
42 Garfield's canine pal
43 Pilots let them down
45 Cushy
46 Catches some Z's
47 __ fugit
49 Gullible
51 Sufficient
53 Knucklehead
57 Horoscope heading
60 Police blotter abbr.
61 Prospector's find
62 World rotator?
63 Fake embroidery?
66 Augury
67 "This way in" sign
68 __ carotene
69 Emcee Parks
70 Nursery packets
71 Flowery verses

DOWN

1 Actor Lorenzo
2 Conscious
3 Odense residents
4 Recolor
5 Critiqued
6 ". . . __ a man with seven wives"
7 __ ordinaire
8 "Candle in the Wind" singer __ John
9 Copal and others
10 Vandalized art work?
11 Put on staff
12 Heinous
13 Kind of estate
18 Movie Tarzan __ Lincoln
23 Whoppers
25 Smog?
26 Showy flower
28 Lumber camp implements
30 Verdi heroine
31 Stumble
32 Makes do, with "out"
33 Float
34 Madame's pronoun
35 Eden resident
37 Divan
41 Scoundrels
44 Its usefulness goes to waste
48 Cumin and cardamom
50 Test tube
52 Actor Greene
54 Courted
55 Livid
56 Ann Richards's bailiwick
57 Poor fellow
58 "Be our guest!"
59 Concluded
60 Thunderstruck
64 Part of a year in Provence
65 Cable add-on

ACROSS

1 Hearth debris
6 Atmosphere
10 Columnist Bombeck
14 Room to —
15 Skater Heiden
16 High time?
17 Critical juncture
20 Parade
21 Some oranges
22 Roasting items
25 Sometimes they get the hang of it
26 Woolly one
30 Carnegie Hall event
32 Where Marco Polo traveled
33 Tomb tenant
34 All fired up?
37 Future brass
41 Modeled, maybe
42 Mountain ridge
43 Peruvian of yore
44 Neptune's fork
46 Physicist Niels
47 Work, work, work
49 Its password was "Mickey Mouse"
51 Trotsky rival
52 Straight shooters?
57 Stops rambling
61 Algerian seaport
62 Broadway groom of 1922
63 Sister of Thalia
64 Bridge seat
65 Bank holding
66 Prepare to shave

DOWN

1 Cleo's snakes
2 Flyspeck
3 "Let the Sun Shine In" musical
4 Sea bird
5 Bristles
6 W.W. I grp.
7 Mausoleum item
8 "Road to —"
9 Beginnings of poetry?
10 Involve
11 Beauty aid
12 Folkways
13 Writer Beattie and others
18 Poet translated by FitzGerald
19 Toledo locale
23 Depended
24 Perfumed

26 Senate output
27 On the briny
28 "Gorillas in the —"
29 Hit a fly, perhaps
31 Mean
34 Host Jay
35 Yen
36 Ivan, for one
38 Church front area
39 Expensive rug
40 Fish in a way
44 Aptitude
45 Weight allowance
47 Pack away
48 "Falcon Crest" star
50 "Egad!"
51 Barge

53 McHenry, e.g.
54 Münchhausen, for one
55 Within: Prefix
56 Common sign
58 Sash
59 Cause for overtime
60 Clucker

4 *by Eric Albert*

ACROSS

1 Colorful salad ingredient
10 Plant pest
15 Throw some light on
16 El __ (Spanish painter)
17 Acting ambassador
19 Mooring rope
20 The sky, maybe
21 Perry's creator
22 Pop's Carly or Paul
25 It's a drag
27 Country rtes.
28 It has its ups and downs
30 Turner of Hollywood
31 "Duke Bluebeard's Castle" composer
32 Super-soaked
33 Literature as art
36 Urger's words
37 Aloha State
38 Ooze
39 Bombast
40 70's sitcom "__ Sharkey"
43 Watered-down ideas
44 Subsequently
45 Teri of "Tootsie"
46 "__ Andronicus"
48 Samantha's "Bewitched" husband
50 Facetious advice in a mystery
54 Indoor design
55 Carouse
56 Birthplace of 16 Across
57 By and large

DOWN

1 "... for __ for poorer"
2 Founder of est
3 Talks Dixie-style
4 Diagram a sentence
5 Competitive advantage
6 Boat's departure site
7 Rocket's departure site
8 It's after zeta
9 Foul caller
10 One more time
11 Schoolmarmish
12 Birthright
13 Bar accessory
14 __ Passos
18 Go with the __
22 Layup alternative
23 Quarantine
24 Be militaristic
26 Manner
28 It can sting
29 Before, in palindromes
30 Actress __ Singer
31 Radar screen image
32 Rouse to action
33 Brief break
34 It's worth looking into
35 Clavell's "__-Pan"
36 Recipe abbr.
39 Mess-hall meal
40 Clint Eastwood's city
41 Kind of scream
42 Obstinate
44 Pelf
45 Miss Garbo
47 Jog
48 Hamlet, for one
49 Nowhere near
50 Fed. medical detectives
51 Sunny-side-up item
52 Lawyer Baird
53 Cambodia's __ Nol

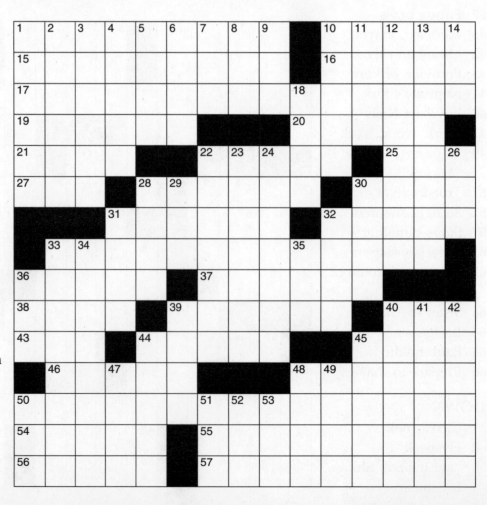

5 *by David A. Rosen*

ACROSS
1 Rumble
6 Not fancy?
10 Difficult obligation
14 "__ of do or die"
15 Bing Crosby best seller
16 Guthrie the younger
17 Hearty entree
20 Kibbutzniks' dance
21 Reverse
22 Must
23 Place to crash
25 Kipling novel
26 Tasty side dish
35 Mortgage matter
36 Words before "in the arm" or "in the dark"
37 Detective's cry
38 Them in "Them!"
39 Common key signature
40 Composer __ Carlo Menotti
41 Cpl., for one
42 Feed a fete
43 Stood for
44 Yummy dessert
47 Cherbourg chum
48 Latin I?
49 Lamb Chop's "spokesperson"
52 Oceania republic
55 Windmill segment
59 Eventual bonus?
62 Cream-filled sandwich
63 Debouchment
64 Internet patrons
65 Blubber
66 Yeltsin veto
67 Koch's predecessor

DOWN
1 Calculator work
2 Radar blip
3 Thieves' hideout
4 They're loose
5 "Yikes!"
6 "The Afternoon of a __"
7 In the thick of
8 First name in perfumery
9 Venture
10 Japanese mat
11 Olympic hawk
12 Bed-frame crosspiece
13 "Mikado" executioner
18 Sport whose name means "soft way"
19 Polo, e.g.
24 Circulars
25 Carpenter's woe
26 French bread?
27 High-priced spread?
28 ". . . and eat __"
29 Subj. of a Clinton victory, 11/17/93
30 Key
31 Midway alternative
32 River nymph
33 The Gold Coast, today
34 "À votre __!"
39 Java neighbor
40 Columbus, by birth
42 "Nancy" or "Cathy"
43 Puss
45 Server on skates
46 Dos + cuatro
49 Take third
50 Take on
51 "__ on Film" (1983 book set)
52 Conniving
53 Coach Nastase
54 Rock's Joan
56 Sphere
57 "Cheers" habitué
58 Alternatively
60 Lady lobster
61 Ungainly craft

by Nancy B. Ross

ACROSS

1 "Charlie's Angels" actress
5 Jimmies
10 One who follows orders?
14 The cheaper spread
15 Campus clubs, for short
16 He jumps through hoops
17 New York cultural site
20 Squirrellike monkey
21 Weird
22 Molly Bloom's last word
23 Smidgens
25 Tempest locale
29 Ambience
30 Vote (for)
33 Woody's son
34 Not on all fours
35 Fido's foot
36 London cultural site
40 Juliette Low org.
41 Dearest ones
42 __ of Samothrace
43 Poetic contraction
44 Bad day for Caesar
45 Moulin Rouge attraction
47 1947 Pulitzer composer
48 1987 Michael Jackson album
49 Swiss capital
52 Universal
57 Milan cultural site
60 Spur
61 More frigid
62 It sticks out of a scabbard
63 Emulate Icarus
64 Suspicious
65 Wordsworth works

DOWN

1 Rich soil
2 Tenor Luigi
3 Bucks, e.g.
4 Coed quarters
5 Press type
6 Jimmies
7 Bridge position
8 __ degree
9 Compass pt.
10 Phoenix source
11 Yellowstone sighting
12 Singaraja's island
13 Vogue rival
18 Tom Smothers' plaything
19 Manufacturer's come-on
23 Quartet after a breakup?
24 Mischievous
25 "T" to ham operators
26 VCR function
27 Sacrifice site
28 Baked Hawaiian dish
29 City where van Gogh painted
30 Of the eye
31 Skier's garment
32 10-to-12 year-old
34 Gutter locale
37 Dickens waif
38 Lymph __
39 Actress Reinking
45 Informer
46 Puts two and two together
47 __ alia
48 Field worker
49 Heat quantities: Abbr.
50 Mr. Saarinen
51 Shankar piece
52 Ballet bend
53 Quick comeback?
54 One of a "Mikado" trio
55 "Winnie __ Pu"
56 Musical that opened 10/7/82
58 Kind of painting
59 Sizzling serve

7 by Morton B. Braun

ACROSS

1 Eve's second-born
5 Selves
9 Recipe direction
14 Venetian traveler
15 Baby's cry
16 Nuts-and-honey snack
17 Syllabus
18 Scottish group
19 Bean or Welles
20 Kind of joint between boards
23 Angers
24 British statesman Sir Robert
25 Pursued
28 It can provide a moving experience
29 "___ La Douce"
33 Pregame rah-rah meeting
34 1948 Hitchcock nail-biter
35 Close
36 Island prison of history
37 Days of celebration
38 Roof projection
39 Hammer head
40 CompuServe patron
41 Joseph of the Senate
42 Viewed
43 "All Things Considered" network
44 Be annoyed
45 Utah's state flower
47 Knot in wood
48 The Iron Chancellor
55 Pre-Columbian Mexican
56 Father of Enos
57 Tennis champ Yannick
58 African antelope
59 Suffix with kitchen or usher
60 Old Russian assembly

61 Race to a base, perhaps
62 Bird feeder fill
63 Observed

DOWN

1 Date with an M.D.
2 Heavy Army knife
3 Verve
4 View from Port Jefferson
5 Hosted a roast
6 Big parties
7 Mideast gulf
8 Alternative to a plane?
9 Kind of leave or dinner
10 Group containing Truk, Belau and Yap
11 Too

12 City in Ukraine
13 Hans Christian Andersen, e.g.
21 1934 chemistry Nobelist
22 Heredity units
25 Holiday paper
26 The Tin Man portrayer
27 "Seascape" playwright
28 Person in a booth?
30 Author of "The Cloister and the Hearth"
31 Expert
32 "You ___ kidding!"
34 Survey data
37 Baseball practice
41 Road shoulder
44 Hurried

46 Avoid
47 Please, to 48 Across
48 Singles
49 Fanciful, as a story
50 Popular cuisine
51 ___ noire
52 Rake
53 Arrived
54 Tatar chief

ACROSS

1 Yahoo
5 Pigeon drop, e.g.
9 Fill one's tank
14 Peace Nobelist Myrdal
15 Rival of Martina
16 Busy airport
17 Freud's home
18 Ticked off
19 Client of 16 Across
20 Princess Margaret's ex
23 Queue after Q
24 Fishing gear
25 Ended a bout early
27 Fishing gear
30 Barbering job
32 Really went for
36 Bakery enticement
38 Tide type
40 Nephew of Caligula
41 1991 Emmy-winning comic
44 Med. sch. subj.
45 Author Dinesen
46 Davis of "Do the Right Thing"
47 Tout's offering
49 Nudnik
51 Highway hazard
52 Uncommon sense
53 Music score abbr.
55 Experimentation station
58 1961 Inauguration speaker
64 Jordanian port
66 Word on a $1 bill
67 Hoedown prop
68 Blender setting
69 Blockhead
70 "If __ You" (1929 hit)
71 Game-show group
72 Tom Smothers amusement
73 Courage

DOWN

1 Cry like a baby
2 Mixed bag
3 Walkie-talkie word
4 Leave time
5 Fight souvenir
6 Eastern region
7 One more time
8 Anti-D.W.I. group
9 Composer of Hitchcock's theme
10 Sounds of satisfaction
11 German coal region
12 "Trinity" author
13 Saucy
21 Attack
22 Giraffe kin
26 Taboos
27 Elephant rider, perhaps
28 Maine college town
29 Best Actor of '39
31 __ Work (rock group)
33 Teammate of Robinson and Hodges
34 "To __ human"
35 B$_{12}$ quantities
37 Photo finish
39 Betraying clumsiness
42 "Fantasia" ballerina
43 "__ I can help it!"
48 Sharon's land
50 Completely
54 Boris Badenov's boss
55 Reindeer herder
56 Water color
57 Stable home
59 Miss Marple discovery
60 Suffix for stink
61 Waikiki locale
62 Chair part
63 Koppel and Kennedy
65 Old-fashioned do

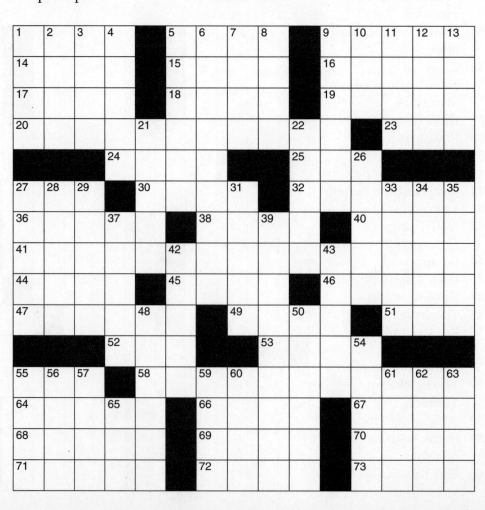

9 *by Janie Lyons*

ACROSS

1 Paint layer
5 Best of old films
9 Plays at Pebble Beach
14 Greengrocer's pods
15 Controversial 70's sitcom
16 Lit
17 Menu appetizer
20 Titter
21 Bambi and kin
22 Hints at the pool table?
23 ___ fixe
25 Ta-ta in Turin
27 Hollywood's Barbara or Conrad
30 Menu entree
35 Lew Wallace's "Ben ___"
36 Word before mother or lively
37 1975 Clavell best seller
38 Slack-jawed
40 Hoover, e.g.
42 Clean, as a computer disk
43 Beaverlike fur
45 Collars
47 Herbal soother
48 Menu side order
50 Carrel
51 G-men
52 Mr. Carnegie
54 Mystery dog
57 Hacker, e.g.
59 Revises
63 Menu dessert
66 Lady's alternative?
67 Kind of log
68 Hammer part
69 1941 Bogart role
70 Sediment
71 Ocean flyer

DOWN

1 Egyptian church member
2 "The Grapes of Wrath" worker
3 Foot part
4 Provide lodging for
5 Vane dir.
6 Walked unevenly
7 Scruff
8 Each
9 Dentist's anesthetic
10 Risqué
11 Stead
12 Parole
13 Televisions
18 Calculator display: Abbr.
19 Crossword diagrams
24 Newt
26 Pines
27 Hallucinogenic drink
28 Bode
29 Seething
31 Toothpaste once advertised by Grace Kelly
32 Type size for fine print
33 Ponders
34 Underhanded fellow
36 View from the Quai d'Orsay
39 Introduced
41 Barbara with two sisters
44 "Straight up" singer Paula
46 Youth grp. founded in 1910
49 Classic Montaigne work of 1580
50 Dock
53 The M-G-M lion
54 Book after John
55 Lollipop was a "good" one
56 Roman get-up
58 Needle case
60 Sunny vacation spot
61 Ruler until 1917
62 Basted
64 Vein find
65 Ran into

ACROSS

1 Not piquant
5 Israelite at the conquest of Canaan
10 Fortune's partner
14 Rustic
15 More than fubsy
16 Part of an été
17 About 17 million square miles
18 Get even, in a way
19 Germany's Oscar
20 Start of an adage
23 Infamous Ugandan
24 "Third Man" director
25 Subservient
28 Mash
30 Computer code
34 Son of Hera
35 Type of window
37 Mason's aid
38 Cornishman
39 Web-footed animal
40 Use a whetstone
41 Four-time Japanese P.M.
42 Mugs
43 Tag words
44 Tithing
46 ABC, for short
47 Making a stand?
48 1905 Secretary of State
50 Shoshone
51 End of the adage
59 Word with fire or no
60 Paris official
61 Pop singer Burdon
62 Some charts
63 Essence
64 Late-night star
65 Fly ash
66 Some homes
67 Crackpot

DOWN

1 Prankster
2 Rummy
3 Anne Nichols stage hero
4 Exciting to the max
5 Welsh dog
6 Incite
7 Wife of Jacob
8 Steep slope
9 Actress Davis
10 Oslo and others
11 Taurus or Aries, e.g.
12 Paw
13 Western Electric founder __ Barton
21 Preternatural
22 Binge
25 Wordless
26 Alpine feature
27 Item in a patch
28 Make powerful
29 Big-band name
31 X'd
32 Type of column
33 Words of explanation
35 "i" piece?
36 Oral stumbles
40 Wood hyacinth
42 Type of gun
45 Like best friends
47 Theta preceder
49 Isle __
50 Patrons
51 Indiana Jones perils
52 Actor Scott
53 Stick in the fridge?
54 Tiny imperfections
55 "Darn it all!"
56 Nabisco product
57 El __
58 Coll. course

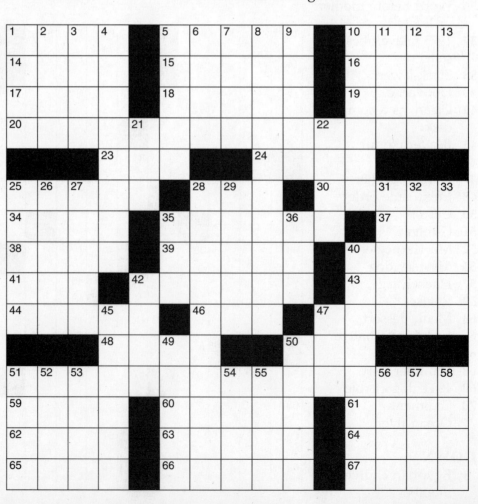

11 *by Nancy A. Corbett*

ACROSS

1 List ender
5 Intrinsically
10 N.Y.C. station
14 Coveted review
15 Love in Limoges
16 "__, Brute?"
17 Part of the eye
18 Rams and Jets, e.g.
19 Newspaperman Adolph
20 "No guarantees"
23 __ Alte (Adenauer)
24 540-1600 on a radio
27 Calpurnia's husband
31 Oner
35 Fluorescent-lamp filler
36 Intoxicating drink of the gods
37 Follower's suffix
38 Unwelcome one
42 Shad delicacy
43 Tight positions?
44 Record
45 Second self
48 Declare
49 Thrall of yore
50 MS. perusers
51 Willy-nilly
59 Concerning
62 Related maternally
63 Assist a prankster
64 __ bene
65 Adder or asp
66 Secure, in a way
67 Not up
68 That is
69 __ Domini

DOWN

1 "The Red"
2 "G.W.T.W." locale
3 Tel __
4 Majesty lead-in
5 Little feet do it
6 Title in Turkey
7 Indulge one's wanderlust
8 Waste reservoir
9 Once, once
10 Bradley University site
11 Another list ender
12 Highest degree
13 Mus' followers
21 Hersey novel town
22 Harem room
25 Control a 747
26 Antiseptic-surgery pioneer Joseph
27 "Lost Horizon" director
28 Tissue gap
29 They may be snowy
30 "Mayday!"
31 Musical form ending a sonata
32 Freeman Gosden radio role
33 Sought office
34 Embark
36 Squealed
39 Society-page word
40 Artist's paste
41 T.L.C. is their forte
46 Nonet, for one
47 Early auto
48 Commercial, in British slang
50 __ Park, Colorado
52 Jeans maker Strauss
53 Writer Bagnold
54 Neck part
55 Miss Cantrell
56 "Voice of Israel" author, 1957
57 Nürnberg no
58 Capital of Manche
59 __ nutshell
60 San Francisco hill
61 I-95, e.g.: Abbr.

ACROSS

1 Smooth wood
5 Treat like a pariah
9 Pin place
14 Mixed bag
15 "Self" starter
16 "Die Fledermaus" maid
17 Stay tuned, Part 1
20 Writer Danielle
21 She shares the wealth
22 Cut (off)
24 — gallop
25 Stay tuned, Part 2
34 "O.K., Ahab"
35 Actress Verdugo
36 Borden bovine
37 "Cool"
39 Gounod opera
41 Marion's finish
42 Island crooner
44 Slangy $100 bill
46 Sniggler's wiggler
47 Stay tuned, Part 3
50 Ankh's cross
51 Midwest Indian
52 Disparages
58 Ogden Nash's feet
62 Stay tuned, Part 4
64 Signal to slow
65 Unguarded, in football
66 Radiate
67 Full of vim and vinegar
68 Word to a refusenik
69 Thanksgiving side dishes

DOWN

1 Lays down the lawn
2 Much
3 Not quite Bo Derek
4 "No kidding!"
5 — Tomé and Principe
6 Hollywood 10 condemner: Abbr.
7 60's spy plane
8 Biblical 950-year-old
9 Gulf of Mexico pirate
10 Cute
11 Aka Edson Arantes do Nascimento
12 Large lodge
13 Minus
18 Boston daily
19 Informal agreement
23 Ill-gotten gains
25 Fish in a John Cleese comedy
26 "— newt . . ."
27 Listed
28 Boxer's asset
29 Operating
30 Reactions to serialists
31 Fall bloomer
32 Given as a source
33 Falls (over)
38 London daily
40 Ballerina's strong points
43 Speaking skill
45 "Roughing It" writer
48 Hippo's wear in "Fantasia"
49 Dramatist Sean
52 Arts degs.
53 "Cope Book" Aunt
54 Arcing shots
55 Author Hubbard
56 Wordsmith Willard
57 The Graf __
59 N.Y. institution on 53d Street
60 Fedora feature
61 Trans-Atlantic speedsters
63 Prov. on Niagara Falls

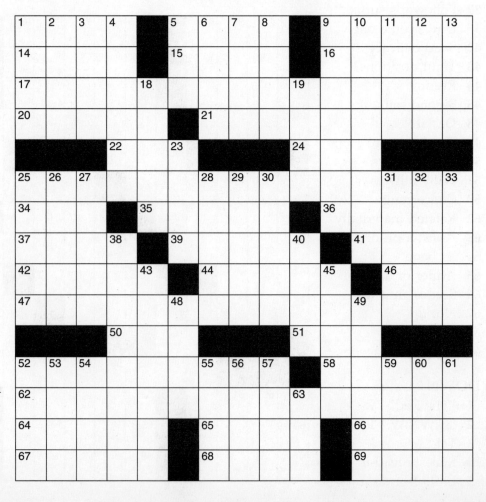

13 *by Albert J. Klaus*

ACROSS

1 "Woe is me!"
5 Inn, informally
10 Dollop
14 Frolic
15 Title holder
16 Burt's ex
17 Jai —
18 Former auto executive
20 Two-pointers
22 Differs
23 Saucer occupants, for short
24 Mozart's "— fan tutte"
25 Ball girl
28 Vacation spot
30 "Jerusalem Delivered" poet
34 Border lake
35 Car in a procession
37 Spring mo.
38 West Point salutatorian, 1829
41 Language ending
42 Off course
43 City two hours south of Lillehammer
44 Spreads the word
46 Bit of voodoo
47 Grueling tests
48 Sword with a guard
50 Louis Freeh's org.
51 Rubbed
54 Ascendant
58 Two-time U.S. Open golf champion
61 Kind of shark
62 Suffix with buck
63 Pentax rival
64 Sicilian rumbler
65 Poet Robert — Warren
66 Exhausted
67 Sunup direction

DOWN

1 Bedouin
2 She gets what she wants
3 Amo, —, amat
4 Modern film maker
5 Leaves in a hurry
6 Wows
7 Jet's heading
8 Mercury and Jupiter, e.g.
9 "Well done!"
10 Actress DeHaven
11 Places
12 — over lightly
13 Kind of crime
19 Mobile unit?
21 Season of l'année
24 Polish producer
25 Cap
26 Having an irregular edge
27 Defame
28 Boil
29 Military chaplain
31 Hot sauce
32 Word with cold or breathing
33 Chocolate snacks
35 Elevations: Abbr.
36 Remark
39 Hardly one with a lilting voice
40 Neoprimitive American artist
45 Unextinguished
47 Kimono sash
49 Paradises
50 Weather line
51 Keep time manually
52 "You are —"
53 Ages and ages
54 Soon
55 Ninth Greek letter
56 Actress Woods and others
57 Pest
59 One who gets special treatment
60 W.W. II hero

14 *by Wayne Robert Williams*

ACROSS

1 Comic Martha
5 Bamboozle
9 Stoppers
14 Height: Abbr.
15 Face-to-face exam
16 Beau at the balcony
17 Town near Caen
18 Chockablock
20 Headlong
22 Resident's suffix
23 Racetracks
24 Dormitory din
28 Radio transimission sites
30 Offspring, genealogically: Abbr.
31 Celtic Neptune
32 Centers
33 Walk-on
34 Chancellorsville victor
35 Western Indian
36 Enmity
38 Sugar suffix
39 Singer Tillis
40 Word after many or honey
41 Conflict in Greek drama
42 French dance
43 A.L. or N.L. honorees
44 "Phèdre" dramatist
46 Flummoxes
48 Spring fragrance
49 Picture blowup: Abbr.
50 Head count
53 Game of digs and spikes
57 Parts of pelvises
58 Greek poet saved by a dolphin
59 Fit
60 Oodles
61 Mississippi Senator __ Lott
62 Branch headquarters?
63 "Auld Lang __"

DOWN

1 Answer: Abbr.
2 Der __ (Adenauer moniker)
3 Cowardly one
4 Changes with the times
5 Carpentry pins
6 Europe/Asia separator
7 Dark shadow
8 Building wing
9 1984 Goldie Hawn movie
10 Look threatening
11 Actress Thurman
12 Solidify
13 Our sun
19 Xmas tree trimming
21 Spoil
24 Interstate trucks
25 Without rhyme or reason
26 "Schindler's List" star Liam
27 Novelist Graham
28 Hitches, as a ride
29 Surpass at the dinner table
30 Natural alarm clocks
33 Hoofbeats
36 About to occur
37 Pulchritudinous
41 Gum arabic trees
44 Garden brook
45 Completely
47 Juicy fruit
48 Takes it easy
50 Contemporary dramatist David
51 King of the beasts
52 Deceased
53 Large tub
54 Hockey's Bobby
55 Golf-ball position
56 Prohibit

ACROSS

1 Protection in a purse
5 Start, as a trip
11 Actor Max __ Sydow
14 Lawyer Dershowitz
15 Dragon's prey
16 Author Levin
17 Ex-heavyweight champ
19 Galley slave's tool
20 "__ been had!"
21 Bad grades
22 "Is that so?"
24 Colonist
26 Rock's __ Vanilli
27 Brit. ref. work
28 Triangular-sailed ships
30 Pencil name
33 Hotel lobby
34 "Ich __ ein Berliner"
36 "Famous" cookie man
37 Little bits
38 Dumb ox
39 Fourposter
40 Linen shades
41 Leafy shelter
42 Small seals
44 Journalist Nellie
45 Get rid of, in slang
46 Deejay's need
50 Los Angeles player
52 Orbit period
53 Lumberjack's tool
54 Singer __ Rose
55 Noble acts
58 __ time (golfer's starting point)
59 Niagara Falls craft?
60 "Java" player Al
61 "__ day now . . ."
62 The "E" of H.R.E.
63 Chocolate-covered morsels

DOWN

1 Baseball's Roger
2 Extant
3 Middy opponent
4 Epilogue
5 Ran the show
6 Almighty
7 Lobster eaters' accessories
8 Hubbub
9 Second drafts
10 Pew attachment
11 A concertmaster holds it
12 Kind of vaccine
13 Not any
18 Ambitionless one
23 Pub drink
25 Stocking parts
26 Yucatán people
28 Name in computer software
29 7D, e.g.
30 Early Beatles describer
31 "Rag Mop" brothers
32 Legendary bluesman
33 Onward
35 Neither's mate
37 It sometimes comes in bars
38 Cassidy portrayer William
40 Uganda airport
41 Boombox sound
43 Jazz date
44 Long-eared pooch
46 Witch, at times
47 Fine cloth
48 Strive
49 Schick et al.
50 Disk contents
51 The yoke's on them
52 Cosmonaut Gagarin
56 Dada founder
57 __ Na Na

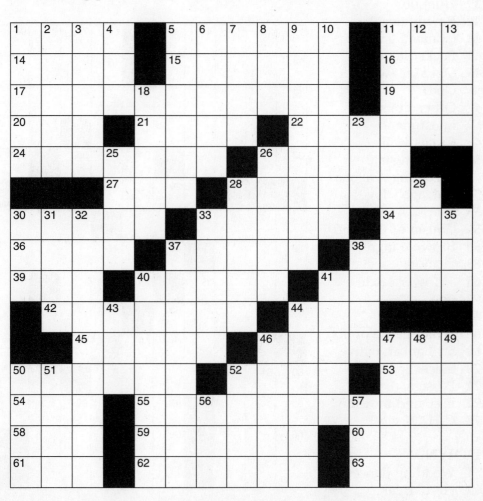

ACROSS

1 Literary Bret
6 From Cardiff
11 Fairy queen
14 Low-cholesterol spreads
15 Winged
16 Señora Perón
17 Rogue
19 Morning dampness
20 Not an expert
21 ___ greens
23 Protein source
24 Chicle product
26 Lemon zest source
27 ___ monkey
30 1945 meeting site
33 Fruit juice blend
36 ___ cit. (footnote abbr.)
38 Canal to the Baltic
39 Hubbub
40 Rowdy one
43 Granada gold
44 Pocket item?
46 Opus ___ (work of God)
47 Off-campus nonstudent
49 Circus walker
51 Mexican state bordering Arizona
53 Zhivago's love
55 Diarist Anaïs
56 Cousin of the emu
60 Brownie ingredients
63 Peanuts
65 "___ ever catch you . . ."
66 Stew
68 Avant-garde prefix
69 Sri Lankan native
70 Since: Sp.
71 Possess
72 Prepared to testify
73 C₄H₈O₂, e.g.

DOWN

1 Wedding dances
2 Hertz rival
3 Satisfy a debt
4 "Just for openers . . ."
5 Suffix with opal
6 Carroll's carpenter's companion
7 Addition
8 Secular
9 Small porch
10 Regatta site
11 Cab symbol
12 State categorically
13 Floozy
18 Bored
22 Washington news source, maybe
25 Vertical dividing bar in windows
28 Cry of glee
29 ___-disant (self-styled)
31 Actress Garr
32 Burn soother
33 Snoozes
34 Abridge, perhaps
35 Do for debs
37 Benin's largest city
41 Bandleader Brown
42 Neither's counterpart
45 Author Paton
48 Coloratura's sounds
50 They're sometimes blind
52 Be finicky
54 Attorney ___
57 Thieves' work
58 Wear away
59 "Mary Tyler Moore Show" co-star
60 Souse
61 "___ Good Men"
62 Oriental combat
64 Ye ___ Shoppe
67 Russian for "peace"

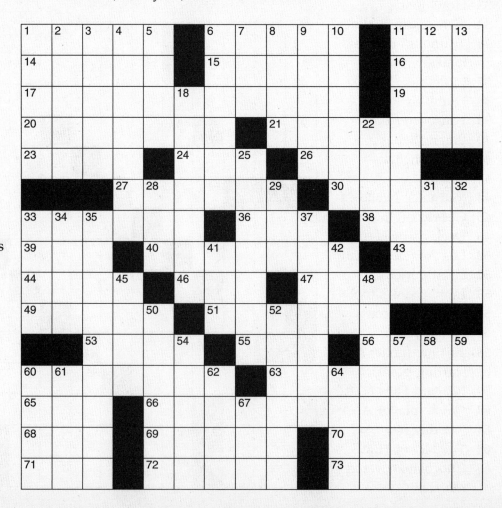

ACROSS

1 Buddy
5 Balance sheet listing
10 Helper: Abbr.
14 New Rochelle college
15 They fly in formation
16 Wife of __ (Chaucer pilgrim)
17 Ordnance
18 Fill with glee
19 Out of the weather
20 Battle in which Lee defeated Pope
23 Sunday talk: Abbr.
24 Activity
25 Fountain treat, for short
26 Battle in which Bragg defeated Rosecrans
31 Singer Coolidge et al.
32 Corner
33 11th-century date
36 Heaven on earth
37 Change
39 Earth sci.
40 Marry
41 Fine poker holdings
42 Hawks
43 Battle in which Grant defeated Bragg
46 John Wilkes Booth, e.g.
50 Tempe sch.
51 Items on a "must" list
52 Battle in which Lee defeated Burnside
57 Retread, e.g.
58 Go along (with)
59 Wrangler's pal
61 Overlook
62 Some are heroic
63 Mideast land
64 Promontory
65 Kilmer opus
66 Niño's nothing

DOWN

1 Spy grp.
2 Baseball, informally
3 Not deserved
4 Not fem.
5 Work to do
6 Infrequently
7 Petticoat junction
8 "Cómo __ usted?"
9 Target MTV viewer
10 Embarrass
11 Nacho topping
12 Rib-eye
13 Ones nearby
21 Dumbarton __ (1944 meeting site)
22 P.D.Q.
23 Item in a hardware bin
27 Fire
28 Nuclear experiment
29 Coffee server
30 Start for fly or about
33 Three-hanky film
34 City once named for Stalin
35 Rick's beloved et al.
37 Herr's "Oh!"
38 "Cry __ River"
39 General Motors make
41 Parcel of land
42 High-hat
44 Words before "I'm yours"
45 Tax
46 "Sweet" river of song
47 Record blot
48 Actress Garr et al.
49 Playwright Clifford
53 Engrossed
54 Mr. Stravinsky
55 Saskatchewan tribe
56 Atop
60 Kind of testing

18 *by Peter Gordon*

ACROSS

1. Bedwear, informally
4. Essen exclamation
7. Move back
13. Sports org.
14. __ tai
15. Ethanol and dimethyl ether, e.g.
17. Germinating
19. One of 38 Across
20. Unchanged
21. Sounds of happiness
23. Hose material
24. One of 38 Across
28. Actress Lupino
29. Distinctive quality
30. Drink cat-style
33. River to the Seine
36. Telecommunications giant
37. Uncommon
38. Theme of this puzzle
42. Missing
43. Dam-building org.
44. Gather
45. Gaze at
46. Afrikaner
47. To and __
48. One of 38 Across
53. Lumberjacks' competition
56. Vote for
57. It is in Spain
58. Concern of 38 Across
61. Beg
63. Fame
64. Nipper's co.
65. Black and tan ingredient
66. Texas city
67. Driver's license info
68. Cobb and Hardin

DOWN

1. Pari __ (at an equal rate): Lat.
2. One of 38 Across
3. Finland, to the Finns
4. "What __, chopped liver?"
5. One of 38 Across
6. Weather data
7. Semi
8. Language suffix
9. Pupil's protector
10. Oscars' cousins
11. Good buy
12. Cubemaker Rubik
16. Antonym's antonym: Abbr.
18. Add color to again
22. Shower's counterpart
25. River in Germany
26. Saturn or Mercury, e.g.
27. Not kosher
30. Pelée output
31. Lover of Aphrodite
32. Bics, e.g.
33. Homeowner's pymt.
34. Sailor's cry
35. Actress Russo
37. More distant
39. Sioux Indian
40. Iris's place
41. Wraparound dress
46. Litters
47. One of 38 Across
48. Type
49. Rathskeller servings
50. "Have __" (interviewer's request)
51. One of 38 Across
52. N.B.A's Thurmond and Archibald
53. Scale notes
54. Eight: Prefix
55. Fill, as bases
59. Yr. parts
60. Singer Sumac
62. Strain

19 *by Harvey Estes*

ACROSS

1 Hunter's prey
5 Batter's woe
10 They're big for conceited folks
14 General under Dwight
15 Resort lake
16 Author Émile
17 Cabdrivers do this
20 Start for step or stop
21 Fix, as in gambling
22 Wild talk
23 Uganda's Amin
24 Show biz routine
28 Rummy cry
30 Repetitious goodbye
32 Simile center
33 "What Kind of Fool ___"
34 Its symbol is five rings
39 Write
40 Optometrists do this
44 Silent communication
45 Tributes
46 Expert
47 Kind of room
48 Animal stomach
52 Stole
53 Battery's partner
57 Show to a seat, informally
58 What you pay at sales
60 Way of Lao-tzu
61 World traveler of note
62 Lip readers do this
67 Conductor Klemperer
68 Friend of Mercutio
69 Cabin wood
70 Unmixed, at a mixer
71 Hanker
72 Busy bodies

DOWN

1 "Get cracking!"
2 Blake of "Gunsmoke"
3 Succeed
4 Before
5 Having a stiff upper lip
6 Har-de-har-har
7 TV band
8 Stock response
9 Each
10 Metrical Pound
11 Flipping
12 Nostalgic
13 Enclosed with an MS.
18 '93, '94, etc.
19 Aquatic zoo
25 Pudding ingredient
26 "Of Thee ___"
27 Big stickers
29 Diamond digit
31 Fine, to a pilot
35 Caustic agent
36 Letter sign-off
37 Slippers for the stubborn?
38 1989 comedy "___ Devil"
40 Page (through)
41 Kiss
42 Victor Herbert work
43 Computer key abbr.
49 Emphasizes, as an embarrassing error
50 Obliquely
51 "Certainly!"
53 Lenten symbol
54 Absolute
55 Imperative to Macduff
56 Overly
59 Dundee dweller
62 Persuaded to marry
63 Not straight
64 Millet's "Man With the ___"
65 Doctors' org.
66 Put ___ fight

ACROSS

1 Funeral stand
5 Lick
8 A little night music
12 Like matzoh
16 Della's creator
17 18th-century monarch, too familiarly?
19 Tributary
20 Residents of Meshed
21 Still
22 Miss Merkel
23 Baby food
26 Items that are piled
29 Overwhelms
34 Shah Jahan's building site
36 Salve base
38 Ennoble
39 Lake Ontario outlet, too familiarly?
42 Indian follower
43 TV's Ricky
44 Tangent's cousin
45 Shenanigans
47 Frond holder
49 It makes towels plushy
50 Indy 500 advertiser
52 Actress Thompson
54 Available, as retail goods
59 Bill collector
63 Architectural refinement, too familiarly?
65 Press for
66 Took orders, in a way
67 By and by
68 Bygone platters
69 Those for

DOWN

1 Bare skin
2 Concerning, at law
3 Robt. __
4 Singer Helen
5 Athletic supporter?
6 Against
7 Indian leader
8 Actress Garr
9 Vicinage
10 Map out
11 Goes down
13 "Do, __, a female . . ."
14 Kind of reality
15 Academic heads
18 Beaver, for one
23 Turkish bigwig
24 In addition
25 Art sale item
27 Wrap name
28 Chafed places
30 W.W. II foe
31 Know-it-all
32 Full assemblies
33 Pharyngeal invader
35 "The King __"
37 Aforetime
40 University of Arizona site
41 Surrenderer
46 Last item?
48 Verdun's river
51 Jail-related
53 Overeager
54 Greenish-blue
55 Crank
56 Utah's state flower
57 Adult-to-be
58 Small cut
60 Letters from Wall Street
61 Parmenides's birthplace
62 Stop lights
64 Como's "__ Impossible"

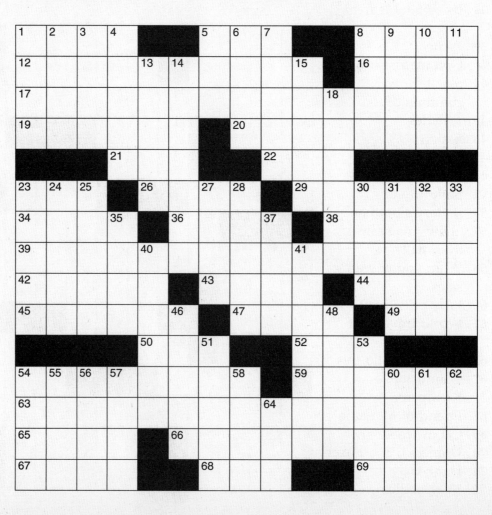

ACROSS

1 Some swabs
6 Ski champ McKinney
12 1964 Hitchcock film
13 Renders drug-free
14 Logical thinker
15 Praises: Var.
16 Lovable
18 Assent
19 River inlet
20 Swiss river
22 Sequel to Buck's "The Good Earth"
23 Group of gangs
26 Bank claims
28 Geo. and Thos., e.g.
29 Adjusts
31 Belles-__
33 "Ars Amatoria" author
35 Word repeated in a Doris Day song
36 Brownies
39 Meal
43 Balkans map abbr.
44 Some boxing jabs
46 Pasta variety
47 Latin I word
49 Drying method
50 "__ the ramparts . . ."
51 Barbara follows it
53 Numbers in parentheses
57 Tough guy of filmdom
59 Break down
60 Oil and water, e.g.
61 Mend a coat
62 Emulated an oenophile
63 Boar or boor

DOWN

1 Libyan strongman
2 Word with blue or believer
3 Atahualpa, e.g.
4 Loading/unloading locale
5 "Flash Gordon," once
6 __-Mex
7 "__ boy!"
8 Electronic synthesizers
9 Guns N' Roses leader
10 Softens
11 Evaluate
12 Not grandiose
13 Master's and others
14 Skin
17 One that gets hit on the head
21 Stage direction
24 Mr. Sikorsky
25 Smith's need
27 Kind of throat
30 Located
32 Shakespeare's "The __ of Lucrece"
34 Pays part of
36 Mogadishu's locale
37 Manners
38 The slammer
40 Pain reliever
41 Dismiss lightly, with "at"
42 Blunt
43 Volcanic rock
45 Asparagus servings
48 Publican's offering
52 Indy champ Luyendyk
54 Once more
55 City southwest of Bogotá
56 Actor Ken or actress Lena
58 Append

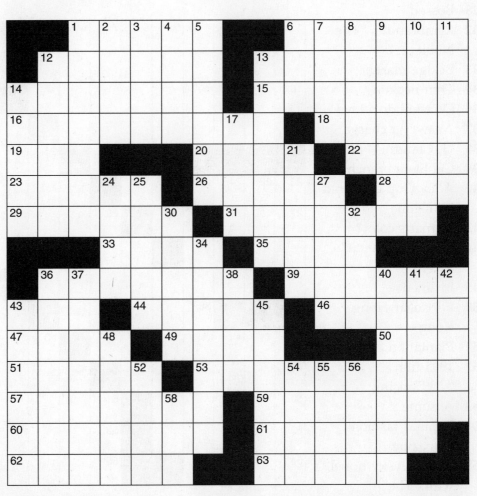

ACROSS

1 It's no loss
10 Grouch
14 Where Croesus's kingdom was
15 Cellular __
16 Rabelais's amiable giant
17 Monks' hour when psalms are recited
18 One skilled in match play
19 Kind of jumper
20 "Brooklyn Bridge" actress Aquino
21 Hint
22 Calls upon
26 One of the Dionnes
27 Skirt style
28 Bossed
32 Rembrandt's "The Noble __"
33 Bridge marker
34 Thin necktie
35 Quasimodo's love
37 Answer a charge
38 "I, Claudius" attire
39 Cal State branch site
40 Alley Oop and Fred Flintstone
43 Hefner's color?
44 "O tempora! __!": Cicero
45 Inclined
50 Port near Hong Kong
51 Plantation crop
52 1985 film "__ Dancing!"
53 Assume
54 Popular fashion magazine
55 Dostoyevsky novel, with "The"

DOWN

1 Hero's tale
2 Peter or Nicholas
3 Melodies
4 Titicaca, por ejemplo
5 Flow (from)
6 Pharmacists' measures
7 Overeager
8 Race track figure
9 Baseball stat
10 Fickle
11 It makes you blush
12 Inca empire locale
13 Assail
15 Connect
19 Marble worker's tool
21 Site of a Margaret Mead study
22 Flower holder
23 Troubles
24 "Anna and the King of __"
25 Dyed-in-the-wool
26 Cheese coatings
28 "Blowin' in the Wind" singer
29 Digits
30 Dash
31 Extinct bird
33 Leafs
36 Lover boys
37 Take steps
39 Railroad flares
40 Monte Cristo title
41 Menotti's "__ and the Night Visitors"
42 Outspoken
43 Does
45 Producer De Laurentiis
46 Picks, with "for"
47 Hot springs
48 Actress Sommer
49 Act
51 Kind of tent

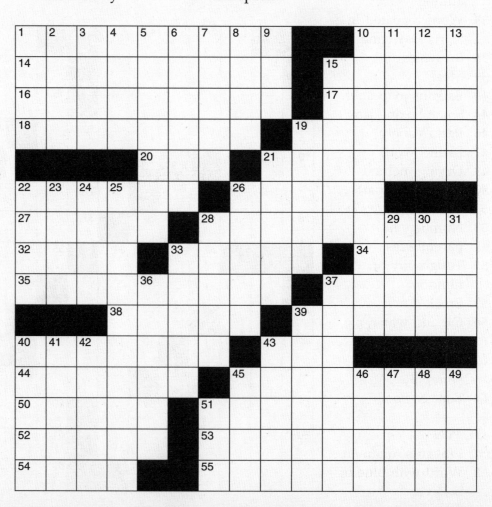

23 *by Daniel R. Stark*

ACROSS

1 Snacks in Santa Rosalía
6 Upright
14 Aligned
16 Elephantine
17 Rainier locale
18 Globe flattener, in a way
19 Interest rate: abbr.
20 Negotiates a puddle
22 ___ Khan
23 Superman's mother
25 Lake resort
26 Galway Bay isles
27 Accommodate
29 ___ openers
30 Positive, for a shutterbug
31 Mugged a snoozer
33 Husky runners
35 Gouda's cousin
37 Berlin one
38 One kind of clutch
41 Sarge, for one
45 Playwright-lyricist Comden
46 Buff
48 Reuniongoer
49 Harry Golden's "___ in America"
50 Watered silk
52 ___ rug
53 Altiplano tuber
54 Where Holstein cows originated
56 Catch some rays
57 Shaven, as a priest's head
59 Fix, as boundaries
61 Rooming-house convenience
62 Foul-ups
63 Quiet firework
64 "Hero and Leander" episode

DOWN

1 Charteris detective Simon ___
2 Alligator pear
3 Old telephone exchange
4 Stop ___ dime
5 Slangy instants
6 Private eye
7 Kind of town
8 Think alike
9 Resins
10 Actress Zadora
11 Least of the Great Lakes
12 Rallying cries
13 Not an easy boss
15 Blockhead
21 Clod
24 More than enough
26 It's south of the Caucasus
28 Lingerie item
30 Tree with edible seeds
32 Apply makeup
34 Aunts and others
36 Ill-fated bullfighter
38 Place for brooding
39 1996 Olympics site
40 Dutch coin
42 Notarize
43 The eldest Titan
44 Most Scroogelike
45 Fair constructions
47 ___-la-la
50 Fable's point
51 Tackles' neighbors
54 "The Incredible ___"
55 Hollow
58 Time of yr.
60 ___ and away

ACROSS

1 __ at Work
4 Diesel-engine submarine
9 Hindu title of address
12 The "A" in U.A.R.
14 Bull: Prefix
15 Pole
16 First name in humor
17 13 Down musical form
19 Kigali's land
21 Soak again
22 Company V.I.P.'s
24 Stately 13 Down dance
26 Americano
28 Carried out
29 Words from Caesar
30 13 Down dance in triple meter
34 Acid
37 Suit to __
38 They often have twists
39 Receipts
40 Neighbor of Leb.
41 13 Down medium for Jean Baptiste Lully
42 Reactor factor
43 Amigo
44 Baby wrigglers
46 13 Down dance, in France
52 English royal house
53 Flood protection
54 Ornamental band
56 13 Down musical form
58 Faithful
62 Female deer
63 __-Bismol
64 Prefix with Disney
65 Snaky shape
66 Deuce toppers
67 Big __

DOWN

1 Miss West
2 Slip
3 60's service site
4 Sundance Kid's girlfriend __ Place
5 Manger locales
6 Literary pen name of old
7 Noisy
8 Woody Herman's "__ Autumn"
9 Give rise to
10 Judged
11 Hot under the collar
13 Highly embellished style
15 Slammin' Sammy
18 Circle
20 Sch. of the Northwest
22 Tart-tongued
23 Stage direction
25 "__ Fideles"
26 First side to vote
27 Old Chevrolet
31 "__ say!"
32 Lon __
33 Western Indian
34 Not now
35 Baby bird?
36 Whom Reps. run against
39 Moderately quick 13 Down dance
41 Made hay?
43 Prayers
45 Drain cleaner ingredient
46 Clearing
47 Former Houston hockey team
48 Climbing plants
49 Marathoner
50 Hang
51 Deplete
55 Writer Anita
57 Inclined
59 Stroke
60 Yorkshire river
61 Long, long ago

25 *by Manny Nosowsky*

ACROSS

1 "Alas"
6 "Chariots of the Gods" author Erich Von __
13 John Denver's "__ Song"
15 Iridescent
16 Jordan River's outlet
18 Extirpates
19 Yodeler's perch
20 Apt to fall apart
22 Astuteness
23 Start of a classic question
25 Twinkle-toed
26 Size up
27 Abram's wife
29 Ship's heading
30 Husky-voiced singer from Vienna
31 Post-kickoff game status
34 Rudolph Valentino, e.g.
36 Kind of suit
38 Israel's Arens
41 "My mamma done __ me"
42 Welles of the Mercury Theater
44 Play money?
45 Fire fighter
47 God of destruction
48 Reagan program: Abbr.
49 1966 musical featuring 30 Across
51 Calif. neighbor
52 Food preservative
54 Get cozy
56 Mark a marker?
57 House Speaker, 1977–86
58 Some car deals
59 Singer James and others

DOWN

1 Former Al-Qubbah Palace residents
2 15 slices, maybe
3 Visored hat style
4 Go to bat for
5 Family tree abbr.
6 Traitorous ones
7 Beatles record label
8 __ a one
9 1969 Nobel Peace Prize winner: Abbr.
10 Of a Plains people
11 Something or someone
12 Lipton competitor
14 Word repeated in a Doris Day song
17 Site of one of Hercules's labors
21 F. Scott Fitzgerald's birthplace
24 Otologist's case
26 Impressionist collection
28 Carpet fiber
30 Resulted in
32 Argentine aunt
33 Mannerism
35 Blowing one's cool
37 "Billy Budd," e.g.
38 Chess or bridge ranking
39 Sir Frederick Ashton ballet
40 Smarts
43 Adam and Eve lacked them
45 Give up
46 Where exes are made
49 Scuttle load
50 Adjust
53 Brother
55 Pick up

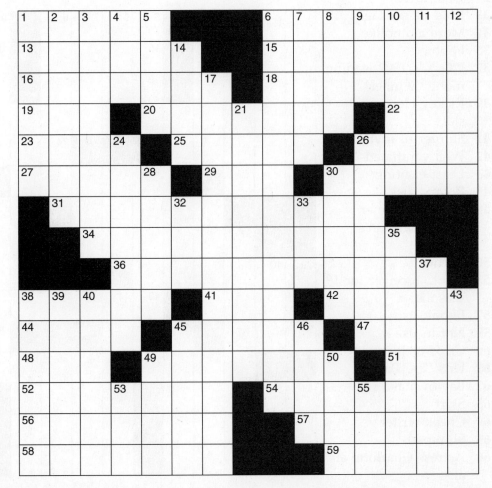

ACROSS

1 Wrongs
5 Stockyard group
9 Sail supports
14 Govt. agents
15 War of 1812 battle site
16 Member of a crowd scene
17 Give stars to
18 Basketball's Chamberlain
19 1993 Formula One winner Prost
20 Old "House Party" host
23 Knocks down
24 Reserved
25 1975 Stephanie Mills musical, with "The"
28 Hot time in Paris
29 Take turns
33 Kind of package
34 More albinolike
35 Phobic
37 P.G.A.'s 1992 leading money winner
39 Rickey Henderson stat
41 Hunter of myth
42 Well ventilated
43 Least exciting
45 Rotary disk
48 Sign of summer
49 Mathematician's letters
50 Throw
52 N.F.L. receiver for 18 seasons
57 Booby
59 Not in use
60 Crips or Bloods
61 Uris' "__ Pass"
62 Baylor mascot
63 Skirt
64 Check writer
65 Slumped
66 Actress Charlotte et al.

DOWN

1 Attack by plane
2 Turkish hostelry
3 Stinging plant
4 Fish-line attachment
5 Axed
6 Dancer Bruhn
7 Small brook
8 Loathe
9 Substantial
10 Wheel shaft
11 Noted film trilogy
12 Angle starter
13 __ José
21 Hebrew for "contender with God"
22 Eponymous poet of Greek drama
26 Temper
27 British alphabet ender
30 Elderly one
31 Gumshoe
32 "__ With a View"
33 Columnist Herb
34 Supplicate
36 Thread of life spinner, in myth
37 Savageness
38 Late actress Mary
39 NaCl, to a pharmacist
40 Truss
44 Deviates from the script
45 Party to NAFTA
46 Exact retribution
47 Enters a freeway
49 Persian Gulf land
51 Trevanian's "The __ Sanction"
53 Green target
54 Madison Avenue product
55 Ardor
56 Boor
57 Cutup
58 Noche's opposite

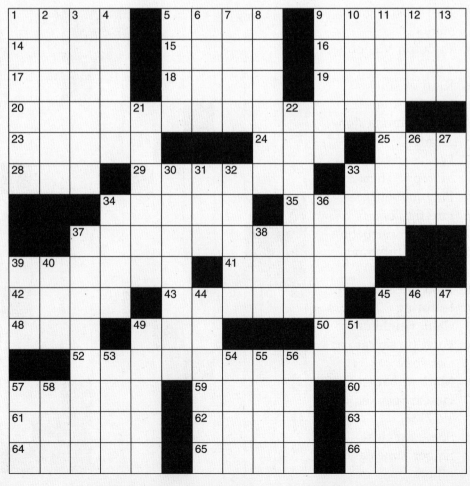

ACROSS

1 Tot's talk, perhaps
5 Encourages
9 First-grade instruction
13 Stinks
15 "Thanks __!"
16 Swing around
17 Like factory workers
19 U, for one
20 Elsie's bull
21 "Mommie __" (Christina Crawford book)
23 "What's __ for me?"
25 Take a potshot
26 Teller of white lies
29 Stage whisper
30 Give the eye
31 Quick bites
33 Advances
36 Baseball's Gehrig
37 Trunk
39 Runner Sebastian
40 Remains
43 Person of action
44 King's address
45 Illegal inducement
47 Mexican dishes
49 Speakeasy offering
50 Saxophonist Getz
51 Candid
53 Waiter's jotting
56 Actress Archer
57 Kind of jury
61 Bucks and does
62 Otherwise
63 Singer __ Neville
64 Lawyer: Abbr.
65 Tackle-box item
66 City inside the Servian Wall

DOWN

1 Tennis shot
2 Run in neutral
3 Body's partner
4 Logician's start
5 Sidekick
6 Sum total
7 Wart giver, in old wives' tales
8 Emphasis
9 On a horse
10 Edit
11 No blessing, this!
12 Shipped
14 Fragrance
18 Marco Polo area
22 Dye color appropriate to this puzzle
24 Vacuum tube
26 Go belly up
27 Borodin's prince
28 Texas' state flower
29 Balance-sheet pluses
32 Golf club V.I.P.
34 Illustrator Gustave
35 Comprehends
38 Patrick Henry, e.g.
41 Bodega
42 Clothing specification
44 Boating hazard
46 Saharan tribesman
48 Newswoman Shriver
49 Intelligence-testing name
51 Actress Thompson
52 Glamour rival
54 River of Spain
55 Leeway
58 "It's no __!"
59 Slippery one
60 Opposite SSW

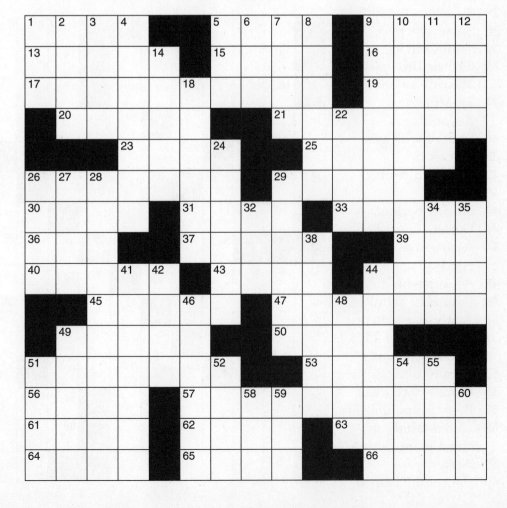

28 *by William P. Baxley*

ACROSS

1 Artistic skill
6 Card game also called sevens
12 Holed out in two under par
14 Warned
16 English essayist Richard
17 Burglar
18 Cools, as coffee
19 Pumpkin eater of rhyme
21 Summer drink
22 Employee health plan, for short
23 Horse trainer's equipment
25 Black cuckoos
26 Long, long time
28 Like some schools
29 Sweetens the kitty
30 Smart alecks
32 Traffic circle
33 Charlie Brown's "Darn!"
34 Ex-Mrs. Burt Reynolds
35 Charge with gas
38 Adorned
42 Vineyard fruit
43 Kismet
44 Snick's partner
45 Detest
46 Alternative to eggdrop
48 A Gershwin
49 Drunk __ skunk
50 Analyze a sentence
51 Actor John of TV's "Addams Family"
53 Locale
55 Money-back deal
57 Boot camp denizen
58 Noted family in china manufacture
59 Arabs
60 Cancel the launch

DOWN

1 "L'état __": Louis XIV
2 Army grub
3 Ripening agent
4 Butler's "The Way of All __"
5 __ Aviv
6 Observed Lent
7 Change the hemline
8 __ do-well
9 "La-la" leader
10 Home of the '96 Olympics
11 Poorer
13 Arranges strategically
15 Smart
18 Sullivan's "really big" one
20 Summers, in Haiti
24 Sharp
25 Clowning achievements?
27 Mexican shawl
29 Top-flight
31 Arena receipts
32 Drive in Beverly Hills
34 Epistles
35 Shocked
36 Pencil ends
37 Knocking sound
38 Forbids
39 Bootee maker
40 Most Halloweenlike
41 Doyen
43 Smithies
46 Dwindled
47 High-muck-a-muck
50 Fir
52 Prefix with masochism
54 Item of office attire
56 Fuel efficiency rater: Abbr.

29 *by Jonathan Schmalzbach*

ACROSS
1 Scroogian comments
5 Grandson of Adam
9 Biblical possessive
12 Sheltered, at sea
13 Spot for Spartacus
14 Carnival ride cry
15 "Ho, ho, ho" fellow
18 Seems
19 Hockey's Bobby, et al.
20 Blue Eagle initials
21 Feasted
23 "My salad days when I was __": Shakespeare
30 Favorite dog name
31 Closes in on
32 The East
33 Word in a price
35 Volcano spew
36 Deli cry
37 Cause for liniment
38 Not-so-prized fur
40 River inlet
41 Bucky Dent slew it at Fenway Park in 1978
45 Zorba portrayer
46 Tennis call
47 Sulk angrily
48 Many Dickens stories, originally
52 Civil War currency
56 Merit
57 Nintendo hero
58 One of the Simpsons
59 Sot's problems
60 Jot
61 Prepares the dinner table

DOWN
1 Mexican peninsula
2 Crooked
3 Maids
4 Moon goddess
5 Misreckons
6 Born
7 Indivisible
8 __ Marcos, TX
9 Arid region of India
10 Chick watchers
11 Thus far
13 Take with __ of salt
14 Utility employee
16 It comes in balls
17 Bad news at a talent show
21 "Bull __" (Costner film)
22 Psyche parts
23 Word in a monarch's name
24 Extent
25 National treasuries
26 Tidy up
27 Teen heartthrob Priestley
28 Undeliverable letter, in post-office talk
29 13th-century invader
34 Monastery head
38 D.C. legislator
39 El Greco's "View of __"
42 Nothing: Fr.
43 Pianist Peter
44 Part of rock's C.S.N. & Y.
47 Brotherhood
48 Comic bit
49 "I cannot tell __"
50 Ultimate
51 Madrid Mmes.
52 Dropout's degree: Abbr.
53 Status letters, perhaps
54 "Say __"
55 Dernier __

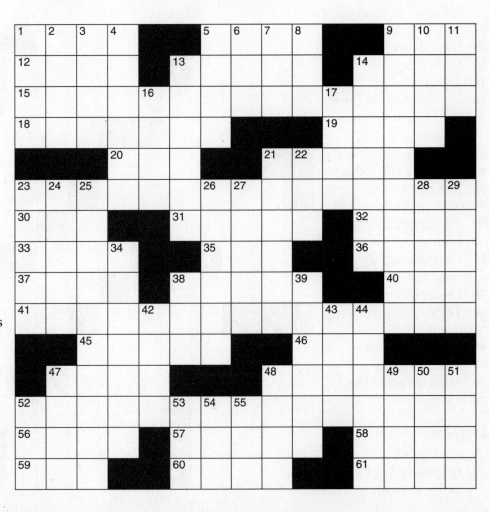

30 *by David J. Kahn*

ACROSS

1 Colo. acad.
5 Start fishing
9 "Dancing Queen" pop group
13 Mata __
14 Tear to shreds
16 Tactic
17 Singer Antoine from New Orleans
19 Intense anger
20 Carty of baseball
21 __ and kin
23 "The Company"
24 Mister twister
28 San Francisco area
29 Antitoxins
30 Laughed, in a way
32 Transfer, as a legal proceeding
36 "Tie a Yellow Ribbon" tree
37 Native land
39 Inform (on)
40 Fantasized
44 Durante's "Mrs."
48 Cosmonaut Gagarin
50 1956 Oscar-winning actress
51 Birthday-suit activity
55 One of L.B.J.'s dogs
56 Munich's river
57 Max or Buddy
59 Till compartment
61 Film hit of 1934
65 Dermatologist's diagnosis
66 Underwater acronym
67 Tevye portrayer on stage
68 Feminist Millett
69 Mikulski and Murkowski: Abbr.
70 Once more

DOWN

1 TV initials
2 Region of heavy W.W. II fighting
3 Heart of the grocery?
4 Champion named 9/1/72
5 __ Magnon
6 Goal
7 Acerbic
8 Acropolis attire
9 Bank loan abbr.
10 Longtime Supreme Court name
11 Humphrey, to Bacall
12 TV's "__ in the Life"
15 Commotion
18 Act like the Apostle Thomas
22 "__ goes!"
25 __ Harbour, Fla.
26 Playoff breathers
27 Machine part
28 "__ she blows!"
30 Food fish
31 A dwarf
33 Syracuse players
34 Floral container
35 Biblical suffix
38 Moist
41 Novelist Rand
42 City bond, for short
43 Secret lovefests
45 Appearance at a sit-down?
46 Suspect's "out"
47 Top-rated TV show of the 60's
49 Baking potatoes
51 Kind of therapy
52 Moi's country
53 "__ my case"
54 "Goodnight" girl
58 Steak order
60 Marie, e.g.: Abbr.
62 Aruba product
63 Nolte's "48 __"
64 Right away

31 *by Robert Katz*

ACROSS

1 Eye site
7 Freshens up baby
14 Canceled
15 P.O.W.'s
16 Partied hearty
17 Fossillike
18 "Liftoff" preceder
19 Early Beatle Sutcliffe
21 Phone button
22 Bottom line
25 Suffix with depend or descend
27 4.0, e.g.
30 "Hey! Jealous Lover" singer
33 Goofs
34 Italian epic poet
36 Showy moths
37 Take in
38 Nursery-rhyme queen's fare
41 Thespian's quest
42 Work unit
43 Shangri-las
44 Timetable divisions
45 Earth and moon, e.g.
47 Letter from Greece
48 Message from the Titanic
49 Satchel binder
53 Willing
57 "__ Lazy River"
59 "__ minute"
60 Twain and others
63 Cloys with adoration
66 Twilight time
67 Voucher
68 Supplies with new hands
69 Iroquoian people

DOWN

1 Computer salesman of renown
2 Maine college town
3 Musical direction
4 Question

5 Plumber's joint
6 Tote board stat
7 Apply lightly
8 __ facto
9 Not under
10 Bundle
11 1977 Streisand hit
12 Abbr. in a military name
13 Compass dir.
15 Nursery-rhyme king's den
20 Gunpowder, e.g.
23 Black numbers
24 '63 film "David and __"
26 Marched
28 Wishes
29 Image in Egyptian art

31 Intersections
32 Tribe of Israel
33 Repeated Jim Varney film role
34 Lifts of a sort
35 Charged at the bench
39 Some Dada works
40 Ovid products
41 Vim
46 Empath's skill
50 __ Janeiro
51 Lark
52 Ziti or fusilli
54 Poet Bradstreet
55 __ Hari
56 German biographer Ludwig
58 Fundamentals
60 Each

61 Oscar-winning Joanne Woodward role
62 Masthead listings, for short
64 Poet's word
65 Boxer's title: Abbr.

32 *by Jonathan Schmalzbach*

ACROSS

1 Granitelike
5 Paris' __ Monceau
9 Paradigm of happiness
13 Melville book
14 Toledo ta-ta
16 "Guys and Dolls" Tony winner, 1951
17 Lose freshness
18 The Rock Island Line?
20 Argus-eyed
22 Pin down, in a way
23 Born
24 Othello, e.g.
25 Police BBQ?
27 Triathlete
30 Next-to-last Greek letter
31 Non compos mentis
32 Fit together
35 Chloroform kin
39 "The __ of Innocence"
40 Men's accessories
42 Parisian season
43 Vitamin start
45 Sandberg of baseball
46 Give __ whirl
47 Showstoppers
49 Propriety
52 Markdown at the marina?
57 Type of luck
58 In the past
59 __ many words
60 Popular women's magazine
62 Mirror, brushes, perfume?
65 Storytelling dance
67 Regular
68 Drinks with straws
69 ". . . unto us __ is given"
70 Laura of "Jurassic Park"
71 Bread grains
72 Jerry-built structure

DOWN

1 In what manner
2 "What __ mind reader?
3 The Pillsbury Doughboy?
4 Pamper
5 Deli meat
6 Punch's cousin
7 Public uprisings
8 Woo
9 Wheels, so to speak
10 Southwest plain
11 Tours ta-ta
12 "Spanish Guitar Player" artist
15 Meet Morpheus
19 Joshes
21 CD-__ (modern "book")
26 Pioneer Carson
27 Muslim priest
28 Francesco Rinaldi competitor
29 Not e'en once
33 Nathan Hale, e.g.
34 Kind of legs
36 Removal of Junior from a will?
37 Part of Caesar's reproach
38 Enlarge, as a hole
40 Morsel
41 Unnecessary
44 Menlo Park monogram
48 Some TV's
50 Hint
51 Nebraska Indians
52 Economized
53 Tequila plant
54 Asocial person
55 With respect to
56 Truckler
61 __ gin
63 Publican's place
64 Actress __ Dawn Chong
66 As well as

33 *by Eileen Lexau*

ACROSS

1 Hazard
9 Rumor
14 Took to mean
15 Prevention dose?
16 Lousy tips
17 Be maître d'
18 "A Chorus Line" song
19 Electrical unit
20 Couple's org.
21 High-pitched
24 Moon valleys
27 One of the Chaplins
28 Fineness
29 Crash sound
31 Dire
34 St. Paul's top
35 See 42 Across
36 1964 Berne best seller (and a hint to seven other answers in this puzzle)
39 Falls off
40 D.J. Jazzy Jeff songs
41 Orders of the court
42 With 35 Across, a cleanser
43 Lean
44 So-so grade
45 Hears tell of
47 Least prevalent
50 Comedian's date
51 Wallops
52 Writer Buruma
54 Went chop-chop?
57 After-dinner drink
60 Breezing through
61 Lifeless
62 Italian summit
63 Matter for the Federal Trade Commission

DOWN

1 Butcher's cut of meat
2 Reply to a knock
3 East, in Berlin
4 School org.
5 Country music's Tennessee Plowboy
6 Lacy dress trimming
7 Judge
8 Track-meet measure: Abbr.
9 Amaze
10 From the sticks
11 Nice article
12 Diamonds
13 Asian holiday
14 U.S.N. rank
20 Computer dot
22 One of Adlai's running mates
23 Toodle-oos
24 Beef roasts
25 Princess __ ("Don Carlos" figure)
26 Anwar of Egypt
28 Nuts
30 N.L. M.V.P., 1954 and 1965
31 Becomes gray
32 Intriguing group
33 Like Uriah Heep
34 __ list
35 Tear
37 Tine
38 Jug
43 George Washington, e.g.
44 Harrah's, e.g.
46 Representative
47 Style of type
48 Twine fiber
49 Flavorsome
51 Relative of lotto
53 Born
54 Son of Noah
55 Umberto of Italy
56 Be lucky in the lottery
57 Turn down
58 Bit of advice
59 Latin I verb

34 *by Brett Blaylock*

ACROSS

1 Game with numbers 1 to 20
6 Crosby to Hope, often
12 Adulterate
13 Deceptive alloys
15 One who's left holding the bag?
16 Pontiac model
17 Definitely not ascetic
19 Gulf War combatant
20 __ ski
21 Thrombus
23 Mini-peninsula
24 Hautboy, e.g.
25 Capital east of Jerusalem
27 Exact point
28 Roy Orbison's "__ Baby"
30 Silo fan
32 George C. Scott feature
35 Fox
37 English martyr
41 French cooking staple
42 Those opposed
44 Wagner's earth goddess
45 Opportunist
47 Chinese: Prefix
48 Spirit
49 Postulate
51 Flagging conversation?
53 Headstrong
55 Pedigreed
56 Personal personnel
57 __ in (curbed)
58 American saint and family
59 Sniggler

DOWN

1 A fiancée of Napoleon
2 Kindergarten book
3 Nerve branch
4 Slavic sovereign
5 People of the Five Nations
6 Something you go by
7 Eight-time Norris Trophy winner
8 __ to say
9 Brown and others
10 Reach in amount
11 More fit
12 Smart
14 Clobber
15 Boy Scouts of America founder
18 January birthstone
22 Tahitian dish
26 Shuttle group
29 Former U.S. poet laureate __ Van Duyn
31 Bell's ringer?
33 __ best friend
34 Master hands
35 Lives
36 Ennoble
38 Hatchery
39 Put on a pedestal
40 Like a newborn
41 Sweetie
43 Funereal, in Folkestone
46 Word on a bill
48 Baby
50 Second leader
52 Away from harm's way
54 Wimple wearer

ACROSS

1 On which Irish linens are made
6 Chase flies
10 Krazy __
13 Fort Knox deposit
14 Part of U.N.C.F.
16 "Foucault's Pendulum" novelist
17 Festive
18 "The Informer" author
20 Not fair
22 Bits of history
23 Ye __ Shoppe
24 Mob
27 Stallone namesakes
28 Vex
29 Muddy
33 Mayberry resident
34 European capital
35 Draw __ on
39 Date
41 Sisal and Bombay, e.g.
42 Bucks for captives
44 Scuffle
46 "Hagar the Horrible" cartoonist
47 Conform
48 Yokel
52 Look for flaws
54 60's hit "Let __ Me"
55 Brewer of 50's pop
57 Presider in the 103d Congress
59 "Duffy of San Quentin" star
62 Bubbling
63 Remote
64 Circumspect
65 Donnybrook
66 To's opposite
67 Alphabet sequence
68 Put __ to

DOWN

1 Some dance contests
2 Josie Hogan creator
3 "Sweet Rosie __"
4 Samuel and Robert
5 Item in a pig's eye?
6 __-Cat (Aspen vehicle)
7 Playboy nickname
8 Lace tip
9 Most somber
10 Larry who played Tony
11 __ of the Apostles
12 G.I. Joe, e.g.
15 Character actor Dan
19 Lock up
21 Hardly a Prince Charming
25 Rainbow
26 Artist Georgia
30 Sire's mate
31 Stat for Alan Greenspan
32 All right
33 Mystery writer Lillian
35 Wall Street operator, for short
36 Kind of graph
37 Rock's Brian
38 Turning
40 Playwright Bogosian
43 Mark of the N.H.L.
45 "__ girl!"
48 13 1/2-ton tourist attraction
49 "Murphy's War" star
50 1940 Rockne portrayer
51 Pulled (in)
53 Blacktops
55 Bygone despot
56 Kind of dollars
58 Spiritual leader
59 Not working
60 Wiliness
61 Big Apple sch.

36 *by Joe Clonick*

ACROSS

1 Started wrongly?
9 Mouse
15 Number after 1?
16 Ravel's "__ for a Dead Princess"
17 Is in the running
18 Unimak Island inhabitants
19 Home folks
20 Adriatic seaport
22 Endangered whale
23 African tyrant and namesakes
25 Like a wolf's howl
26 Furnish
27 Legal landmarks
29 Digital clock's light emitter
30 La Plata locale: Abbr.
31 Gary Cooper-ish?
33 Like "The Persistence of Memory"
37 6-0, courtesy of Steffi
38 Immortal Pirate
40 French sea
41 It's bound to show the way
42 Site north of Frederick, Md.
47 Emblem on an English shield
48 Fabulous finish?
49 Stories
50 Health org.
51 Film makers' equipment
53 Certain degrees: Abbr.
54 Crumples
56 Aeronautical inclination
58 Army command
59 Casts an absentee ballot

60 Designer Norman Bel __
61 TV address, in short

DOWN

1 Cut the mustard
2 Cheap jewelry material
3 Anyone's game?
4 Angkor __
5 Noted rapper
6 Host of a short-lived talk show
7 Swirls
8 Utah's early name
9 Outpouring
10 Hearty accompaniment?
11 "__ Gotta Be Me"
12 Upset
13 Double __
14 Junk-mail addressee
21 A rug
24 1984 Jeff Bridges role
26 Not loose
28 Manitoba Indians
29 Went under
32 Puts a wrap on
33 No-goodnik
34 Superlative
35 Fed the Colt again
36 Maj.'s superior
39 Frostbite preventers
43 École employee
44 Scroll-shaped ornament
45 Decrees
46 Have an aversion to
48 Acts hangdog
51 Early actress Eleanora
52 God of destruction
55 Downcast
57 Name in voyeurism

ACROSS

1 Spit the kabobs
7 __ Noël (holiday figure)
11 Nosy Parker
12 Accommodating
14 At her small condo, actress Glenn was __
17 "The __ Progress"
18 1903 Nobelist
19 "Go, team!"
20 Time for les vacances
21 Mount
22 Foreign-exchange cost
23 Novelist Buntline
24 French friend's pronoun
25 Failing
27 Hot spots
29 Levels
30 In her corset, actress Beatrice was __
34 Operetta composer
35 Kind of cake
36 Cowcatcher
38 Before time
39 Friday, e.g.: Abbr.
42 "__ may look on a king": Heywood
43 Hold forth
46 Broadway's "High __"
47 Cal. pages
48 Kind of bar
49 V sign
51 The holiday gathering at actress Betty's was __
54 Bolt down
55 Click beetles
56 Retreats
57 Watch mechanism

DOWN

1 Natural
2 Chaffed
3 Axis end
4 Army addresses
5 Guitarist __ Paul
6 Making a stand?
7 Scotland yards?
8 Republic since 1948
9 Unloyal sort
10 Make it keep going, and going, and . . .
11 Lorelei
12 Unvarnished
13 Finished second
15 Canadian prov.
16 Brake equipment
21 Recital works
22 Put on __
24 Miss America prop
26 Clean
27 Deadly reptile
28 Skittish
30 Dugongs
31 Drubbed
32 Did not move decisively
33 Wash
34 Source of fine fleece
37 Gin hounds
39 Bee's target
40 Tyke's four-wheeler
41 Lock
44 Ethnic group
45 "__ du lieber!"
48 Knock for a loop
49 Rel. of college boards
50 Cigar's end
52 Italian __
53 Réunion, e.g.

38 *by Ed Pegg Jr*

ACROSS

1 "__ Without a Cause"
6 Musical scale letters
11 Joker
14 Smell
15 Of great scope
16 Electric __
17 Proverb
18 Old-fashioned picture taker
20 Elevator name
22 Victory symbol
23 Norse Zeus
24 Candidate Landon
26 Was sore
28 Having divergent lines
29 Backside
31 DNA shapes
33 Letter getter
35 Seize
36 That lady
39 Make into a spiral
40 Book after Deuteronomy
42 Opposite of SSW
43 __ Mahal
45 12, at dice
46 Leisurely study
48 Eric of "Monty Python"
49 October gems
52 __ Rouge
54 Olive __
55 Sushi go-with
56 National anthem contraction
57 Author Irwin
59 Intercom
62 Smoldering spark
65 Unfashionable
66 "__ a Rainy Night" (1981 hit)
67 On top of
68 Formerly named
69 One of life's certainties, in a saying
70 Deep-__ (discarded)

DOWN

1 Type of computer chip
2 Historical time
3 Ticket booth
4 Discharge
5 Keats poem
6 Recede
7 Beg shamelessly
8 Trapped
9 European freshwater fish
10 Medicine watchdog: Abbr.
11 Uncared-for, as a lawn
12 Eagle's nest
13 Liver or thyroid
19 Extinct birds
21 Rhodes __
24 Jingle writers
25 Greg Evans cartoon
27 Use voodoo on
28 Crate up again
30 __ Jo, of the '88 Olympics
32 Coaxes
34 Mosquito marks
36 Train for the ring
37 __-burly
38 Artist's prop
41 __-fi
44 Diner music maker
45 "Kapow!"
46 Entreaty
47 __ Tuesday
49 Director Welles
50 Irritate
51 Not obtuse
53 Three-toed birds
56 Neighbor of Ark.
58 Both: Prefix
60 Acumen
61 Illiterates' signatures
63 The day before
64 Ruby

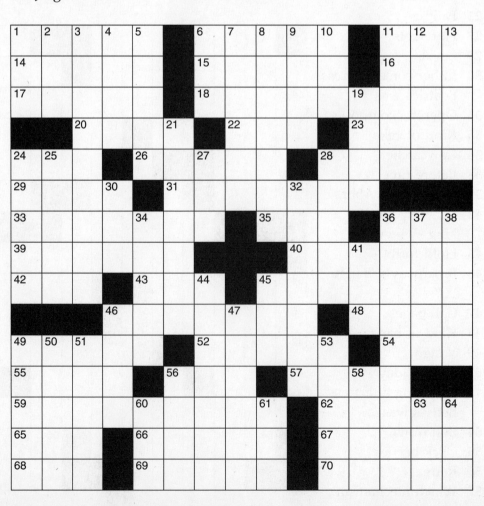

39 *by John Greenman*

ACROSS

1 Fitzgerald's forte
5 Shortening
9 "__ little piggy . . ."
13 Impetuous
14 Sunburn remedy
15 Rule the __
16 Agitate
17 Have on
18 Simone's school
19 Epithet for a TV set
22 Jeanne or Thérèse: Abbr.
23 Believer in God
24 Podunk
30 Eucharistic plate
31 Lascivious looks
32 Set-to
35 On __ with (equal to)
36 High in pitch
37 Mongol monk
38 Bandman Brown
39 Baseball's Doubleday
41 Bank patron
42 Fixation
44 "Queenie" author Michael
46 Get a move on
47 Gambler's tormentor
53 Beau __
54 Flub
55 Eye layer
57 Take back to the car pound
58 Axlike tool
59 60's vocalist Vikki
60 German river
61 "Let's Make a Deal" choice
62 Make a cable stitch

DOWN

1 Last year's jrs.
2 Marcus Porcius
3 M __ Mary
4 Farm machine
5 Maker of cases
6 Not aweather
7 Abbey or Tobacco, e.g.
8 Suffix for 41-Down
9 Alarm bell
10 Catcalls
11 Wee atoll
12 Ending for hip or hoop
15 Extends a subscription
20 School founded in 1440
21 Fragrance
24 October birthstone
25 Place for a necklace clasp
26 Hellenic H's
27 Obliqueness
28 Moray pursuer
29 Aquarium fish
32 Sitarist Shankar
33 Bodement
34 Voting district
37 Politician with a limited future
39 Hurricane of 1992
40 Smile broadly
41 Word before deep or dive
42 Demosthenes, e.g.
43 Impatient one
44 Bumped impolitely
45 Spanish direction
47 Grimm villain
48 "Yipes!"
49 Old fogy
50 Dolt
51 Netman Lendl
52 Garr of "Tootsie"
56 Trump's "The __ of the Deal"

ACROSS

1 Outbuildings
6 Hobgoblin
10 "__ sesame"
14 Mischievous sprite
15 Selves
16 Nuclear reactor
17 Ahead of the times
19 Prefix with marketing
20 Sleep stage
21 Accurate
22 Made an incursion
24 Medicine that's not all it's promised to be
26 Bewails
27 Fictitious
30 Trigonometric function
32 Sashes
33 Oil city of Iran
34 Memorable period
37 Melts
40 It may be penciled in
42 Ott or Gibson
43 Appraised
45 Inland sea east of the Caspian
46 Rephrased
48 Lord Peter Wimsey's creator
50 Caper
52 Uproar
54 Evades
56 __ of arms
57 Small amount
60 Woodwind instrument
61 Restaurant special
64 Add-on
65 Swearword
66 Valletta is its capital
67 Not the pictures
68 Nautical chains
69 Stocking material

DOWN

1 Box
2 Busy place
3 Word with eye or final
4 Gunga __
5 Resolve
6 __ Arts
7 Monstrously cruel
8 The Almighty
9 River to the North Sea
10 Right to purchase
11 Secondary residence
12 Actress Burstyn
13 Desiderata
18 Electric power network
23 Astound
24 Noted lioness
25 Take new vows
27 Froth
28 French ecclesiastic
29 Love letter
31 Low island
33 Fall bloomer
35 Bellow
36 Piercing tools
38 Instant
39 __ one's words
41 Reddish-brown horses
44 Give a little learning
47 Reader's __
48 Miner's nail
49 Cooling-off time
50 Take as one's own
51 Aristocratic
53 Closet pests
55 Espy
57 Kewpie, e.g.
58 Prefix with graph or crat
59 Breakfast fiber source
62 Ballad
63 Blue bird

41 *by Ernie Furtado*

ACROSS

1 Dogpatch's creator
5 Palindromic term of address
9 Talked, old-style
14 Nose tweaker
15 Willa Cather's "One of __"
16 With sickly pallor
17 Dream
18 Till's bills
19 Rags-to-riches writer
20 Start of an old motto
22 List ender
23 Shooter ammo
24 Part 2 of motto
26 Take-__ (accompaniers)
29 __ of one's own medicine
30 Part 3 of motto
31 Bulldog
32 Twosome
36 Martinique, e.g.
37 Environmentally minded, for short
39 Hook shape
41 "Don't Bring Me Down" rock group
42 Miami's county
44 Blanche in "The Golden Girls"
46 Part 4 of motto
48 Particle
50 Conquering hero
51 Part 5 of motto
54 Aerialist's safeguard
55 Theater people
56 End of motto
61 Sightseeing sight
62 Golfer Isao __
63 Singleton
64 Ball
65 A night in Paris
66 Exterior: Prefix
67 Blackthorn shrubs
68 1949 erupter
69 Creep through the cracks

DOWN

1 Search thoroughly
2 Together, musically
3 On hold
4 Make believe
5 Heath
6 Godmother, often
7 Rings of color
8 Orig. texts
9 Mower's trails
10 Mouth parts
11 White, informally
12 Last name in fashion
13 Nest for 21-Down: Var.
21 See 13-Down
22 "Me" types
25 Thumb-twiddling
26 Fatty __
27 Refrain part
28 1985 Danielle Steel best seller
33 Regretfulness
34 Choir voice
35 Koh-i-__ (famed diamond)
38 Pinch reaction
40 Cut of meat
43 Nitty-gritty
45 Just managed
47 Streets
49 Medea's ill-fated uncle
51 Miss Muffet edible
52 Business as __
53 Zoo heavyweight
57 Related
58 Comic Rudner
59 Spot
60 "Avast!"
62 Actress Sue __ Langdon

ACROSS

1 Mercury or Mars
4 Good old boy
9 Double-crosser
14 1979 film "Norma __"
15 W.W. I battle site
16 Pomme de __ (French potato)
17 Modern bank "employee": Abbr.
18 "__ in Venice"
19 Feeling regret
20 Night photographer's work, with "a"?
23 Common connectors
24 Bother
25 Wears well
27 Kind of budget
32 Dustin, in "Midnight Cowboy"
33 Actress Ward of "Sisters"
34 Exist
35 Like an inept photographer's subject?
39 Christina's dad
40 Snoop Doggy Dogg songs
41 Plays
42 Indy and Daytona
45 Classified
46 Sleep stage: Abbr.
47 Family member
48 Photojournalists' choices?
54 "__ Paradiso" (1966 film)
56 Catalyst
57 Mining area
58 "__ of robins in her hair"
59 San __, Calif.
60 Chemical suffix
61 Mill, to a cent
62 Embellish
63 __ Guinea

DOWN

1 Fat, in France
2 Vow
3 Floor model
4 Owing to
5 Defeats
6 Imps
7 One of the March sisters
8 Netman Arthur
9 Road, in Roma
10 Reflex messenger
11 Composer Satie
12 Prince Valiant's son
13 Fraternity party staple
21 "Jerusalem Delivered" poet
22 __ Lama
25 Author Esquivel
26 Greek
27 Computer sounds
28 Swiss range
29 Trigger
30 Fumbled
31 Grades below the curve
32 Surf sound
33 Open carriage
36 Chaplin persona
37 Shadow-y surname?
38 __-frutti
43 One of the Gallos
44 Affluence
45 Spoiler
47 Vinegar: Prefix
48 British gun
49 Lady of Spain
50 "Holy moly!"
51 Unrestricted
52 Supreme Court complement
53 Brood
54 Topper
55 Single

43 *by Jonathan Schmalzbach*

ACROSS

1 Send a Dear John letter
5 Antarctica's ___ Coast
10 Stain on Santa
14 Medicinal herb
15 "Golden" song
16 Clinton Transportation Secretary Federico
17 Prefix with bucks or bytes
18 Ad: Part 1
20 Ad: Part 2
22 And others
23 Lennon's lady
24 Clinches
25 Ad: Part 3
28 Ad: Part 4
33 Beats
34 Judge
35 Dogpatch diminutive
36 Cabbies' credentials: Abbr.
37 Jabbed
38 Radio knob
39 And so forth, for short
40 Singular person
41 Gladiator's place
42 Medium in which this puzzle's ad appeared
45 Furnishes for a time
46 Twilights, poetically
47 Richmond was its cap.
48 Queen Victoria's husband
51 Ad: Part 5
55 Sponsor of the ad
57 Snead and Spade
59 15 miles of song
60 Floor pieces
61 Wasatch Range state
62 Prepared to drive
63 Unclogs
64 Glazier's section

DOWN

1 Predicament
2 "___ a song go . . ."
3 CBS's eye, e.g.
4 Genteel snack spots
5 Topper's first name
6 Wings
7 Peculiar: Prefix
8 Clear
9 Downcast
10 Quite an impression
11 Trompe l'___
12 "Dedicated to the ___ Love"
13 Noted Chaplin follower
19 Shoshoneans
21 Responsibility
24 Buries
25 Shiftless one
26 ___ Bandito of commercials
27 New Mexico's state flower
28 Offenses
29 "The Old ___ Bucket"
30 Martian or Venusian
31 Article of food
32 Actress Raines and others
37 Indicates
38 Concocts
41 In addition
43 Adjudged
44 "Buona ___" (Italian greeting)
47 Judit Polgar's game
48 Help a crook
49 Bait
50 Spreadable cheese
51 Tempest
52 Browning locale
53 "Do I dare to ___ peach?": Eliot
54 Muscat's land
56 Fashionable
58 That girl

44 *by Harvey Estes*

ACROSS

1 Annie, for one
7 Sandwich often on toast
10 "__ 'em!"
13 Took refuge
15 __ rights (police suspect's entitlement)
17 Bomber type
18 Noted Richard III portrayer
19 Congressional funding?
21 Memory unit
22 R. E. Lee's land
23 Three-time World Cup medalist
27 Many a time
29 It borders Tenn.
33 Declaration
36 Taj Mahal, e.g.
39 Most-wanted poster letters
40 Vatican Museum holdings?
43 __ out a living
44 First name in game shows
45 "Brace yourself!"
46 He played Fred on "Sanford and Son"
48 Trading-bloc inits.
50 Particles
51 Make __ story (lie)
54 Famous sewer
57 Vacation slides?
64 Tank gas
65 Forked over
67 Nineveh's nation
68 "Great Expectations" miss
69 Ben in the film "Ben"
70 O.K.
71 Well-__ (rich)

DOWN

1 Cries
2 Campus mil. grp.
3 __-bargain
4 Jalopy
5 Make up on the spot
6 Harebrained
7 Coll. V.I.P.
8 Shade of purple
9 Stumbles
10 Irritated state
11 Bit of brainwork
12 Baseball's Yastrzemski
14 Pic
16 Birdy?
20 Table scraps
23 On __ (theoretically)
24 Call forth
25 Ran at an easy pace
26 Lamb producer
28 Stroller passenger
30 Freighter filler
31 Ohio city
32 Pours
34 Provide weapons
35 Caustic
37 55 letters?
38 Fancy neckwear
41 Start to dominate
42 One at the beginning
47 Hardly svelte
49 Two-door vehicle
52 Admiral in the Arctic
53 Nickname in the Senior P.G.A.
55 Tennis kill
56 Bash, biblically
57 Boom or box
58 Nocturnal bear
59 "Make the __ of it"
60 Votes for
61 "Zip-__-Doo-Dah"
62 Undulate
63 Christmastime
66 Itsy bit

ACROSS

1 Spring runner
4 Pole at sea
9 Dieter's measure
13 Robust drink
14 Delete-key function
15 TV tease
16 Golf ball's position
17 Sedaka and Simon
18 Play the fink
19 "Falstaff"
22 Marked down
23 "The Woman in the Dunes" author
24 It's big in London
25 Hard or soft approach
27 Scout's group
30 Quatrain's pattern
33 Seville snack
35 Sister of Charlotte
37 "The Misfits"
40 Barkin of "Sea of Love"
41 Genealogist's work
42 It may be cured
43 Monaco cube
44 Speech site
46 Actress Carrie
48 Cobbler's tool
49 Imperfect bridge holding
53 Homer #521
59 Blotter entry
60 Waugh and others
61 Eunuch's unit
62 Disk-shaped marine fish
63 Challenger's quest
64 Political abbr.
65 Hound's quarry
66 Semicircular recesses
67 Wordsworth's "We __ Seven"

DOWN

1 Military blast
2 Refuge seeker
3 Duke and earl
4 More than forgetful
5 Favors
6 Tout's post
7 __ Mujeres, Mexico
8 Chester Gould femme
9 Smooth-skinned edible
10 Learning method
11 It makes the mundus go round
12 Actress Washbourne
15 Gordian knot, for one
20 Show amateurish interest (in)
21 Chess's Mikhail
25 Works with Riddick Bowe
26 Facility
27 Belly flop, e.g.
28 Lamb of yore
29 "No way, Sergei!"
30 Elderly
31 Java neighbor
32 Up to snuff
34 Choral voices
36 Tick of time
38 On edge
39 Seaquarium arm
45 Like
47 Swains' requests
48 Like Pegasus
50 Now, in Nogales
51 Autumn beverage
52 Marchers' camp
53 Wear's partner
54 Chase of Tinseltown
55 Pre-rehab Pinocchio
56 __ Hari
57 Underdress
58 "__ Do It" (Porter tune)

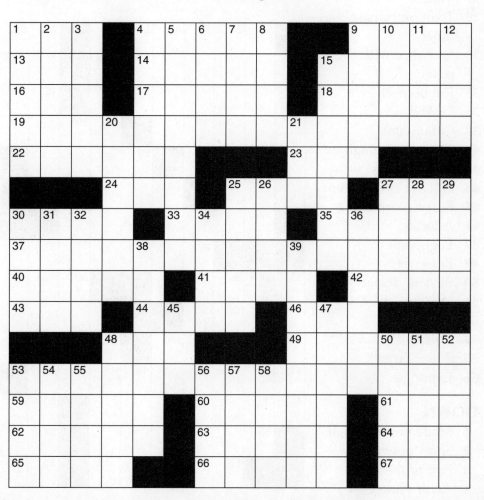

ACROSS

1 Kind of fair
7 10th-century English king
12 Walden Pond habitué
13 One found in the stacks
15 Bandit's cry
16 Fine-wooled sheep
18 Beehives, for instance
19 From 8 to 11
21 Venison
22 Alda of "M*A*S*H"
23 "Cheaper by the __"
24 Baseballer Maglie
25 View
26 Antique autos
27 Vain
29 Temporary hair tinter
30 Romance with the past
33 Rubberneck
36 Linked
39 Catamount
40 Thumbs through
41 __ out (relax)
43 Not very competent
45 Furry companions
46 Allocate
47 Leggy one
49 Passengers
50 Birders' society
51 Duds
53 __ piece
54 Volunteers
55 Super buys
56 Expunge

DOWN

1 Mademoiselle's hat
2 Short poems
3 Fire of the mind
4 Actor Parker
5 Letter after sigma
6 Most limber
7 King's fur
8 Consider
9 Rose up, in dialect
10 Newspaper part
11 Inhabitant
12 Dropping sounds
14 Lovers
17 Sixth __
20 Searched thoroughly
22 Old radio favorite "Easy __"
25 __ gin
28 Delight beyond measure
29 Splits
31 Dawdled
32 Teeth holders
33 Bright star in Virgo
34 Mechanic's job
35 Revised
37 Hillary's conquest
38 Political thaw
40 Shells out
42 Hero's exploits
44 Shinbone
46 Actress Van Doren
48 Lifeguard's beat
49 Satisfy
52 One, in Aberdeen

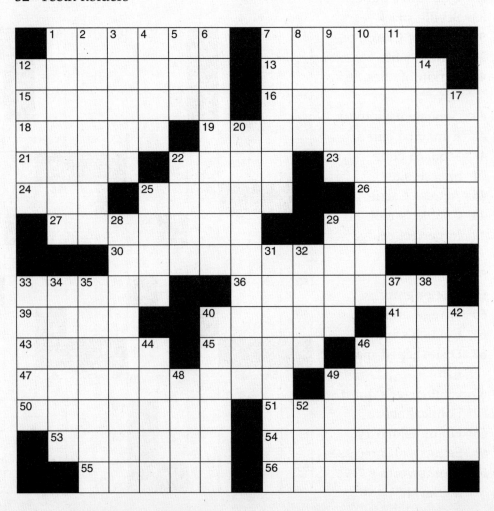

47 *by Trip Payne*

ACROSS
1 Wrought-up
6 City near Phoenix
10 Melodramatic cry
14 Cottonwood, in Spanish
15 Burns one up
16 Perambulate
17 One past his prime
20 On the other hand
21 Essentials
22 Summer top
23 Skedaddle
24 Wish
25 Least significant
28 Bluesman Robert
29 Coffee-break brake
32 Independently
33 "You there!"
34 Relief pitcher's feat
35 Hot time
38 Makes like
39 Man with a lift
40 Échecs piece
41 N.Y.C. cultural site
42 Litigant
43 Most fit
44 Sir overseas
45 Biter
46 Plays the zither
49 Picked up on
50 __ Vicente, Brazil
53 It won Hepburn an Oscar
56 One of the O'Neills
57 Iditarod terminus
58 World's largest cobalt exporter
59 Attributes
60 Gumption
61 Register

DOWN
1 Lots
2 Tissue addition
3 Santa drawer
4 Dennis the Menace, e.g.

5 Site of a May 1942 battle
6 Chop finely
7 Work units
8 Dry
9 Camels' destinations?
10 Marquis protagonist
11 Hel's father, in myth
12 Maintain
13 Faxed
18 "Yeah, sure!"
19 Brit's phrase
23 Wards (off)
24 Instructors, for short
25 Mary Stewart's "__, Will You Talk?"
26 Waive one's rites?
27 Physician-turned-wordsmith

28 The Mighty Clouds of Joy, e.g.
29 Farr of "M*A*S*H"
30 Hot spots
31 Nice topper
33 Daisylike bloom
34 Silvery fish
36 Elton John's first hit
37 Make citified
42 Penultimate round
43 From square one
44 Great shakes?
45 "The Maids" playwright
46 Quash
47 What you used to be
48 Flat rate
49 __ Valley, Calif.
50 The joint

51 Prefix with space or stat
52 Mr. Hershiser
54 Postal Creed word
55 Children's author Agle

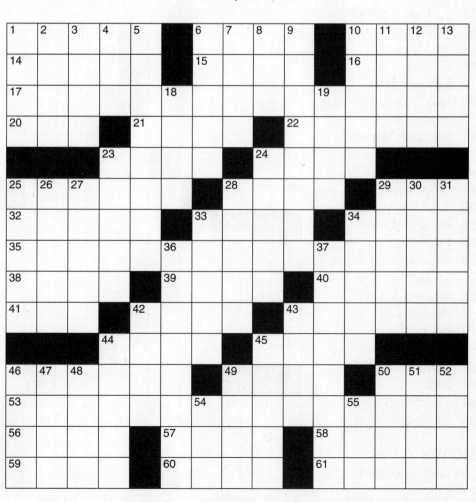

48 *by Manny Nosowsky*

ACROSS

1 Challenge authority
6 Acronym since 1960
10 Off one's trolley
14 Napoleon, twice
15 Shake makers
17 Guys may be attached to them
18 Appendectomy, for one
19 Mimic
21 Covers with a blanket
22 Subject of a Thomas Gray ode
23 Panama, e.g.
25 Physicist's __ jar
29 Hearing aid?
30 Divine __
32 Compelled
33 Superficial pretenses
35 __-Day vitamins
36 Words on romance by Virgil
40 Similar
41 Schoolwork
42 Hold, as one's attention
44 Musical "repeat" sign
45 Calendar mo.
48 More expensive
50 "Get the point?"
51 Marginal mark
52 Give it __
54 Bad weather for a sailor
56 Dessert for the mistaken?
60 Loose
61 Kind of booth
62 Gods' blood
63 Moist
64 Watch over
65 Energetic

DOWN

1 Convene after a break
2 Combo bet at Belmont
3 King's neighbor
4 First name in rock
5 Majesty preceder
6 Bernardo's bear
7 Acts on the basis of 36-Across
8 Churchill successor
9 Sing door-to-door
10 Famous standard maker
11 Mr. Onassis
12 Referee's decision
13 Nine-digit ID: Abbr.
16 Shot the breeze
20 Zoo critters
24 Ten-percenters
26 Honorific of Spain
27 Stuntman Knievel
28 "Hud" Oscar winner
30 Kind of room
31 Walk wearily
33 With worthiness of respect
34 Nets
36 Kitchen staple, once
37 Steinbeck emigrant
38 Brando's "__ Zapata!"
39 Pierce Arrow competitor
43 Nikola the inventor
45 At __ door
46 "thirty-something" character
47 Stick in the salad?
49 Mitchell hero
51 Not a whiz kid
53 Andy Griffith's TV son
55 "Jeopardy!" is one
56 Shrouded
57 Purpose
58 Trim
59 Finale

ACROSS

1 Use a letter opener
5 Dadaist poet Tristan
10 Bus. bigwigs
14 Bear of "very little brain"
15 Grant portrayer
16 Emerald City princess
17 Cogwheel comparison?
20 Skewers
21 Nuke
22 Tool for Bo-Peep
23 Focuses
25 Emmy winner Arthur
26 Totaled car, perhaps?
33 Made a touchdown
34 Got ruined in the wash
35 Manche capital
36 Sci-fi regulars
37 Quieted with Quaalude
40 "Do — say!"
41 Brews
43 Palm (off)
44 Financial success
46 Inflamed toe cause?
49 Big Ben?
50 Mayberry boy
51 Math discovery
54 Nameless one
56 Nolan Ryan was one
60 Mega-marathon?
63 Arabic name starter
64 Christmas Eve flier
65 Eye at the beach
66 Botch
67 Into pieces
68 Source of abundance

DOWN

1 Spring spots
2 Dropped, maybe
3 Isle near Mull
4 Bob Dylan back-up group
5 Make lace
6 Famed cop slapper
7 Anatomical loop
8 Glean
9 Dadaist painter Hans
10 Aiken and Hilton
11 Basso Pinza
12 "Typee" sequel
13 Dropped, maybe
18 Stage remarks
19 Bakery worker
24 Words before "TV" or "each other"
25 Crams
26 Hat-tipping cartoonist
27 Start
28 Curmudgeons
29 Eliot's "Jennyanydots" e.g.
30 Author Calvino
31 The Folger Lady, Mrs. —
32 Jet, at Orly?
33 Levi's mother
38 Bashes
39 Defense mechanism
42 Swimming classes?
45 Hides
47 Dennis the Menace's dog
48 Word with baby or schuss
51 Surrey carriage
52 "Mike and Ike" creator Goldberg
53 Heavy load
54 It's most useful when it's cracked
55 Prefix re honeycombs
57 Buster Brown's bulldog
58 Kaiser, e.g.
59 Like Nash's lama
61 Public works inits.
62 S. & L. accrual

50 *by Cathy Millhauser*

ACROSS

1 "Alice in Wonderland" figure
6 Disney classic
11 Overcrowding antidote, initially
14 In __ (prenatal)
15 Film director Resnais
16 Different ending
17 God
18 Minolta rival
19 Carrie married to Cavett
20 Modern choice #1
23 Former Swedish P.M. Ullsten
26 Ventnor or Vermont, e.g.: Abbr.
27 Sassoon creations
28 Modern choice #2
33 Theda "The Vamp"
34 Example, for example
35 Modern choice #3
42 Triple-layer treat
43 Cocoon-stage insect
45 Modern choice #4
51 Leading
52 She sang "At Seventeen"
53 Give a wave
54 Modern choice #5
59 That, in Spain
60 Suitor
61 Hoople or Houlihan
65 P.R. concern
66 "Unsafe at Any Speed" author
67 Logical starting point
68 First degs.
69 Plumbing tool
70 Gait problems

DOWN

1 Holy city of Iran
2 Tony winner Hagen
3 Comic book squeal
4 "__ Tu" ('74 hit)
5 Illinois State University site
6 Angel
7 Jai __
8 Jazz flutist Herbie
9 Life story: Abbr.
10 Greenhorn
11 Showy flower
12 Welcome culmination
13 Valleys
21 Caesar's salad ingredients?
22 "Arabian Nights" flyer
23 Globe
24 Riffle
25 Earthy prefix
29 Egypt and Syr., once
30 __ the other
31 Milne marsupial
32 It's "hard" for the French
36 "Do-si-do" dos
37 Muff
38 Car monogram of yore
39 Jupiter's mother
40 Courage
41 Bee's charge, in Mayberry
44 Shtick
45 Cycle parts
46 Word in a children's title
47 Contemptuous utterance
48 Coyote State capital
49 Shaver
50 Varmint
51 Bitter
55 Like Robinson Jeffers's stallion
56 End notes?
57 Need a bath
58 Approach the terminal
62 Lord of fiction
63 Alley from Moo
64 Apt. ad info

51 *by Sidney L. Robbins*

ACROSS

1 Women's mag
5 One-liners
9 Soccer legend
13 Egg-shaped
14 TV oldie "Green —"
16 Vientiane's land
17 Building code requirement
19 Prod
20 Pilgrim John
21 Most pleasant
23 Madam's mate
25 July 4, 1776, e.g.
26 Opposite of vert.
29 W. Hemisphere org.
32 Mr. Arnaz
34 The lowdown on dancing?
36 Kind of car or sandwich
38 Use a crayon
41 Ratted (on)
42 Armbone
43 By oneself
44 Writer Hunter
45 Hauls
46 Stimulate, as curiosity
47 Measure out
48 Provence city
50 Stalin ruled it
52 "The Bridge of San Luis —"
53 Stephen of "The Crying Game"
54 Late tennis V.I.P.
57 Dawn goddess
59 Lustrous fabric
61 "Faust," for one
65 Shocked sound
67 Summer treat
70 Matures
71 Go 1-1 in a doubleheader
72 Letterman's "Top Ten," e.g.
73 Model's position
74 "Auld Lang —"
75 Not so much

DOWN

1 Divan
2 "Hear no — . . ."
3 Cooking fat
4 Hightails it
5 Oil alternative
6 U.N.C. and U.Va. grp.
7 In a lofty style
8 Artist's brown
9 +
10 Bulldozer
11 Captain's record
12 Language suffix
15 Church offshoot
18 Arthurian lady
22 Slippery one
24 Sum up
27 Not quite spherical
28 Los Angeles motorist King
29 Of the eyes
30 Magnetism
31 Shades
33 By oneself: Prefix
35 News entry
37 Home port
39 Burden
40 Hall-of-Famer Pee Wee
49 Was in session
51 Motel vacancy
55 Does needlework
56 Mounds
58 "How do you — relief?"
60 Church nook
62 Writer Wiesel
63 Flagmaker Betsy
64 Picnic pests
65 Cumberland, e.g.
66 In the past
68 One for Wilhelm
69 Numbered rd.

52 *by Joel Davajan*

ACROSS

1 Atop
5 Clubbed
10 Motes
14 New York Cosmos star
15 Chou __
16 Oklahoma tribesman
17 Lord Nelson site
20 Part of an electrical switch
21 Zeroes
22 Hectored
23 Sans verve
24 Medicament
27 Winter woe
28 Ottoman official
31 The Donald's ex
32 Fly like Lindbergh
33 Aits in Arles
34 Prepare for an Indian attack
37 Raison d'__
38 30's actress Grey and others
39 Nighttime noise
40 Beam
41 Sponsorship
42 Feeds a furnace
43 Belgian river
44 Baseball union boss Donald
45 Like llamas
48 Sends quickly
52 Ships' drop-off location?
54 Sea flyer
55 Gnawed away
56 Composition closure
57 Crazy bird?
58 Monopoly payments
59 Formerly

DOWN

1 Goes (for)
2 __ Beach, Fla.
3 Airline to Jerusalem
4 Testimonial
5 It's hummed
6 1973 hit by the Rolling Stones
7 Covered
8 The "E" in E.N.T.
9 Prohibit
10 Wampum
11 I-70's western terminus
12 Ilk
13 Golf course 18
18 Of some electrodes
19 Printer's spacer
23 Tree trunks
24 Potato preparer
25 "Requiem for __"
26 Take the plunge
27 Lawyer Roy M. and others
28 "Take __ at this!"
29 Type
30 Bridge of __ (Euclid proposition)
32 Way up?
33 Blissful state?
35 Produce
36 Wheezing cause
41 Birthright seller
42 TV listing
43 Modern-day Sheba
44 Tops
45 Ex-steelworkers chief
46 Fiery fiddler
47 1962 Bond villain
48 Solar disk
49 Mr. Stravinsky
50 Lawyers' degrees
51 Install in office
53 "__ you sure?"

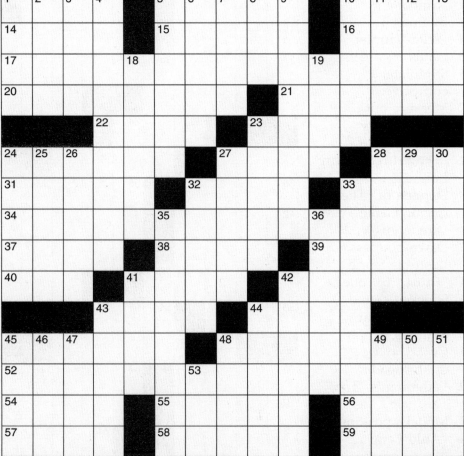

ACROSS

1 Child's getaway
5 Nurse's stick
9 Malpractice target
14 Margarine
15 Part of a cash register
16 Sam or Tom, e.g.
17 Businessperson's oxymoron
20 Crowbar
21 Runner Devers
22 Sums
23 "Get __!"
25 Cut up
27 Vipers
30 Indignant person's oxymoron
35 Actor Erwin
36 Breezy
37 Refer (to)
38 Dinner bird
40 Command to Fido
42 Jewish dinner
43 Mideast language
45 Flood survivor
47 W.W. II grp.
48 Oxymoron for a homely person
50 Cheek
51 Riches' opposite
52 Took a powder
54 Jacob's brother
57 Bare
59 Speechify
63 Coffee drinker's oxymoron
66 Passé
67 Within: Prefix
68 Model married to David Bowie
69 Steeple
70 Slumber
71 Library item

DOWN

1 Monk's hood
2 Lotion ingredient
3 Former talk-show host
4 Fireplace equipment
5 Penn, e.g.: Abbr.
6 Belly dancers
7 Edison's middle name
8 Mathematician Pascal
9 Sine __ non
10 Straighten out
11 Sarcasm
12 Dolt
13 Barbies' mates
18 Enrage
19 Bow of silents
24 Black bird
26 Three-time Super Bowl–winning coach
27 Tin Pan Alley org.
28 One of the Beatles
29 Chrysalises
31 In competition
32 Lindley of "The Ropers"
33 Creativity
34 Indoor balls
36 Writer Loos
39 Busybody
41 Stashes
44 Caesar's swans
46 Certain vote
49 Shylock
50 Magellan, e.g.
53 Lee to Grant
54 Concludes
55 It's seen in bars
56 Against
58 Unit of force
60 BB's
61 Word after "go!"
62 Sea eagle
64 Humorist George
65 "Oh, darn!"

54 *by Joel Davajan*

ACROSS

1 Christiania today
5 Noggin tops
10 Hind's mate
14 Hullabaloo
15 Open-eyed
16 "Damn Yankees" vamp
17 Ike was one
20 Track officials
21 Testify
22 "Rule, Britannia" composer
23 Early Briton
24 Social groups
27 Garlic relative
28 Asian holiday
31 Culture mores
32 Coxswain's crew
33 __ Marquette
34 G.I. newspaper
37 Cures leather
38 "That's interesting"
39 Opt
40 Two-by-two vessel
41 Reared
42 Worth
43 Shed
44 Escape
45 Roman villa locale
48 Apollyon adherent
52 Biblical beacon
54 Seller's caveat
55 Backcomb hair
56 Mechanical memorization
57 Smoker's sound
58 Mead research site
59 Animal team

DOWN

1 Switch settings
2 Eye opening
3 Kind of flow
4 Bell workers
5 Thin metal disks
6 Cognizant
7 Salts
8 Dr.'s graph
9 Most rundown
10 Nodded
11 Pamplona runner
12 Hale of "Gilligan's Island"
13 10 on the Beaufort scale
18 Pressure
19 Spoon
23 Intrinsically
24 Jai alai basket
25 It makes scents
26 Part of the evening
27 Put on cargo
28 Dakota digs
29 Upright
30 Blood and acid, e.g.
32 Beginning
33 Bohemian beers
35 Berlin events of 1948
36 Recap
41 Machetelike knife
42 Wimbledon champ Gibson
43 Code name
44 1980 DeLuise flick
45 Royal Russian
46 "__ girl!"
47 Ski spot
48 Coal stratum
49 Hotcakes acronym
50 Bristle
51 Revenuers, for short
53 "__ sport"

ACROSS

1 John Denver's "Christmas in __"
6 "Tuna-Fishing" painter
10 Among
14 "__ Eyes" (1969 song)
15 Actor Richard
16 Bounty rival
17 Refinement
18 Witticisms
19 Vigor
20 1950 Sinatra hit
23 West Bank org.
24 "Just a __"
25 Three strokes, perhaps
28 Actress Sommer
31 Shares
36 Feared test
38 Troubles
40 Weaken
41 1955 Sinatra hit
44 Improve
45 Rig
46 Shut off
47 Beachwear
49 Relax
51 Audit conductor, for short
52 Guy's date
54 Eternity
56 1961 Sinatra hit
64 "Warm"
65 Minnow eater
66 Driving hazard
68 Petruchio's mate
69 Shillelagh land
70 10th-day-of-Christmas gift
71 Swerve
72 Henna and others
73 Follow

DOWN

1 Blue-chip symbol
2 Lively dance
3 Chihuahua change
4 Bar, in law
5 Compass part
6 Half begun?
7 Excited
8 Stucco backing
9 Foot part
10 Swear
11 Ryun's run
12 Basil's successor
13 Niels Bohr, e.g.
21 The Man Without a Country
22 More aloof
25 Propels a gondola
26 Bouquet
27 Bird "perched upon a bust of Pallas"
29 Toddlers
30 Dramatist Rice
32 Goddess of discord
33 Raccoon kin
34 Lawn tool
35 Is apparent
37 Impart
39 Ditto
42 Saw
43 Elevated
48 Stood up
50 Kind of switch
53 Distrustful
55 Run site
56 Prepares the presses
57 Plumber's concern
58 Behind
59 Ale
60 Pennsylvania port
61 Roadhouses
62 They go into locks
63 Relative of Hindustani
67 Volte-face WNW

ACROSS

1 "Spare tire"
5 Ferris wheel, e.g.
9 Shares quarters (with)
14 Furor
15 Airline to Haifa
16 Point with intent to shoot
17 General Bradley
18 Yarn irregularity
19 Roman goddess of flowers
20 Notorious 30's criminal
23 Smoker's intake
24 Subterfuge
25 German physicist Georg
28 Skin problem
31 Chinese veggie
35 F. ___ Bailey
36 Shankar's strings
38 Unaccompanied
39 Notorious 30's criminal
43 Killer whale
44 Massenet opera
45 Links position
46 Some flights
49 Janet of Justice
50 Mark's competitor
51 Quite ready
53 Road warning
55 Notorious 30's criminal
62 By radio, e.g.
63 New York Public Library figure
64 Cheater's aid
66 Rubbish
67 War god
68 He wrote "My Way" for Sinatra
69 Misogynist
70 Communications leader?
71 Walter ___ Hospital

DOWN

1 To's opposite
2 Reader's aid
3 Seaweed derivative
4 Special Forces cap
5 Put in a straitjacket
6 Not wisely
7 Smear
8 Pipe joint
9 Church drawing
10 Subject of the Teapot Dome scandal
11 Melville novel
12 ___ Tyler Moore
13 Native African village
21 Ankle bones
22 Pup's sound
25 Actor Edward James ___
26 Love, on bumper stickers
27 Muslim's holy place
29 Watch part
30 "Horrible" comic character
32 Parrot's moniker
33 North, of Irangate
34 Senior leader
37 Ancient letter
40 O'Neill play, with "The"
41 Balderdash
42 Hillock
47 Ransacker
48 Baden-Baden, e.g.
52 Razzle-dazzle
54 Filmdom honor
55 City near Bristol
56 Atmosphere
57 Englishman, in slang
58 Cork's locale
59 "The First ___"
60 Normandy river
61 Winged Victory
65 Spoiled

by Harvey Estes

ACROSS

1 They have pins at one end
6 Military bigwigs
11 Put in chips
13 Pan-fried
15 Mary Tyler Moore's old boss
16 Queen Victoria's family
17 Strikes out, perhaps
18 Nautilus habitat
20 Unflattering
21 Cub groups
22 Rock music's Tears for __
24 London essayist
25 Calendar periods: Abbr.
26 Posthumous Forster novel
28 Persuaded
29 San Francisco pants-maker
31 Ancient fly prison
33 Troubles
34 The hunted
35 Offer an apple in Eden
37 Threadbare
40 Spending limit
41 Taunted
43 Quangtri locale
45 Last words
47 Bearded
48 "The __ Report" (1976 best seller)
49 Buddy of Irene Ryan?
51 Record number?
52 Hay holders
53 Carbon attachment
55 They're sometimes tickled
57 Put under
58 Bond, once
59 Smarts
60 Lacks

DOWN

1 Painters' equipment
2 Con
3 Egg containers
4 Some eagles
5 Use the peepers
6 Ewe said it!
7 Scores of diamonds
8 Make up
9 Barber's town
10 Less upscale
11 Like abandoned gardens
12 "Hunches in Bunches" author
13 Lamb Chop's voice
14 More than misgivings
19 Shoots an average score
22 Deducted style points from
23 Like Capone's face
26 Ralph of "Happy Days"
27 Touch up
30 Canyon edge
32 Party letters
34 Political tract
35 Purr-fect pets?
36 Show piece
37 Station that went on the air in 1978
38 Like one 1992 Olympics team
39 Ragamuffin's attire
40 Sorority possibles
42 Gave a rap
44 Topsy-turvy
46 L.B.J., e.g.
48 Lena of "Stormy Weather"
50 Picky people pick them
52 Like a star for a 46 Down
54 River to the Irish Sea
56 Bismarck's predecessor

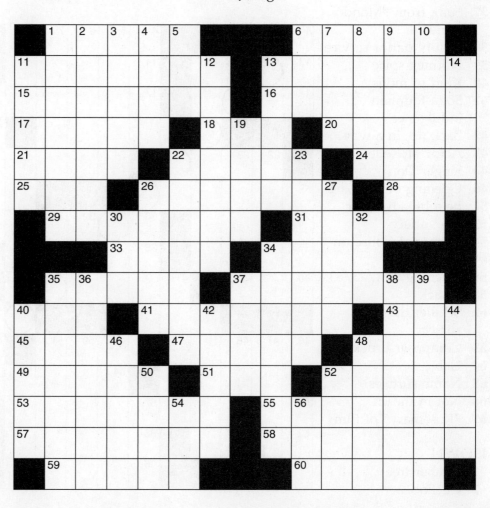

ACROSS

1 Swiss river
4 New Orleans's Vieux __
9 Child shot
12 Pique
14 Mix 'n match collections
15 Fisher's boat
16 Rhapsodic
17 Opening of 4/11/91
19 "My Cup Runneth Over" singer
21 Church teachings
22 Pitch
24 Opening of 3/13/47
26 Dialect
28 Beatles' "__ Mine"
29 Responsibility
30 Pope of 1775
34 Kitchen item
37 Song from "Mondo Cane"
38 Beauty parlor service
39 Nutmeg spice
40 Kind of money
41 Soda fountain indulgence
42 Back up, in a way
43 Actor McKellen
44 Singer Don
46 Opening of 3/26/64
52 Be a breadwinner
53 Flu variety
54 Memorial Coliseum player
56 Opening of 4/23/63
58 Smack
62 Schiller drama subject
63 Composer Bruckner
64 Gab
65 Name suffixes
66 Not in the __
67 "Rosemary" of film

DOWN

1 Timber tree
2 Cuckoo
3 Oil drilling equipment
4 Robin Cook best seller
5 Out on __
6 Stage stand
7 Martini's partner
8 Snake
9 In concealment
10 Advertising ploy
11 Theater critic Kenneth
13 1979 Midler film
15 Electron tube
18 "Turandot" librettist
20 Sixth-century date
22 Eastern capital
23 Often illegal auto maneuver
25 "__ Hell Harry"
26 Magnificence

27 Out of jail
31 "...kerchief and __ my cap"
32 Berlin connector
33 Retirees' agcy.
34 Flutter
35 Vast expanse
36 "Roberta" composer
39 Bunkum
41 "Just __"
43 Together
45 Medium grade
46 Crash diets
47 Poe family
48 Nobel physicist Bohr
49 Soames Forsyte wife
50 Certain Jamaican
51 Broadway cars
55 Parking mishap
57 Comics prince

59 "__ Woman" ('72 hit)
60 Astr. or biol.
61 Some popular music

DIAGONAL

1 Opening of 5/4/93

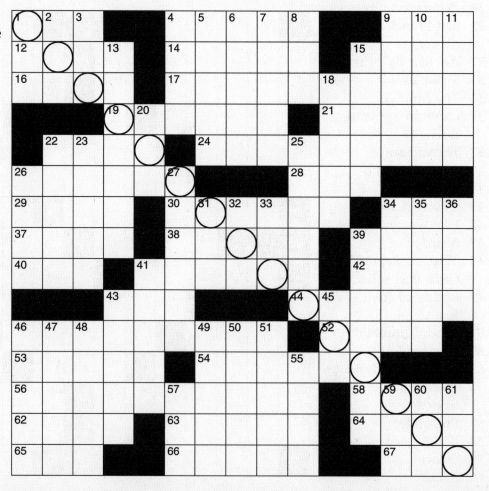

ACROSS

1 Name from 50's TV
9 Baseball's Doubleday
14 Romberg product
15 Filmdom's Lawrence
16 Infant's game
17 Infant's shoe
18 Showed fear
19 Stupidity
20 Sting
24 Mal de ___
26 Words of enlightenment
27 Mars sighting
29 Bestow
32 Blow the cover of?
34 Puts back
38 ___ Juana
39 Urban noise maker
41 Take this out for a spin
42 University founded in 1253
44 Locust
46 Exhortation
48 Pitcher Ryan
49 "___ of you . . ."
52 Ear-related
54 "The ___ From Brazil"
55 Defective stop sign?
58 "I ___ You Babe"
60 Yogi's cartoon sidekick
61 Blubbered
66 Like spring flowers
67 Battery type
68 Physicist Freeman
69 Innkeeper

DOWN

1 Person with a collar?
2 One rung on the evolutionary ladder
3 Spike, for one
4 Biblical vessel
5 Coach Bryant
6 Up
7 High
8 Vietnamese money unit
9 Accelerator item
10 Sticks
11 Dostoyevsky's "___ From the Underground"
12 Beethoven dedicatee
13 Singer Della
15 ___-Wan Kenobi
19 Star in Cygnus
20 Rabbits' tails
21 "Pagliacci" husband
22 Menachem's peace partner
23 Deface
25 Agony
28 Item of love?
30 Bk. of Revelation
31 Poison
33 Pioneering video game
35 Writer Calvino
36 TV show since 1/14/52
37 Wings have them
40 Wambaugh's "The ___ Field"
43 Bogey
45 Male swan
47 1980 Richard Gere portrayal
49 Hooked in a way
50 Definitely not a brain surgeon
51 Chemical compounds
53 Kind of tour
56 Continue
57 South Africa's ___ Paul
59 "___ does it!"
61 Phooey's cousin
62 Novelist Rölvaag
63 Medium for Matisse
64 Ending with acetyl or butyl
65 ___ Spiegel

60 *by Harvey Estes*

ACROSS

1 Tiller's place
4 Flop's opposite
9 Merchant R. H. __
13 Money maker
14 Dessert bean
15 Newton knighted in 1705
17 Keg contents
18 "Help!" star
19 1959 Ritchie Valens hit
20 Behave
23 Multicolored
24 __ Palmas, Spain
25 On an errand, maybe
26 Mortgage interest
27 Purple Heart, e.g.
30 "Low bridge! Everyone down!" canal
31 Officeholders
32 Circle of angels
33 Belief system
35 Is meticulous, with 53 Across
41 Abbr. in car ads
42 Many millennia
43 Word in an obit
44 Garroway of 50's TV
47 Itty-bitty map
49 "Interview with the Vampire" author
50 E.T.'s ship
51 "Life __ beach"
52 Alta. neighbor
53 See 35 Across
59 Kind of wave
60 Scrub a tub, maybe
61 Bolivian export
62 Triangular treat
63 Be a ham
64 It's in the bag
65 NASA green lights
66 Make current
67 Catching of thoughtwaves

DOWN

1 First bone donor
2 Tagalog speaker
3 Most microscopic
4 Seafood dish
5 Water artery
6 An embarrassing problem to face?
7 Is in a slump
8 Celebration
9 The original Goldfinger?
10 "Unto us __ is given"
11 Openness
12 American in Habana
16 Brahman, for one
21 Study
22 Pronounced
26 Topper
27 Lack of oomph
28 Edifice extension
29 Spoils, with "on"
30 Trio of mommies?
32 Chance
34 Family nickname
36 Equal a bet
37 Ground-breaker
38 Sweet liqueur
39 Striped apparel, often
40 Heart of Billy Williams
44 Heating pipes
45 "Out of __"
46 Spelling exercise?
48 Gamal of Egypt
49 Fan noise
51 Sailors' keys
52 Litter
54 Went to the bottom
55 Ne plus ultra
56 Diving bird
57 Guitar's ancestor
58 Piece of cake

ACROSS

1 1975 Wimbledon champ
5 ___ nova
10 High-ranking NCO
14 Oscar winner for "Moonstruck"
15 Sit up for
16 Ron Howard TV role
17 Irving Berlin song
20 Woolgatherer?
21 Winter forecast
22 Sioux Indians
23 "Gimme a G . . . ," e.g.
25 Org.
26 Word in Amtrak's slogan
28 N.H.L. legend Gordie
30 Wide's partner
33 "La Bohème" role
34 Louisiana inlet
35 One in France
36 Andrews Sisters hit
40 Speaker's pauses
41 Writer Cecil of "The Straight Dope"
42 ___ me tangere
43 Q followers
44 Strength, in Variety talk
45 Favor
47 Confused thoughts
49 Secretaries may file these
50 Alpha's opposite
52 Unified
54 Profit by
57 Andrew Lloyd Webber song, with "The"
60 Astound
61 Chisholm, e.g.
62 Tense
63 1/17/94 honoree
64 First-year law school class

65 "Rule, Britannia" composer

DOWN

1 Highest point
2 "Pygmalion" author
3 Beatles recording
4 Goof
5 Tried to save a sinking ship?
6 Steinbrenner to the Yankees
7 Wise
8 Search (through)
9 From ___ Z
10 Loses feathers
11 "Mary Poppins" tune, with "A"
12 Take's partner
13 Golfers' gadgets
18 River in Belgium
19 Revolted
24 "Aquarius" musical
25 Gone, but not forgotten?
26 Dinosaur DNA preserver
27 Coffin stands
28 Injures
29 Court cry
31 "Twisted" body part
32 Broadcast anew
34 Boast
37 "The Human Comedy" author
38 "Zip-___-Doo-Dah"
39 Like Nash's "lama"
45 Juries
46 Nothing: Fr.
48 Ripening
49 Like a pitcher's perfect game
50 Siberian city
51 Conductor Riccardo
52 60's hair style
53 Asterisk
55 Avoid
56 Cigar ending
58 Giant Mel
59 "Make ___ double"

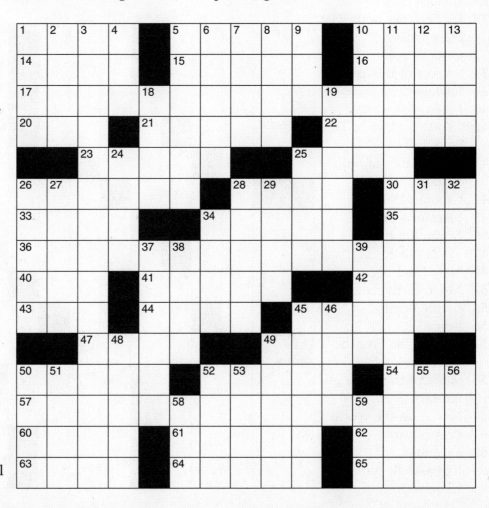

ACROSS

1 Say "I do" again
6 March starter
9 Diplomatic skills
14 Dwelling place
15 U.N. member
16 Honolulu hello
17 Scrabble, anagrams, etc.
19 Bottoms of graphs
20 Disney dog
21 Madam's mates
22 Mosque chiefs
23 Ave. crossers
24 "I've been __!"
25 City on the Brazos
27 Ear cleaner
29 __ race (finished first)
30 Lived
33 Oaxaca waters
35 Dictionaries and thesauruses
37 Organic soil
38 Subject of this puzzle
39 Lockup
40 Preambles
42 "You __ Have to Be So Nice"
43 "The Sultan of Sulu" author
44 Crooner Williams
45 Jokester's props
46 Nightclub bits
47 Tricia Nixon __
48 New Deal org.
51 Move furtively
54 Barely open
56 Bewail
57 Start of the French workweek
58 Some of them are famous
60 Not __ in the world
61 Prayer part
62 __ nous
63 Ex-baseball commish Ueberroth
64 Light time
65 Lucy's landlady

DOWN

1 Singer Lou
2 Enemy vessel
3 T H I S
  H E R E
  I R O N
  S E N T
4 Whirlpool
5 B.A. or Ph.D.
6 Like August weather, perhaps
7 Client
8 Computer access codes
9 City vehicle
10 Battle depicted in "The Last Command"
11 Hip joint
12 Not us
13 Freshness
18 Quickly: Abbr.
24 Towel word
26 Connectors
28 Housebroken
29 Circumlocutory
30 Poet laureate, 1843–50
31 Similar
32 Mil. officer
33 __ Romeo
34 Well-mannered
35 Incoherent speech
36 Off Broadway award
38 Is obstinate
41 More erratic
42 Humanitarian Dorothea
45 Where a cruise calls
46 Previn or Kostelanetz
47 Disk jockey Kasem
49 San Diego pro
50 Photographer Adams
51 Masher's comeuppance
52 Politico Clare Boothe __
53 __ the finish
55 Al Hirt hit
56 __ Blanc
59 Itsy-bitsy

63 by Sidney L. Robbins

ACROSS

1 Hypothetical eccentricities in time
6 Competition
10 Jail unit
14 "__ man with seven wives"
15 Miss Cinders of old comics
16 Singer Guthrie
17 Brightly sunburned
19 Leaning
20 60's space chimp
21 Heroic legends
22 Teen woe
23 Beelzebub
24 Aware of
25 French painter Jean
29 Hesitation sounds
30 __-di-dah
31 Sports sites
33 Mr. Whitney
35 Slippery one
38 Calms medically
40 Car gear
42 Mount St. Helens spew
43 "How dry __"
44 Cylindrical
45 Self
47 Pass receiver
50 "M*A*S*H" character
51 Flake material
52 Boors
54 Cordial
55 They get smashed
56 Clumsy ships
60 One of five
61 Oscar winner for "Sayonara"
63 Lease
64 __ Stanley Gardner
65 Boundary
66 Advantage
67 Philosopher A. J. __
68 Versifiers

DOWN

1 Use Western Union
2 Prayer's closing
3 Effect a makeover
4 School orgs.
5 Airline to Stockholm
6 Cash back
7 Sour brew
8 Under-the-sink item
9 Sups
10 Poolside hut
11 Greenland settler
12 Grassy plain
13 Mislay
18 Botanist Gray
23 Depot
24 Hardy and North
25 Pedro's house
26 Silver holders
27 It misleads
28 Broadway's "Three Men __ Horse"
32 Ocean
34 Permit
36 This, in Barcelona
37 Amorous gaze
39 Place of refinement
41 Baseball stat
46 Reproductive cell
48 Kind of soup
49 Not so clever
51 Exposed
53 Houston sch.
54 Had been
55 Length x width, for a rectangle
56 Prefix with sphere
57 Judicial cover?
58 Mend, as bones
59 Speedy planes
62 Spigot

by Julian Ochrymowych & Amy Goldstein

ACROSS

1 __ Rica
6 Job for Perry Mason
10 Career summary
14 Top grade
15 "__ We Got Fun?"
16 Son of Seth
17 Jockey's handful
18 Govt. agent
19 Mounties: Abbr.
20 Meaningful silence
23 Prominent features of Alfred E. Neuman
24 Carnaval site
25 Shrimpish
27 University of Maryland player
29 Stumble
32 Antigone's sister
35 Mongolian desert
36 The Monkees' "__ Believer"
37 1987 Edward James Olmos film
40 Actor Chaney
41 Minor profits?
42 Guinea pig or groundhog
43 Emily Dickinson's hometown
45 Air freshener scent
46 Nixon and Schroeder
47 Black-eyed item
48 Shows approval
52 Film in which Hayley Mills played twins
56 Ballet leap
58 One of the Menendez brothers
59 Gaucho gear
60 Elliptical
61 Look
62 Last word of fairy tales
63 Cravings
64 Flexible Flyer, for one

65 Ex-press secretary Dee Dee

DOWN

1 __ diem (seize the day)
2 Puccini product
3 More like a fox
4 Filament material
5 Org.
6 Tabby treat
7 "We __ please"
8 Breeze
9 Mediterranean spouter
10 Against
11 Stimulus
12 Mix of westerns
13 Venomous viper
21 Debts
22 Greek vowel

26 It's south of Saudi Arabia
28 Sign a check
29 Stylish, in the 60's
30 Basque, e.g.
31 Hair splitter
32 Mallorca, por ejemplo
33 Lively dance
34 Whisky-vermouth cocktail
35 Mdse.
38 Place to meet following a tennis match
39 Pick out of a lineup
44 Mertz and Merman
45 Looked too soon
47 Cracker Jack bonus
49 Speechify
50 Library gadget

51 Trains, in a way
53 Cribbage counters
54 Asia's __ Sea
55 Streetcar
56 "The __ Luck Club"
57 Night before

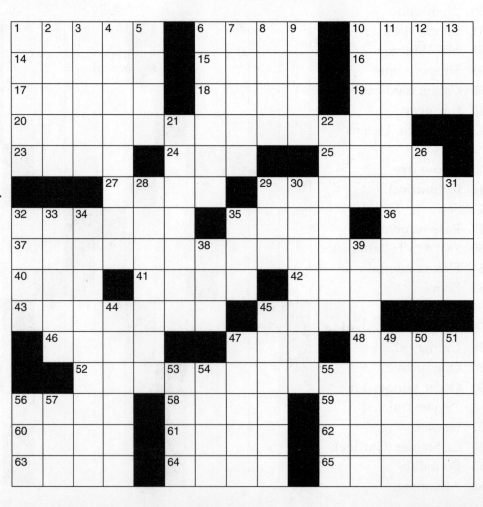

ACROSS

1 "St. John Passion" composer
5 In vogue
9 Carpet variety
13 Nepal's location
14 Leftovers dish
15 Prowess
16 "Lost Horizon" paradise
18 Public sentiment
19 "Message received"
20 Songwriter John
21 Long, deep bow
25 More than a snack
27 First look
30 1901 Churchill novel, with "The"
34 With masts fully extended
35 Imprint on glass
37 Posted
38 Puny pup
39 Dweller in Gulliver's Houyhnhnmland
40 Wash
41 Deuce topper
42 Skater Heiden
43 Idolater
44 Snow remover?
46 Seven Cities of Cibola seeker
48 George Takei TV/movie role
50 Confuses
51 Shore bird
54 Soprano Nixon
57 Dik Browne Viking
58 Town visited by Tommy Albright
63 Subtle twist
64 Like elbowing, e.g.
65 Paris landing site
66 Aromatic herb
67 Prepared brandy
68 Start for "of honor" or "of silence"

DOWN

1 __-relief
2 Ski wood
3 "The Company"
4 Solo of "Star Wars"
5 Plating material
6 Nixon chief of staff
7 Sunny vacation spot
8 Mojo
9 King Kong's home
10 Saber handle
11 To boot
12 __ Burnie, Md.
15 Aborigine's weapon
17 Woodworker's concern
21 City attacked by Cleon
22 Fabric with a raised pattern
23 Near ringer
24 "Jaws" locale
26 Canyon sound
28 Bring up
29 Work __
31 Action star Steven
32 Blitz
33 Typing pool members
36 Designer Chanel
39 Make oneself heard in the din
43 Lecterns
45 "Tumbling Tumbleweeds" singer, 1935
47 Traveled far and wide
49 Eclipse shadow
51 Kind of splints
52 Butler's quarters?
53 Operatic prince
55 "...as a bug in __"
56 Sally of NASA
59 Medic
60 Spanish gold
61 Timeworn
62 TV comic Louis

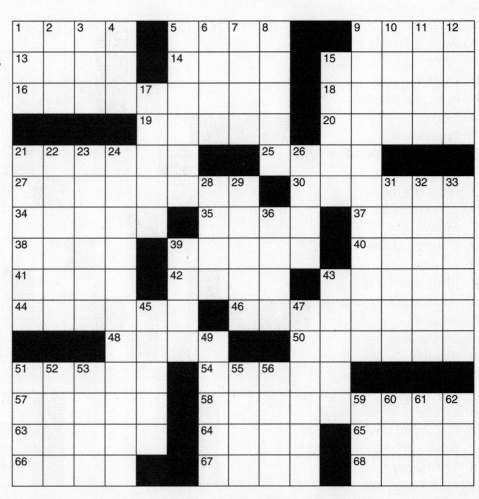

66 *by Charles Arnold*

ACROSS

1 Guzzles
7 Bebop
11 Certain muscles, informally
14 Dislocate
15 Woodwind
16 Varnish resin
17 Ancient ascetic
18 Letter writing: Abbr.
19 Japanese admiral Yuko
20 Battleship
23 Mesmerized
27 "Or __!" (veiled threat)
28 "Torero Saluting" painter
29 Rioting
31 Despicable
32 Greek market
33 Mitigates
35 Actor Matheson or Allen
38 Dictionary
40 Rogers's partner
42 Wily
43 Topple
45 Fudd of cartoondom
46 Director's cry
47 Bee activity
49 __ Downs (English racetrack)
52 Contented sound
53 __ fixe
54 Bluff, with a gun
57 Nuclear defense grp.
58 Russia's __ Mountains
59 Slanted
64 Petition
65 Scoop (out)
66 To wit
67 "__! We Have No Bananas"
68 Whirlpool
69 Like Parmesan

DOWN

1 Neighbor of Ont.
2 Raises
3 "__ Gratia Artis" (M-G-M motto)
4 Enemy
5 Dear, as memories
6 Two-track
7 Oedipus's mother
8 Lodging
9 Swedish painter of "At the Granary Door"
10 "Fiddler on the Roof" star
11 Straighten
12 Wash up
13 "Waverley" novelist
21 Burstyn and Barkin
22 Labor org.
23 Iranian dollars
24 Theater backer
25 Stand-in
26 Actress Garr
30 Transistor predecessor
31 "__ Misérables"
34 Cronus, to Romans
35 Meek
36 "*The* woman" for Sherlock
37 Traffic sign
39 Choose
41 Prefix with meter
44 Just as much
46 Bill's partner
48 Vexing
49 Emerson piece
50 Aspect
51 Noted White House resident
52 Multicolored pattern
55 Slender nail
56 Sirius, e.g.
60 Drs.' org.
61 Tennis call
62 __ de France
63 Dancer Charisse

ACROSS

1 Forlorn
4 Poker actions
10 Is appropriate
14 Actress MacGraw
15 State boldly
16 British title
17 Cover
18 Animated myope
20 Type of lily
22 Neighbor of Switz.
23 Oriental tea
24 Plant with cup-shaped flowers
26 Skirt opening
27 Communists
28 Clamorous advertising
32 Part of a book
34 Down the __
35 Word of rejection
36 Escape vehicles
37 Misprint
38 Mr. Kadiddlehopper
39 In the past
40 False temptress
41 Targets of 40 Across
42 Ta-ta
44 Fictional plantation
45 Gypsies
46 Cold dessert
49 One of the Borgias
52 Rimsky-Korsakov's "Le Coq __"
53 Rival of Brown
54 Aussie hopper
57 Actor Cariou
58 First name in mysteries
59 Flair
60 Any person
61 Son of Seth
62 Small piano
63 The "o" in Cheerios

DOWN

1 Latin beat
2 1979 sci-fi hit
3 Musical instrument from Down Under
4 Collide head-on
5 Vietnamese and Nepalese, e.g.
6 Point of contention
7 Match parts
8 Afore
9 Tot toter
10 Allegiance
11 Venetian troublemaker
12 1982 Disney film
13 Work long and hard
19 Works long and hard
21 Portents
25 Pindar piece
26 Wooden shoe
28 Beast of burden
29 Uproar
30 S-shaped curve
31 Resistance units
32 Tiff
33 Okefenokee resident
34 Small combos
37 Strunk and White's "The __ of Style"
38 Transport
40 Botanist's concern
41 West of Hollywood
43 Big quackers
44 Seat of power
46 Philosopher Kierkegaard
47 Russian writer Bonner
48 Religious principle
49 Ontario tribe
50 Merit
51 Town near Caen
52 Dream pictures artist
55 Hiatus
56 Legendary Giant

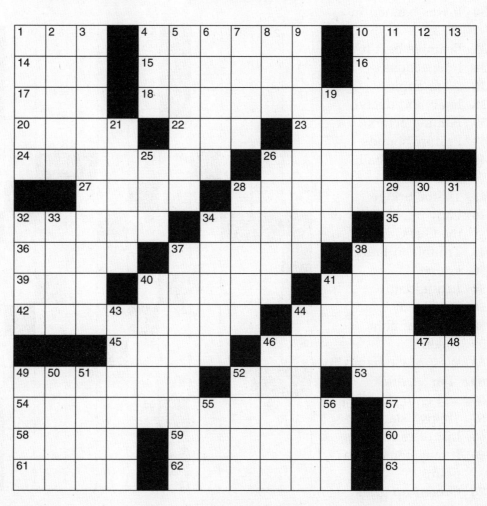

ACROSS

1 It goes from stem to stern
5 Ten Commandments word
10 Companion of Ollie
14 Dancer Pavlova
15 Champing at the bit
16 A billion years
17 Con game
18 Vacant
19 Soap unit
20 Stoves that don't work?
23 "Diamonds __ a girl's . . ."
24 "Gidget" star
25 Perform perfectly
28 Hägar the Horrible's honey
30 It was banned in 1973
33 Beatniks beat it
34 Interjections
36 __ in apple
38 Iamb and dactyl
39 Filming actors?
43 Pasture sounds
44 Carl of baseball, informally
45 Tic-toe bridge
46 Lady __, founder of the Girl Guides
48 Trouble in France
50 Frame
54 Itch initiator
56 Partake of
58 Calendar abbr.
59 Arson?
63 West of Gotham City
65 "I'm __ duck"
66 __ hemp (fiber plant)
67 "I Spy" star
68 List of candidates
69 It may come with points
70 Grown-up grigs
71 Biblical king with 10 wives
72 Muffs

DOWN

1 North African fortress
2 Concert cry
3 Filling surrounder
4 "Mrs. Battle's Opinions on Whist" writer
5 Île de la Cité site
6 The __ Man (tarot card)
7 Actor John
8 First name in supper club entertainment
9 Drift
10 Not at a distance
11 Logician
12 Flight approval
13 22° 30'
21 Baking potato
22 Lump
26 "Rock of __"
27 Young 'un
29 Thrilled response
31 Tony of "Who's the Boss?"
32 License
35 Pen
37 Trans-Atlantic flier
39 Emerson, the __ of Concord
40 Game originally called "fives"
41 Descartes conclusion
42 Fashion
43 Sot's spot
47 Big __, Calif.
49 Not staccato
51 A sew-and-sew?
52 Hubbub
53 Is foppish
55 Grind
57 Kind of attraction
60 Run in place
61 About
62 No __ (register button)
63 Plane downer
64 Like threatening bills

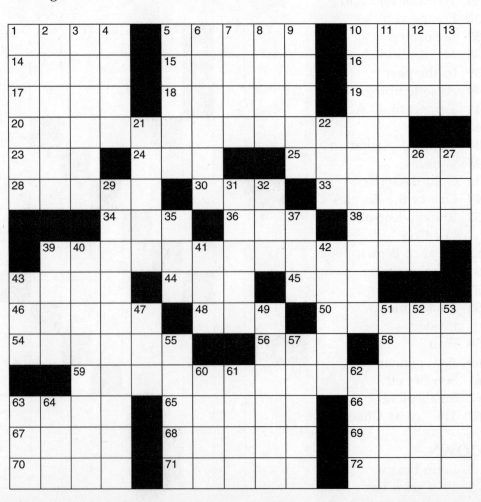

ACROSS

1 Speleology topic
5 Plane egresses
10 Pedestal topper
14 C.I.A. profiler Philip
15 Paradigm
16 Savvy about
17 Canine laryngitis?
19 Mutant heroes of modern comics
20 Not gross
21 Gain
22 Fanciful
24 Doubtful story
25 Fancies up
26 Record lists
29 Uses a cheat-sheet
30 "The Many __ of Dobie Gillis"
31 Watkins __, N.Y.
32 Gridiron period
36 Candid
37 First-aid contrivance
38 Stage curtain
39 Encircle
40 Way with words
41 Sneak preview
42 Posh
44 Like some hair
45 Words preceding film credits
47 Kingsley et al.
48 Warned with a horn
49 South of France
50 Shocking word
53 The least concern
54 Experimental canine?
57 Adjective for an antique store
58 TV exec Spelling
59 Hors d'oeuvre spread
60 Former empire
61 Acknowledge
62 Like certain trays

DOWN

1 "Three Coins in the Fountain" lyricist
2 Chills
3 Third piece of three
4 "A mouse!"
5 Richard Sheridan play, with "The"
6 Be gaga over
7 Chow __
8 Lobbying acronym
9 Winter sport
10 Canine underwear?
11 Frighten to the core
12 Cut flowers
13 "West Side Story" beau
18 Lady Gregory cohort
23 Deprive (of)
24 Stylish canine?
25 "__ You Glad You're You?" (1946 hit)
26 Stop (up)
27 Snake dancers
28 Maintain
29 Succeed, informally
31 Endocrine, e.g.
33 Loads
34 Juice flavor
35 Rations
37 Not get hit?
41 Dither
43 Miniature
44 Failing business's woe
45 Trunk items
46 Gangsters
47 Plains critter
48 Commandment word
49 Vidal's Breckinridge
50 "Gil __"
51 Courtroom ritual
52 Comply with
55 Contemptuous cry
56 Bath, for one

ACROSS

1 Tick off
5 Jerry Herman musical
9 Scarf
14 Tennis's Ivanisevic, often
15 "Fatal Attraction" villain
16 Bust finds
17 Diner's card
18 1953 Leslie Caron role
19 Long time
20 #1 song for Robert Palmer
23 At that point
24 Bookbinding leather
25 At regular intervals
28 Innocent one
29 Entirety
32 Communion table
33 TV's "Batman," e.g.
34 Oil of __
35 Learning method that "works for me"
38 "Indecent Proposal" director Adrian
39 Jokesters
40 One quadrillionth: Prefix
41 Vane dir.
42 Ill will
43 #, & or %
44 Either star of "Tea and Sympathy"
45 To you, to Yves
46 Empty-calorie lover
52 Craze
53 Novel featuring Doctor Long Ghost
54 Bear in the sky
55 Keats or Wordsworth
56 Mash preceder
57 Sardine containers
58 Wash
59 Light submachine gun
60 Noted Renaissance name

DOWN

1 Doll's cry
2 Like some tea
3 Ward (off)
4 Yuletide snack
5 Ice cream treat
6 Xenophobe's fear
7 Pinochle combo
8 Turnoffs
9 It fell in 1979
10 Attach, as a feed bag
11 King Harald's father
12 Folk tales
13 Slalom shape
21 Beloved
22 Energy
25 Humorist Mort et al.
26 Artful dodges
27 Pay the penalty
28 "Tootsie" Oscar winner
29 Out on __
30 Milk: Prefix
31 Popular disinfectant
33 Checking places
34 "Hold on . . ."
36 Happy, for one
37 1934 song "The Very Thought __"
42 Goddess of Hades
43 One of the Virgin Islands
44 Filled turnover
45 Give __ of one's own medicine
46 Nonsense song of 1918
47 Hand or foot
48 Exclude
49 Mr. Kristofferson
50 Does not exist
51 Life of Riley
52 Crowd around

ACROSS

1 Enjoys at leisure
5 Lucifer
10 Likely
13 "Flower Song," e.g.
14 Harden
15 A Guthrie
16 Start of a quip
19 Part of a flick?
20 French holy women: Abbr.
21 First
22 Egg: oval::__: pyriform
23 Supports
25 1973 Elton John hit
28 Burnt, in cooking
29 Environmentalism: Abbr.
30 Large: Prefix
31 "The Conqueror Worm" writer
34 Middle of the quip
38 Foreign exchange listing
39 Come to __
40 O.K. Corral figure
41 Unstable
42 Elegant
44 Know-it-alls
47 Highlander
48 Treasured violin
49 Repugnance
50 "Whiffenpoof" syllable
53 End of the quip
57 Rotunda resting place
58 Prospero's sprite
59 Kind of ox
60 TV "clutter"
61 Curt
62 Arguments for

DOWN

1 "Völsunga __"
2 Infuriates
3 Material for a topi
4 Had a session
5 Kind of anguish
6 Choler
7 Wash sites
8 Dernier __
9 That girl
10 Spinning
11 Argue
12 Lincoln's in-laws
15 "For want of __ the horse was lost"
17 Understanding words
18 Black __ (sensational 1947 murder case)
22 Tiresome one
23 Coaxes
24 Boxlike sleigh
25 Slightly wet
26 Be heartsick
27 Time for mad dogs and Englishmen
28 Nuts
30 Grades
31 Vegetables
32 Not just mine
33 Glimpse
35 Kind of food
36 Capital
37 Kind of cutlet
41 Lecher
42 Kine
43 Lascivious look
44 Brazilian dance
45 "The way of a man with __": Proverbs
46 Windmill arms
47 Rubbernecks
49 He's got it coming
50 Smudge
51 To boot
52 Bids
54 Topper
55 Long start
56 Little dickens

by Fred Piscop

ACROSS

1 Land for development
6 Small nail
10 __ Observer (1992 mission)
14 Move like a chopper
15 Greek liqueur
16 Wanted G.I.
17 __ Gay
18 Comics canine
19 __ fide (in bad faith)
20 Heirloom tool?
23 Carte start
24 Run an art show
25 Red giant, e.g.
28 TV's "__ Academic"
31 N.L. cap monogram
32 Schlemiel
33 Knock for a loop
35 Casino request
39 President Lincoln's tools?
42 Hightail it
43 Hummer's instrument
44 Month in which D.D.E. was born
45 Astronaut Grissom
47 Cornell's Big __
48 Disturb, with "up"
49 Peloponnesian War participant
52 Antipollution grp.
54 Secret military tool?
59 100 kurus
60 __ du Lac, Wis.
61 Puts out
63 In a frenzied fashion
64 Former Hawaii Senator Hiram
65 Annual visitor
66 Kind of loaf
67 __-eyed
68 Actress Georgia

DOWN

1 Word ignored in indexing
2 Gossipy Barrett
3 Admit
4 Home of the 1962 Mets
5 Park way
6 Flub, as a grounder
7 Wife of Boaz
8 Conqueree of 1521
9 Goofball
10 Class to which all of us belong
11 Look for
12 Esther of "Good Times"
13 Dispatch
21 Attaches
22 Joint: Prefix
25 Drenches
26 1 on the Mohs' scale
27 Way off
29 Transported
30 Until now
33 Our longest bones
34 Level
36 Commandment starter
37 Certain raingear
38 C.P.R. specialists
40 1945 blast site
41 Augured
46 Doesn't tip
48 Lunatic
49 Goo
50 Word of mouth
51 Play for __
53 Bel __ cheese
54 Decked out
55 __ time (right away)
56 1988 Dick Francis thriller, with "The"
57 Throw barbs at
58 Kitchen addition?
62 Pitcher Maglie

ACROSS

1 Cleo player
4 Nods
7 Healing waters
10 Bottom-of-letter abbr.
13 Greek nickname
14 "Barney Miller" regular Jack
15 1964 Murray Schisgal play
16 Vietnam's My __
17 Place for coming to grips?
18 Prom flowers
20 Toast word
21 Oven for a singer?
23 Peking finale
24 Mr. Buchwald
25 Sign maker
27 "Damn Yankees" team
30 "__ well . . ."
32 Pope's "An __ on Man"
33 Immensely
34 Man's name meaning "red"
35 "Le Coq __"
36 Amenable
37 Big name in top 40
40 Backbiter?
43 Govt. help for mom-and-pop stores
45 "Alice" role
46 Radar reception
47 Come about
49 "Runaround Sue" singer
50 Get in return
51 Skipper's command
53 Jazz's __ Winding
55 Oxlike critter
56 Sea for a singer?
61 First name in tyranny
62 More sluggish
63 By way of
64 Literary monogram
65 Long spell

66 Exactly right
67 Charley Weaver's Mt. __
68 Author Harper
69 __-Cat (arctic vehicle)
70 Kidnapping grp., 1974
71 Bandleader Brown

DOWN

1 Religious leader
2 It's south of Georgia
3 Tubular pasta
4 Award for "Wings"
5 Actress friend of Prince Andrew
6 Take up like a sponge
7 Quenches
8 Washington waterway
9 Staved off
10 Grain for a playwright?
11 Revulsion
12 Like apple juice
19 Forte for an actress?
22 Flavor sensor
26 Arcane
27 Annoyer
28 Menu phrase
29 Voyage for an actor?
31 Mauna __
38 "Xanadu" rock grp.
39 Rare aquatic
41 Half a dance
42 Keystone figure
44 Plowed lands
47 #1 hit for the Chi-Lites, 1972

48 Wicked one
49 Family name of F.D.R.'s mother
52 Squash
54 It comes straight from the heart
57 Puppies' barks
58 Baudelaire's "The Flowers of __"
59 Orderly
60 Senate votes

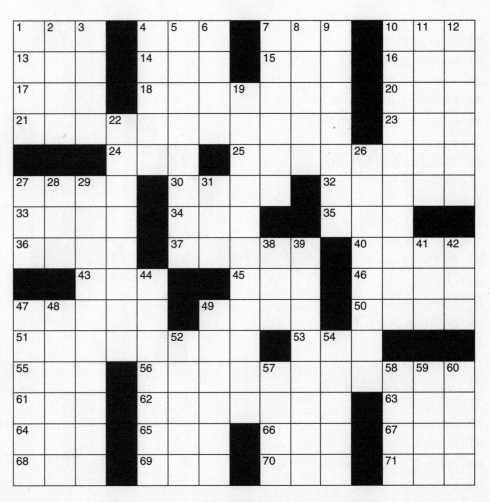

ACROSS

1 Jam maker
8 Mounds of arms
14 Facsimile
15 Tour follower
16 Occupy
17 Treadmill
18 They may try you
19 RR depot
21 Borders
22 Look up and down
23 "No bid"
25 Curve between musical notes
26 "Agnus __"
27 Crustacean catcher
29 Before
30 Scopes Trial defender
32 Fit into the schedule
34 Coal container
35 Razor-billed bird
36 Reindeer relative
40 Like this answer
43 Constellation next to Scorpius
44 Membership fee for 39 Down?
46 Shipping letters
48 "__ Was a Rollin' Stone" (1972 hit)
50 Picker-uppers
51 Stories
52 Uses a knife
54 Sullivan Award grp.
55 Sommelier's offerings
56 "Four Quartets" poet
58 Temporary
60 Sprays, perhaps
61 Ruin, as plans
62 Naguib's successor
63 Originally

DOWN

1 Shooter supporter
2 Took back
3 Highest orbital points
4 Get wider
5 Whopper juniors
6 Henri's here
7 Dupe
8 Bathing suit top
9 Bit
10 Takes to the street edge
11 Uniform attachment
12 Visualize
13 Is incensed
15 Comprehends
20 Drink opener
23 Resolve, as differences
24 Consoles
27 Kid corrals
28 City on the Loire
31 Baseball stat
33 Ring result
36 Where nautical rope is wound
37 Uzbek lake
38 Duelers' equipment
39 W.W. II craft
40 Masters tournament location
41 Freeloader
42 Cracker toppers
45 Certain code carrier
47 Ruthless ruler
49 Book containing legends
51 Florentine painter
53 Spot
55 "Star Trek" Klingon
57 Finish'd
59 Youngster

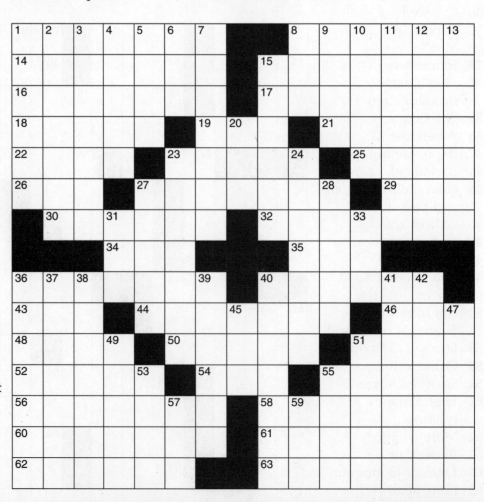

75

by Bob Klahn

ACROSS

1 Apple competitor
4 Gambler Holliday
7 Fifth-century pope
12 Green
14 The "S" in T. S. Eliot
16 Men of La Mancha
17 Farmer's tipcart
18 Cartridge type
19 Aviatrix, for short
20 Point of no return?
21 Hidden theme of this puzzle
24 Last word of "Finnegans Wake"
25 Make an appeal
26 White House monogram
27 Outfit
29 Make an appeal
30 Miners' sch.
32 Out of sorts
33 Friend of 21 Across
35 Affected by pollen
38 "Clan of the Cave Bear" heroine
39 Chosen number?
42 Anwar's successor
43 Pickpocket
44 Slangy hello
45 New York eng. sch.
46 Like 33 Across's apple
50 Suffix meaning "small one"
51 Pack animal?
52 Laid-back
53 Quick to blush
56 London barrister
58 Game officials
59 Making out
60 Hot time in Chile
61 Umpteen's ordinal?
62 Green lights

DOWN

1 Hosp. hookups
2 Doctors often carry them
3 Franciscus TV drama of the 60's
4 "Dream Lover" singer
5 With no letup
6 Price abbr.
7 Material
8 Pro follower
9 Dog, for short
10 Proof goof
11 Minimal ante
13 A bit obtuse
14 Maze word
15 Droopy-eyed
19 Corset result, perhaps
21 Where fat cats get thin
22 "I'm glad that's over!"
23 Sealy rival
28 N.H.-Vt. neighbor
30 Open
31 Whirligig
32 Actor Gerard
33 Boxer's title, briefly
34 Short shot?
35 Daphne and hazel
36 It's like home?
37 Bomber Boomer
39 Beethoven's only opera
40 Sight saver?
41 Peaked
43 Cockpit display
44 Mrs. Rockefeller
47 Former capital of Bolivia
48 Underground event
49 ___ gland
54 It ended in 1806: Abbr.
55 Two or go follower
56 X
57 Football linemen: Abbr.

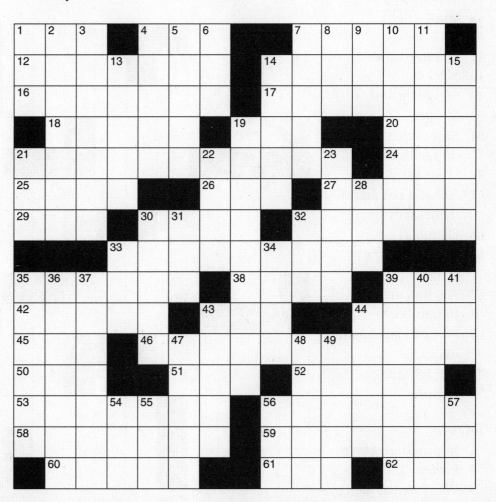

ACROSS

1 Wealthy person
5 Takes advantage of
9 "The Forsyte ___"
13 Likeness
15 Kind of stick
16 Sheriff Tupper of "Murder, She Wrote"
17 Social hangout
19 Sea swallow
20 Home turnover
21 Knock out of kilter
23 Illuminated
24 Terminator
25 Bear up there
29 Steep slope
33 Crier of Greek myth
35 Wakens
39 Bettor's challenge
43 Show fright
44 Weird
45 Followed orders
48 N.Y. Police ___
49 Exodus priest
53 Mauna ___
55 Responded unintelligibly
58 "Last stop! ___!"
62 Abner's pal and namesakes
63 Diamond coup
66 Relative of the clarinet
67 Auction actions
68 Indian boat
69 Part of Halloween makeup
70 Church nook
71 Endure

DOWN

1 Informal greetings
2 Eastern V.I.P.
3 Wind instrument?
4 They'll be hunted in April
5 Big sports news
6 Loudly weep
7 "Holy moly!"
8 Kind of loser
9 Beelzebub
10 Change
11 Watkins Glen, e.g.
12 "Lou Grant" star
14 Lod airport airline
18 Nobelist Wiesel
22 Esteem
25 German link
26 Kind of squad
27 Lemonlike
28 Singer Lane
30 Cuomo's predecessor
31 Son of Prince Valiant
32 Australian hopper
34 Long Island town
36 Tool storage area
37 Limerick site
38 Barber's cut
40 Wane
41 Bullring shout
42 Receive
46 Pass
47 Cabbage patch item
49 Visibly happy
50 Caribbean getaway
51 "___ has it . . ."
52 Start
54 Actor Guinness
56 Old lab burner
57 Trapdoor
59 Milky gem
60 Arm bone
61 Pueblo town
64 Employee card and others
65 Still and all

ACROSS

1 Dumbfounded
5 Acquire, as expenses
10 Singer Campbell
14 Colombian city
15 Hughes' plane, Spruce __
16 1890's Vice President __ P. Morton
17 1959 Rodgers and Hammerstein hit
20 "You can __ horse to . . ."
21 Bridal path
22 Predicament
24 Obote's successor
26 1956 Comden-Green-Styne collaboration
33 On __ (counting calories)
34 Man with a title
35 Russian space vehicle
36 Pride and envy, e.g.
37 Old hat
38 "Aurora" painter
39 Kind of cap or cream
40 Radio host of note
41 First U.S. saint
42 1930 Gershwin musical
46 Sigmatism
47 Achy
48 Whiz kid
51 Blotto
54 1983 Herman-Fierstein musical
60 "Metamorphoses" poet
61 Wish granters
62 TV's Oscar
63 Hitches
64 Mill material
65 Murder

DOWN

1 Part of a play
2 Star of TV's "Wiseguy"
3 "Waiting for the Robert __"
4 Puts out of commission
5 Desert critter
6 Persona __ grata
7 How some packages are sent: Abbr.
8 R. & R. org.
9 Ring leader?
10 Sticking together
11 Decreasingly
12 Demonic
13 Garibaldi's birthplace
18 Keats or Shelley
19 Popular street name
23 Invent
24 Snaps handcuffs on
25 Gentle, as breezes
26 Grounds
27 Kingly decree
28 Passenger ship
29 Gobble
30 "__ man with seven . . ."
31 Curtain material
32 Nine-to-five routine
37 Conks out
38 Mutinied
41 __-comic (play type)
43 Long narratives
44 Alan, Larry or Stephen
45 Tap-dance
48 Crushing news
49 Four-star review
50 __ rain
52 Admiral Zumwalt
53 Actress Moore
55 Chicken's counterpart
56 Atmosphere: Prefix
57 Prefix with lateral
58 Omicrons predecessors
59 Thesaurus listing: Abbr.

ACROSS

1 One who reunes
5 Bic or Parker products
9 Lox's partner
14 Computer offering
15 Face shape
16 Shade of white
17 No ifs, __ or buts
18 Soho so-long
19 Lounges lazily
20 Start of a quip
23 Consumed
24 Israeli airport
25 __ chango (magician's command)
29 "That was close!"
31 Horror film frightener
34 Oscar de la __
35 Mimi Sheraton subject
36 Obstinate one
37 Middle of the quip
40 Hor.'s opposite
41 __ of March
42 French avenue
43 It's north of Calif.
44 Chance __ (meet accidentally)
45 Not present
46 Columbus univ.
47 One, in Orléans
48 End of the quip
55 His beloved was Beatrice
56 Old newspaper section
57 Hide
59 Rags-to-riches writer
60 Roughneck
61 Bombeck, the columnist
62 Hops brews
63 Sea eagle
64 Cooper's was high

DOWN

1 Internists' org.
2 Give temporarily
3 Remove, as a knot
4 Daydream
5 Spud
6 Dodge
7 European defense grp.
8 Dross
9 Swell, as a cloud
10 Have nothing to do with
11 Course game
12 A Gardner
13 Fleur-de-__
21 Old Nick
22 Coasters
25 Utah city
26 Allude (to)
27 __ nous
28 Editor's mark
29 Part of NOW
30 Breaks up clods
31 Company B awakener
32 "...in tears amid the __ corn": Keats
33 Ism
35 Rover's playmate
36 Tormé and Gibson
38 Raise the end of
39 Cacophonous tower
44 Does a groomsman's job
45 Whosoever
46 Bewhiskered animal
47 Author Sinclair
48 Fabric texture
49 "Come Back, Little Sheba" playwright
50 Prod
51 Rating a D
52 Aboveboard
53 Florida's __ Beach
54 Pollster Roper
55 A tiny bit
58 Ecru

ACROSS

1 "West Side Story" girl
6 200 milligrams
11 Low island
14 1968 song "All ___ the Watchtower"
15 River to the Missouri
16 Fuss
17 Seaver's nickname
19 Robert Morse Tony-winning role
20 House cleaner, in England
21 "Absolutely"
22 Legal profession
24 Queen Victoria's house
26 Freight charge
27 Half-wit
28 Better than a bargain
29 Polynesian carvings
33 "Hail, Caesar!"
34 Netman Nastase
37 Sheepish
38 Cup's edge
39 Battery part
40 Anti-prohibitionists
41 Disfigure
42 Get extra life from
43 Portaged
45 Patriotic uncle
47 Rocket's cargo
49 Crib-sheet contents
54 Earthy colors
55 Veneration
56 Hand-cream ingredient
57 "Harper Valley ___"
58 Decorative shrub
61 Sock in the jaw
62 Address grandly
63 Coeur d'___, Idaho
64 Flood relief?
65 Pave over
66 Coiffed like Leo

DOWN

1 "Concentration" objective
2 Hello or goodbye
3 Type type
4 Opening
5 Stone, for one
6 Kitchen gadgets
7 Garage-sale words
8 Spitfire fliers, for short
9 Work up
10 Electronics whiz
11 Western spoof of 1965
12 "What ___" ("I'm bored")
13 "___ Sixteen" (Ringo Starr hit)
18 Package-store wares
23 Skater Zayak
25 Place for posies
26 Call back
29 Wrecker
30 "___ had it!"
31 News locale of 12/17/03
32 Shoe part
33 Auto option, informally
35 Wallet contents, for short
36 Shoebox letters
38 Alan or Cheryl
39 Kind of buildup
41 Gauge
44 Inertia
45 Finn's pal
46 Once again
47 "Where's ___?" (1970 flick)
48 Part owner?
50 Half of a Western city name
51 Pulitzer-winning novelist Glasgow
52 TV exec Arledge
53 Basted
55 Cinema canine
59 ___ out (missed)
60 Descartes's conclusion

80 *by Stephanie Spadaccini*

ACROSS

1 Casper or Balthazar, e.g.
6 Rope material
10 Chorale part
14 Florida city
15 Jai __
16 La Scala presentation
17 NO UNTIDY CLOTHES
20 Walking on air
21 Macadam ingredient
22 __ Cruces, N.M.
23 Prepared
24 Harem
26 Subordinate Claus
29 Apocalypse
31 Gene material
32 Seldom seen
34 "QB VII" author
36 Lump of jelly, e.g.
39 GOVERN, CLEVER LAD
43 "You said it!"
44 Writer Shere
45 Approve
46 W.W. II grp.
48 Agrippina's son
50 German pronoun
51 Answer to "What's keeping you?"
55 Mount near ancient Troy
57 Item in a lock
58 "I" affliction
59 1990 Bette Midler film
62 BLATHER SENT ON YE
66 Neighborhood
67 Le Mans, e.g.
68 Conductor Georg
69 Back-to-school time: Abbr.
70 Bouquet
71 Friend of Henry and June

DOWN

1 Word on the Oise
2 Long (for)
3 Food critic Greene
4 Arm bones
5 Fried lightly
6 Actor Charles of "Hill Street Blues"
7 Overhead trains
8 Not shiny
9 A captain of the Enterprise
10 Dance, in France
11 On __ (doing well)
12 1979 treaty peninsula
13 Authority
18 Alternate road
19 Los Angeles suburb
24 Obviously pleased
25 Big name in viniculture
26 Physics unit
27 Zhivago's love
28 "It Came __ Outer Space"
30 Mezz. alternative
33 "It's true," in Torino
35 French resort town
37 Forest florae
38 __ B'rith
40 Fingernail polish
41 Realism
42 Salon selection
47 Rossini character
49 Potemkin mutiny site
51 Jots
52 Skiing's Phil or Steve
53 Tiptoe
54 Air Force arm: Abbr.
56 Illinois city
59 Cassandra
60 Falana or Montez
61 Opposing
63 Dracula, sometimes
64 Sgt., e.g.
65 Frozen Wasser

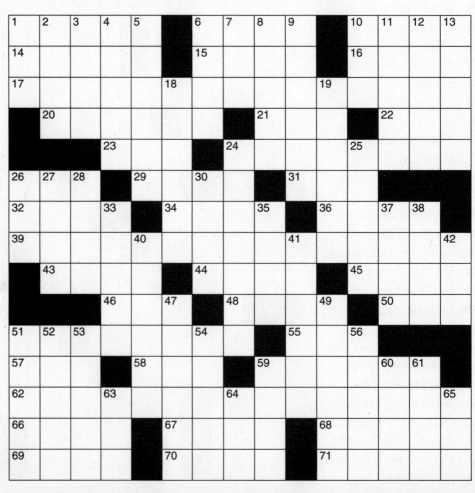

81 *by Randolph Ross*

ACROSS

1 Funny pages favorite
11 Composer Satie
15 Exciting adventure
16 "I came," to Caesar
17 Recruiter's objective
18 Professional suffixes
19 Three after B
20 Cousin of "Eureka!"
21 Shows how
23 Stout
24 Hawaii's state bird
26 Screen's partner
27 Post
29 Show anger, in a way
32 According to
33 They make a bloom blossom
35 Satisfied subscribers
37 Profligate
40 Tubular pasta
43 Victoria's Secret selections
47 Blown-up photo: Abbr.
48 Discovery of 1781
51 Stevedore's, e.g.
52 Philatelist's item
54 Little pest
56 One over due
57 Shade maker
60 Twosome
61 Season in St. Lo
62 Turner and Pappas
63 Way back
66 Furniture wood
67 Crudity
68 Guinness Book suffixes
69 Creator of 1 Across

DOWN

1 Start of a Gardner title
2 C.B.ers' names
3 Brennan and Ford
4 Calendar abbr.
5 Match play?
6 Chung's former partner
7 Singer Nina
8 Real ending in London
9 1978 Yankee hero
10 Renowned costume designer
11 Bounce
12 Amend
13 Whole amount
14 "Pow!" places
22 Quakers
25 Loop for a lobe
28 Oscar __ Renta
30 Like Gen. Schwarzkopf
31 Prefix with cycle or sex
34 Gym exercises
36 TV host, 1955–82
38 N.Y.C. div.
39 Bambi's aunt
40 Break
41 Pipe openings
42 Show anger, in a way
44 Hospital personnel
45 Feature of many court buildings
46 Increase the angle of elevation
49 Without cause
50 Long, bony fish
53 Mardi Gras sights
55 Friendly Islands
58 First ed.
59 Actress Olin
64 Dutch painter Gerard __ Borch
65 Thrash

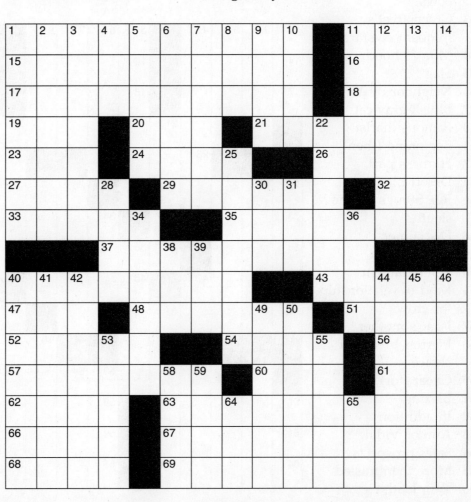

82 *by Norma Steinberg*

ACROSS

1 "Major Barbara" playwright
5 Sierra Club founder John
9 Phrygian king
14 Per capita
15 __ facto
16 "Have __ day!"
17 Proctor's cry at the end of a test
18 Pierce
19 Coast
20 Imprisoned feline's call?
23 Cornucopia
24 "Star-Spangled Banner" contraction
25 Avaricious
28 Nostalgic song for cows?
33 Greenstreet's frequent co-star
34 Monk's hood
35 Flag
36 Neighbor of Afr.
37 Bluish-gray cat
40 Famous diarist
41 Beginning (then)
43 Harness part
44 Desert plant
46 Rex Stout's canine sleuth?
48 Disclaimer
49 Kind of shot
50 Temperament
51 Kind of relationship for crows?
57 Isaac's mother
58 Pierre's breakfast choice
59 Cheer (for)
61 Blazing
62 In addition
63 Author Vidal
64 Sales prospects
65 More than misled
66 Tom Joad, e.g.

DOWN

1 Get __ (ready)
2 Reagan Secretary of State
3 Wile E. Coyote's supply company
4 If
5 1990 Kathy Bates film
6 Author Sinclair
7 "...ere __ Elba"
8 Kind of cop
9 Old word for a harasser
10 Get by will
11 Parisian house of design
12 Plat portion
13 Comment before "I told you so"
21 Computer add-on
22 Cons
25 Learn through research
26 Awaken
27 Goof
28 Pattern
29 TV lawyer __ Marshall
30 Leonardo's hometown
31 Author Jong
32 Of the kidneys
34 Singer Laine
38 Whiff
39 "__ newt..."
42 Word before march
45 Experience
47 Fancies
48 Tipped, in a way
50 Verdun's river
51 Eatery
52 Kathleen Battle offering
53 Holiday season
54 Takeout shop
55 Kitchener
56 Actress Spelling
57 Former baseball all-star Bando
60 Driver's aid

ACROSS

1 Sibelius's "__ Triste"
6 Where pins are made
10 Masochist's start
14 "Tempest" spirit
15 Late king of Norway
16 Popular rapper
17 Impractical idealist
19 Venus's home
20 Legal add-on
21 "__ goes" ("Slaughter-house-Five" refrain)
22 Casserole tidbit
24 Port, e.g.
26 Son of __
27 Gardner of "Mogambo"
28 Hollywood comer
31 Butler portrayer
34 First king of Israel
35 Leprechaun's land
37 French state
38 Father: Prefix
39 Oscar-winning song of 1958
40 "The Wind in the Willows" character
41 Deadlocked
42 Peacocks do it
43 Hook and crew
45 Kind of ball or card
46 He talked horse sense
47 Super-remedy
51 Hamlet's weapon
54 Jolts
55 Copacabana locale
56 Send forth
57 Performer of prodigious feats
60 Set of type
61 Sea into which the Amu Darya flows
62 Persian
63 Deuce topper
64 Caravel of 1492
65 Strong tastes

DOWN

1 "Star Wars" villain
2 Went up
3 Like some pads
4 Et __ (footnote abbr.)
5 Slippery
6 Spirit
7 Scads
8 Make antimacassars
9 Bad influence
10 Cruel employer
11 Folic, e.g.
12 "Heigho! the derry oh" setting
13 Tribe in the Winnebago nation
18 Early center of Celtic learning
23 Sharing adjective
25 Daydreamer
26 Take __ for the worse
28 Makes replete
29 Navy battle site of 1813
30 Comics bulldog
31 Masterpiece
32 Superior to
33 Site of a "Road" film
34 Redeemed
36 "Delta of Venus" author
38 Immature adult male
42 Livelihood
44 Art today
45 Bridle
47 Arum lily
48 Nordic
49 Chinese weight
50 Actress Anderson, et al.
51 Deprived, poetically
52 Subject in Virgil's "Eclogues"
53 Furniture wood
54 Don __
58 "Exodus" role
59 Blue Eagle agcy. of the 30's

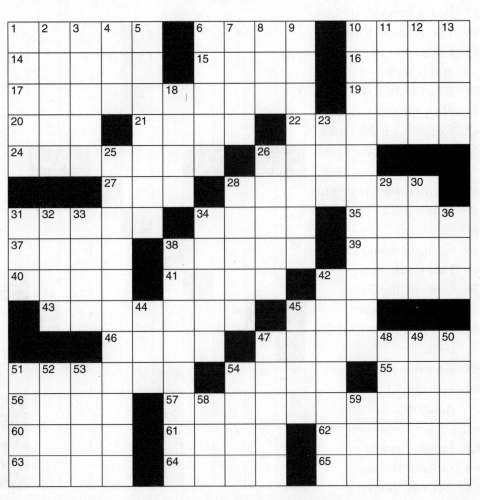

ACROSS

1 Fight locale
6 Rhyme scheme
10 Fitzgerald specialty
14 Lonesome George
15 Third Vice President
16 Nope
17 Of one of the senses
18 Neck of the woods
19 Linger
20 Hot stuff
22 No contest, e.g.
23 NASA affirmative
24 Suitor
26 Man with a horn
30 Can't stand
32 Hideouts
33 Untrustworthy sort
34 Former nuclear agcy.
37 Being broadcast
38 The Rumba King
39 Colleague of Scotty and Spock
40 Road material
41 Showed the world
42 Keepers of the flame
43 Obsolete typewriter necessity
45 Memorable shepherd
46 Public fuss
47 "__ you!"
48 Congressional caucus
49 Hot stuff
56 Coin in the Trevi
57 Nobelist Wiesel
58 Herbert Hoover, by birth
59 Reckons
60 Hirschfeld's daughter
61 __ garde
62 Letter closing
63 Lincoln in-law
64 Actress Evelyn

DOWN

1 Arab nobles
2 Lopsided win
3 Iberian river
4 "Hud" star
5 Attentive
6 By surprise
7 Ambience
8 __ Rabbit
9 Pentagon pooh-bah
10 Inferior
11 Hot stuff
12 Isherwood collaborator
13 "Take __ Train"
21 __ to mention
25 Taipan frypan
26 Like crazy
27 Superboy's girlfriend
28 Hot stuff
29 Sportscaster Cross
30 Hot stuff
31 Bit of wampum
33 Beyond question
35 Sommer of the screen
36 Zodiacal border
38 Window type
39 Sample soup
41 Outlaw
42 Apple Computer co-founder
44 Slant differently
45 Spelldown
46 Bad news on Wall Street
47 Place
48 Give away
50 Miscellany
51 Barnum's soprano
52 Robert Indiana painting
53 On vacation
54 It's blowin' in the wind
55 Some carpenters

ACROSS

1 Bit of lowlife?
6 Unyielding
10 Spacewalk, e.g.: Abbr.
13 "Reflections on Violence" author
14 Occupied with
15 Lose it
16 Brit's potato chip
17 Headliner
18 Hunt hint
19 Example
21 Riddler of old
23 Burnish
24 Careening
25 Use face cream
27 "Perpetual Peace" writer
28 First name in daytime talk
29 Brit. ref. work
30 Mr. Bones, in a minstrel show
33 Hard-rock band named for an inventor
35 Train schedule abbr.
37 French pupil
38 Nahuatl speakers
40 Cable TV inits.
42 Oklahoma city
43 Writer Hubbard
44 Guides
46 Refute
47 By __ and bounds
48 Bearlike
49 Set apart
53 Flip talk
54 Spice
56 Missile depots
57 Comic Kamen
58 Art Deco master
59 Bar, legally
60 "__ luck?"

61 Env. enclosure
62 Expressionless

DOWN

1 Spore sacs
2 Daybreak
3 Discordia's counterpart
4 Readers' perusal
5 Woolly fabric
6 They're thrown at meets
7 Became a member
8 __ glance
9 Abandon
10 Hitch
11 Boast of
12 High point
15 Spielberg film
20 Don't do it

22 Smooth
25 At the home of
26 Sans esprit
28 Concerned citizens' org.
31 Alamo competitor
32 Hammett detective Beaumont
34 Flip __ (decide randomly)
36 Kind of ballot
39 Signs of a cold
41 Wood sorrels
45 Literary works
46 Einstein
48 U.S. Grant's school: Abbr.
50 Countertenor

51 Saturday TV fare, slangily
52 Glimpse
55 Paleozic, e.g.

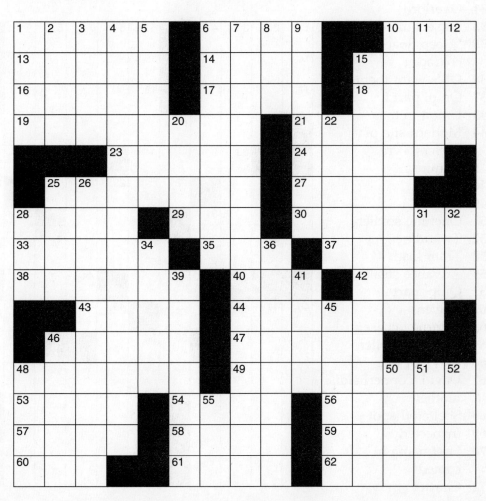

86 *by Harvey Estes*

ACROSS
1 Taj Mahal, e.g.
5 Leader from Talah Minufiya
10 Braces
14 Spy in a 1962 exchange
15 Wide open
16 "Listen up," old style
17 Chuck-a-luck equipment
18 Defunct award
19 Villa Maria College site
20 Start of a quip
23 Copied
24 Davis's home: Abbr.
25 Carmichael's "__ Buttermilk Sky"
26 Chaps
28 Scrap for Rover
31 Overlord
33 Subject of equitation
35 "Deep Space Nine" character
36 QB's want them
37 Quip, part 2
43 Union initials
44 Modern site of ancient Tyre
45 Minute __
46 Lower
49 Mount
51 Onetime soldier
52 Twaddle
53 Tram load
55 Advance stealthily
57 Quip, part 3
62 Mavens
63 Attorney chaser
64 Garden dweller
66 May, for one
67 David Copperfield's mother
68 Sheltered spot
69 Inspected
70 First name in comedy
71 Coaster

DOWN
1 Jot
2 Final copy: Abbr.
3 Repairer
4 Censor, in a way
5 Vegetarian football game?
6 Family data
7 Dungeonlike
8 By the item
9 Rides herd on
10 Pronoun in a wedding vow
11 MOMA work
12 Field-guide listing
13 Make fun of mercilessly
21 "Is it soup __?"
22 Carnival day
26 Marcus Loew founded it
27 Debussy's "Le Jet d'__"
29 Writing on an urn
30 Irrelevant facts, slangily
32 Locale in a Beatles song
34 Go soft
36 Disposable
38 On the other hand
39 Fish-line material
40 Flying cross, e.g.
41 More than aloofness
42 Partygoer
46 Ballet movement with the toe
47 Manhattan type
48 "Becket" co-star, 1964
49 Word in a detergent ad
50 Chic
54 Unwelcome tenant?
56 Decodes
58 Gone, with "up"
59 Fraternity
60 Bring home
61 Moolah
65 Kind of school

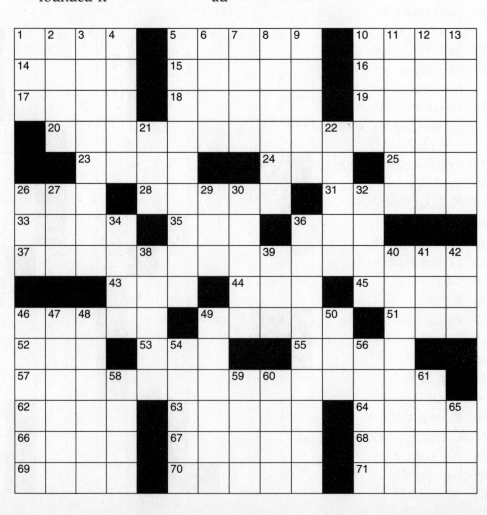

ACROSS

1 "... more than one way to skin —"
5 Supply a party
10 Beast of burden
13 Fads
15 Speak publicly
16 Caltech rival
17 Cereal "fruit"
19 "— of these days, Alice ..."
20 Outdoor
21 Spiritual punishment
23 Meadow
24 Jockey Cordero
25 Civil War flash point
32 Nom de crook
33 Upset
34 Small dog, for short
37 Split
38 Grew ashen
40 Coffee, informally
41 Hat-room fixture
42 Salon offering
43 More painful
44 U.S. commodore in Japan, 1853–54
47 Letter-shaped metal bar
50 Señor Guevara
51 Lovebirds' destination, maybe
54 Paul of "Casablanca"
59 — Altos, Calif.
60 County of Northern Ireland
62 Had a little lamb?
63 First name in cosmetics
64 Novelist Françoise
65 Roll of bills
66 Looks (to be)
67 Unattached

DOWN

1 With the bow, in music
2 Bellyache
3 Malarial symptom
4 Part of T.V.A.: Abbr.
5 Hooded snakes
6 Exist
7 Diamond cover
8 To be, to Satie
9 "— the Fox" (classic fable)
10 In the midst of
11 From the time of
12 Girder material
14 — of justice
18 Yesterday: Fr.
22 "— luck?"
25 David's instrument
26 Downwind, nautically
27 Wedding sine qua non
28 Add to, unnecessarily
29 Smut
30 Prior to, in poems
31 Crimson
34 Henry VIII's VIth
35 "Reply completed," to a ham operator
36 Queen of Scots
38 Word before bull or stop
39 Grasshopper's rebuker
40 Baseball's DiMaggio
42 Mexican snacks
43 Isn't miserly
44 Cosmo, e.g.
45 Reverberations
46 At what time?
47 Wedding acquisition
48 Flora and fauna
49 Let up
52 Type of wine
53 Kitty starter
55 Kind of estate
56 Therefore
57 Major rug exporter
58 Unit of force
61 Rep. foe

ACROSS

1 Bend
5 Exchange
9 Polite form of address
13 Actor Calhoun
14 Make __ for (argue in support of)
15 Ray of Hollywood
16 This puzzle's mystery subject
19 "The Joy Luck Club" author
20 Fuzzy
21 Rule
22 Yield
23 Dubbed one
24 1951 movie with 16 Across
31 Stumble
32 River to the Caspian
33 Veterans Day mo.
35 Daly of "Gypsy"
36 Competition for Geraldo
38 Trig function
39 Wynken, Blynken and __
40 They're sometimes wild
41 Earth mover
42 1957 movie with 16 Across
47 Thumbnail sketch
48 16 Across's "Cat on __ Tin Roof"
49 Étagère piece
52 County north of San Francisco
54 Neighbor of Ind.
57 1946 movie with 16 Across
60 "__ known then what . . ."
61 Cancel
62 "A" code word
63 Greek portico
64 Use épées
65 Half a fortnight

DOWN

1 Stew
2 "Damn Yankees" seductress
3 Green land
4 __ Affair
5 Play's start
6 He coined the term "horsepower"
7 Pallid
8 Caress
9 MGM's Louis B. and others
10 "__ know is what . . ."
11 Sick as __
12 Dawn
14 Put up with
17 Novelist Waugh
18 Disney mermaid
22 Horn, for one
23 Iranian chief, once
24 Letter abbr.
25 Richard of "Bustin' Loose"
26 Newswoman Ellerbee
27 Tend to
28 Refrain syllable
29 Confederacy's opponent
30 Three trios
34 Exceedingly
36 Eight: Prefix
37 Through
38 Latched
40 Law professor Hill
43 Airline to Spain
44 Outpouring of gossip
45 Bit of fall weather
46 Miss O'Neill
49 Publisher Adolph
50 Sloop
51 Defense means
52 Diner's guide
53 First-class
54 Man or Ely, e.g.
55 16 Across's "__ With Father"
56 Plumber's concern
58 Travel (about)
59 16 Across's "The Last Time I __ Paris"

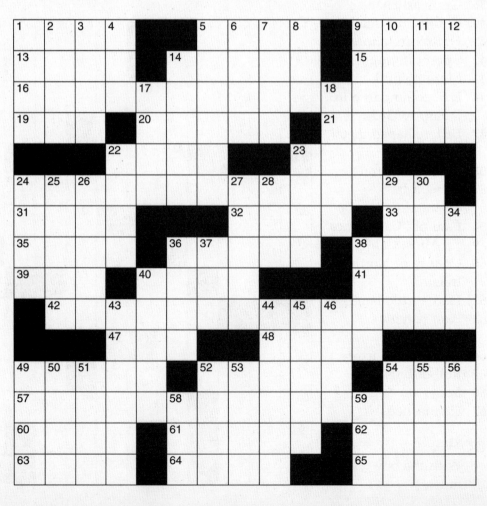

89 *by Joel Davajan*

ACROSS

1 Unhappy
5 Man with the world on his shoulders
10 Israeli carrier
14 "Mona __"
15 Scarlett's love
16 Comic Rudner
17 What we celebrate on July 4
20 Honor, with "to"
21 Form 1040 amount
22 Buntline and Rorem
23 Sean Connery, e.g.
24 Duke's home
27 Fifth Avenue name
28 Catch in the act
31 Gaucho's rope
32 Golfer Ballesteros
33 Old Russian assembly
34 What we celebrate on July 4
37 Bronze and Iron
38 Some intersections
39 Think
40 Stag party attendees
41 Scorch
42 Ranch
43 Tools locale
44 __ de foie gras
45 Book after Nehemiah
48 Fortification
52 What we watch on July 4
54 A lulu
55 Miss Brooks portrayer
56 Muck
57 Witnessed
58 Stocking material
59 Some whiskies

DOWN

1 Happy
2 Green shade
3 Employed
4 Seasons, as meat
5 Teen hangout
6 Dean Martin's "__ Amore"
7 __-majesté
8 Arm of the Treasury Dept.
9 Ill
10 Construct
11 Island near Venice
12 Mighty mite
13 Costly cloth
18 Hangover soother?
19 Son of Seth
23 Baseball and hockey stats
24 Father of Hector and Paris
25 Danny of the N.B.A.
26 Weighed down
27 Passover feast
28 Blue entertainment
29 Hotpoint rival
30 Sang to the moon
32 Golf legend Sam
33 Doctor's instrument
35 Intangible
36 Egypt's __ Church
41 "Good night, __" (old TV phrase)
42 Briny
43 Like Samson, once
44 Kind of truck
45 Heroic poetry
46 "Auld Lang __"
47 It's better known for its bark than its bite
48 Third degrees, usually
49 Seaman's shout
50 Nod off
51 Rams' dams
53 Dernier __

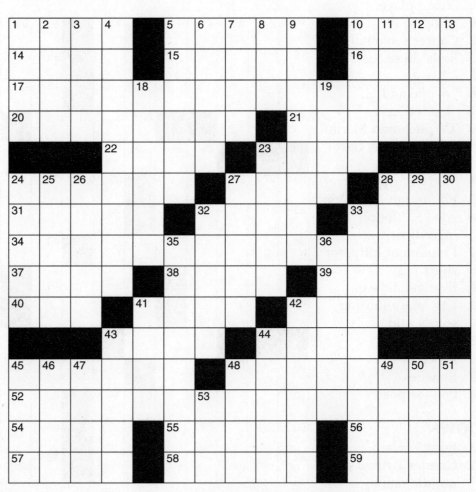

ACROSS

1 On the __ (very angry)
8 For the well-to-do
15 November winner
16 Savannah's place
17 "Evil Ways" band
18 Bar members
19 Dynamite's kin
20 Christian Science founder
22 Popes "An __ on Man"
23 __ way (incidentally)
25 Murals and the like
26 Free-for-all
29 Play callers
31 Ill-fated sibling rival
35 Put on a pedestal
36 Ark builder
37 Singer Falana
38 String player
40 "Hop to it!"
42 Cancer's symbol
43 Reds' Rose
45 2:1, e.g.
46 "A-one and __"
47 "I smell __"
48 TV pitchman Merlin
49 "A Christmas Carol" boy
51 Study of optometry?
53 Edinburgh dwellers
56 Aloe __ (lotion ingredient)
57 Retirement kitty, for short
60 Evangeline, e.g.
62 Last-place finisher, so it's said
65 Unyielding
66 Fence in
67 Reneges
68 Quotes poetry

DOWN

1 Frontierward
2 Chester Arthur's middle name
3 Monthly due
4 %: Abbr.
5 __ loss for words
6 Belief
7 Edith + Holly
8 Hideous
9 Black-eyed one, perhaps
10 Farmer, in the spring
11 Billy + Lucille
12 "Rock of __"
13 Italian bread
14 Word before come and go
21 Car for test-driving
23 Alexander + Timothy
24 Abominable Snowman
25 Tennis's Arthur
26 Islamic center
27 Bring to bear
28 Steven Bochco TV drama
30 Patti + Lana
32 Boxing matches
33 Borden bovine
34 Instructions to Macduff
39 Lunch meat
41 "Star Trek" counselor
44 Record
50 Basketball's Thomas
52 "Common Sense" author
53 "Saint Joan" playwright
54 Sign over
55 Reverend Roberts
56 Animal docs
57 "__ You Babe"
58 Misleading move
59 Senate votes
61 SSW's reverse
63 New Deal grp.
64 Yale player

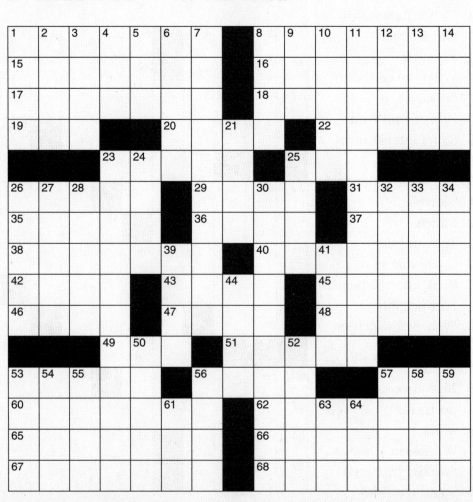

ACROSS

1 Kindergarten instruction
5 Onetime La Scala tenor
11 Shake up
14 Brook
15 Unlocked
16 Hollywood's Thurman
17 Star of "The Invisible Man"
19 Hoover, for one
20 Zeus or Jupiter, e.g.
21 School grp.
22 Wood-shaping tool
23 Fleur-de-___
25 Mr. Sondheim
27 Not left in the lurch
32 "The Time Machine" people
33 Speckled horse
34 Poet Wilfred
36 Meanies
39 Religious offshoot
40 Pay by mail
42 Onetime Texaco rival
43 Not on the level
45 Talkative Barrett
46 Prefix with plasm
47 Not cleric
49 Two-pointer, the hard way
51 Comes out
54 Kin of calypso music
55 Beats it
56 Piggie
58 Orientals, e.g.
63 Belief
64 Star of "The Vanishing" (1993 version)
66 Bedlam site
67 Spoke from the soapbox
68 Pull off a coup
69 Author Beattie
70 Choir voices
71 Minus

DOWN

1 Electrical paths
2 Gyp
3 Ali, once
4 Coin that's not a coin
5 One who shares a masthead billing
6 ___ financing (car ad phrase)
7 Sow's opposite
8 Rightmost column
9 A century in Washington
10 ___ bodkins
11 Star of "Without a Trace"
12 Flabbergast
13 Japanese noodle soup
18 Kewpie
22 Orbiting points
24 Betsy Ross, e.g.
26 "Don't Bring Me Down" rock band
27 Nocturnal bear?
28 They might be heard a thousand times
29 Star of "Missing"
30 All broken up
31 Disband, postwar
35 Hirschfeld hides them
37 This, in Madrid
38 Chimney grit
41 Ale mugs
44 Barrister's headgear
48 The "c" in etc.
50 Actress Lemmons
51 "My Fair Lady" lady
52 Stoneworker
53 Divans
57 Newts
59 False god
60 Dickensian chill
61 Eerie loch
62 Concorde et al.
64 Book after Esther
65 A stingy fellow?

ACROSS

1 Clicker that might be used on a trawler?
9 London elevator
13 Tibetan V.I.P.
14 Plume source
16 Starter at an Italian restaurant
17 Quick on one's toes
18 Shoshonean
19 Health resort
20 Department store employee
21 Behan's "__ Boy"
23 George Sand, e.g.
24 Gene Kelly's "__ Girls"
25 Loving touches
26 German coal region
28 Propelled a punt
29 Amtrak listing: Abbr.
30 One of the Astors
31 Is interested
32 Caddies carry them
33 Bank account amt.
34 Vatican City dwellers
35 Jetty
36 It causes a reaction
38 Great noise
39 Sparta was its capital
40 Have the chair
44 Resounding, as a canyon
45 TV knob abbr.
46 Statehouse V.I.P.
47 Left the chair
48 Cheese at an Italian restaurant
51 "Put up your __!"
53 Élan
54 Solemn hymn

DOWN

1 Piece of a poem
2 Change, as hems
3 Capuchin monkey
4 Racetrack informant
5 Confirmation slaps
6 Twangy
7 Ambulance attendant: Abbr.
8 Philosopher's universal
9 Scholarly
10 Eliza's 'enry
11 Chicken dish
12 Distance gauge
13 Paint unskillfully
15 Brewer and Wright
20 Parisian papas
22 Kill, as a dragon
23 Turns white
25 Meltdown areas
26 City south of Palo Alto
27 Salad ingredient
28 __ New Guinea
30 Throw off the scent
31 Some lose sleep over it
32 Baking pans
34 Most runtlike
35 Polish dumpling
37 Yankee great Skowron et al.
38 Herds
40 Call up
41 Jim Croce's "__ Name"
42 Gift getter
43 Holiday nights
48 Cushion
49 Baseball hitter's stat
50 Household god, in Roman myth

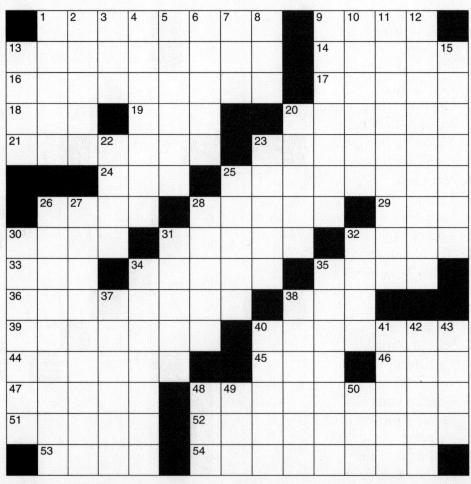

93 *by Glenton Petgrave*

ACROSS

1 Twain character
7 To the extent that
14 Lacking nothing
15 Closet
16 Blinker
17 Art of arguing
19 Traditional areas of knowledge
20 Defraud
21 High-paying easy job
22 Geraint's love
23 "__ Johnny!"
24 Part of an equine family tree
25 Room with an easy chair
26 Become entrenched
27 __ Aviv
28 Football team
30 Part of elopement plans
32 Egg on
33 Fuzzy fruit
35 Holds back
38 Accolade
40 Conflict
41 Negotiations
42 D.C. summer time
45 Flag
47 Wall decoration
48 Blackthorn fruit
49 Derive (from)
50 Thin
51 Sign of life
52 Table
54 Rodeo rope
55 One on a walkout
56 Repay
57 Hobo's garb
58 Business news

DOWN

1 Prepared potatoes
2 "Who'll volunteer?"
3 Of the same mother
4 Stacked
5 Goddess of discord
6 Danger signal
7 Unlined tablet
8 Hot
9 Kith and kin
10 Live
11 On/off routes
12 Nimbleness
13 Ties down
18 Refine
20 Procreate
23 Busy place
26 Socialist Eugene
29 Amateur
30 Terrible __
31 Fit out
33 Czar-era bourgeois
34 Sorts
35 Food that's hole-some?
36 Most acidic
37 Short melody
38 Breadwinners
39 Commotion
41 Merchant
43 Medicinal amount
44 Be indecisive
46 Brainy
47 Much the same
48 More confident
51 Blacktop
53 Be in session
54 Escape

94 *by Arthur S. Verdesca*

ACROSS

1 Entertain from house to house
6 Sirs' counterparts
12 Horse show locales
14 Slow musical pieces
16 Kind of license or justice
17 Measles variety
18 W.W. II German bomber
19 "From the __ of Montezuma"
21 Pascal's law
22 Part of H.R.H.
23 Fixed, as a gauge
25 Reposed
26 Iris's place
28 Chichi
29 Place for belt-tightening
30 Flooring of marble chips
32 Ibsen play
33 Singer Laine
34 Kind of suit
35 Strait of Dover port
38 Women's wide-legged pants
42 __-garde
43 District
44 Orient
45 Shower attention (on)
46 Jeans
48 Third-millennium year
49 "__ Along Little Dogies"
50 Gist
51 Drum accompanying a fife
53 Academy Award category
55 Strainers
57 Quietus
58 Pluck, as eyebrows
59 Juicer
60 Iris with a fragrant rootstock

DOWN

1 Prisoner
2 Alarm, e.g.
3 Stink
4 Like some beer
5 My __, Vietnam
6 "A Christmas Carol" specter
7 Not for kiddies
8 Small flatfishes
9 Questionnaire info
10 "Pizarro Seizing the Inca of Peru" artist
11 Recital singer
13 Sonata's third movement, often
15 Louisiana 11
18 Folded up
20 Respecting
24 Demolishes
25 Founder of Taoism
27 Esoteric
29 Avast, on land
31 Got off
32 Robot, in Jewish legend
34 Most like the Marx Brothers
35 Sponged
36 Dodger
37 Trellis
38 Singer Lily
39 Africa's fourth-longest river
40 Seeps
41 Pen
43 Early American publisher Peter
46 Stupid
47 Beef cattle
50 Where Anna Leonowens taught
52 Affirm
54 Japanese drink
56 W.W. II battle site, for short

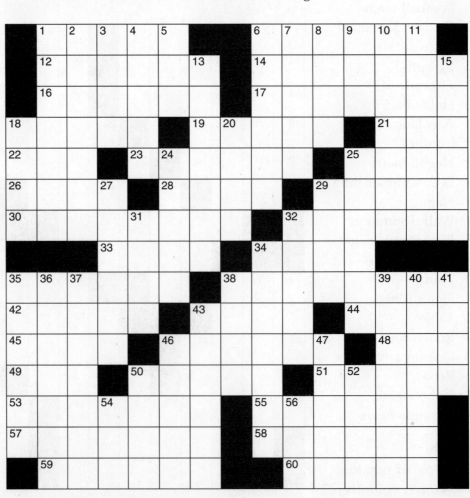

ACROSS

1 Garden tool
6 "Gimme Shelter" band, with "the"
12 Explain visually
14 Brecht's "Mother —"
15 With 16 Across, Canadian speech
16 Anagram of 15 Across
17 Kind of fingerprinting, nowadays
18 Pollen holder
20 By way of
21 Left-fielder Ron
23 "For" words
24 Screen —
25 Dubai royalty
27 Lush
28 Suffix with kitchen
29 Reminisce
31 Siege site
34 Midafternoon on a sundial
35 Suffix with sonnet
36 Make no change
41 Iced dessert
45 Heavy reading?
46 One for the road
48 La Scala locale
49 Banned apple spray
50 Error's partner
52 Druggie's nemesis
53 Ukr. neighbor
54 Land of ancient Smyrna
55 Earl Grey, e.g.
56 With 58 Across, hires recording artists again
58 Anagram of 56 Across
61 — list
62 Enrage
63 Satrap
64 Ad signs

DOWN

1 Like Rushdie's verses
2 Tour org.
3 T.W.A. info
4 Kind of wheel
5 Hams it up
6 Boils
7 Malaysian gent's title
8 Table scrap
9 Ingénue's trait
10 Self-ish folks
11 Upper chambers
12 Ebbets Field player
13 — only
14 Regain consciousness
19 Beginning (then)
22 With 24 Down, instructor's turf
24 Anagram of 22 Down
26 Coasted
30 Back talk
32 Person in stripes
33 Four years, for a President
36 Headlined
37 The second T in TNT
38 Accumulates
39 Puzzle direction
40 Follow
42 Typewriter rollers
43 Price cutters, in a sense
44 Box up
47 — bran
50 Believe it
51 Singer Frankie
54 Currency premium
57 Rascal
59 Enlisted V.I.P.
60 A superior of 59 Down

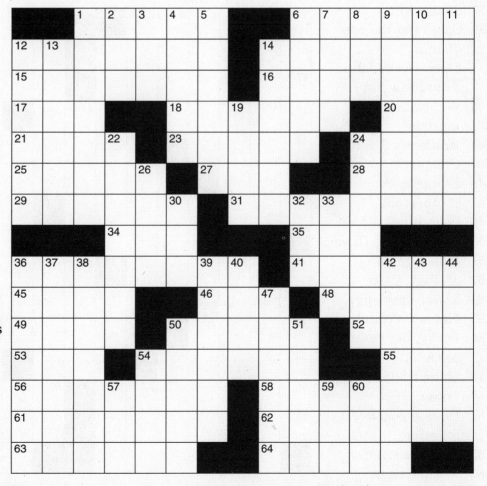

ACROSS

1 "Star Wars" group
7 __ card (wallet item)
13 "Walk on the Wild Side" singer
15 Puget Sound city
17 Feeler
18 "L'École des Femmes" writer
19 Retard
20 "Make __ double!"
22 Introvert
23 Sticky strip
24 Static __
26 Thurmond of hoops
27 __ flash
28 Hang on the line
30 Medicine amounts: Abbr.
31 Some shooters
33 Singer Kitt
35 Subject of the book "Perjury"
36 Open-weave fabric
37 Examine again
40 We're all in this together
44 Addison's "__ to Creation"
45 Leathernecks
47 __ anemone
48 High time?
50 Tar from the Thames
51 Italian bread
52 __ Park, Colo.
54 Masc. alternative
55 Niamey's country
56 Lucky, like sesame seeds?
58 Shiite leader
60 Loose
61 Double negative follower
62 Not worn out
63 Ran the show

DOWN

1 Adjustable
2 Four-time Super Bowl QB
3 Housed in
4 "The Forsyte Saga" lady
5 Overhead expense
6 Poet's adverb
7 On __ (when wanted)
8 Ab __ (from the start)
9 Dudley Do-Right's love
10 M-G-M or TriStar rival
11 Show historically
12 Seventh-inning activity
14 Newspapers
16 Mother of Calcutta
21 Advice
24 Glassware
25 Grant's opponent, 1872
28 Jeffersonian belief
29 1979 Richard Gere film
32 Any miss
34 Artist Lichtenstein
36 Center, for one
37 Beaus
38 Six-time Emmy-winning actor
39 With a will
40 Quiet, expressive one
41 Pioneer pilots
42 Golden
43 Long in the past
46 Rummaged in an arsenal?
49 Vassals
51 Digs
53 Alphabetize
55 Second starter
57 Majors in acting
59 Chew the fat

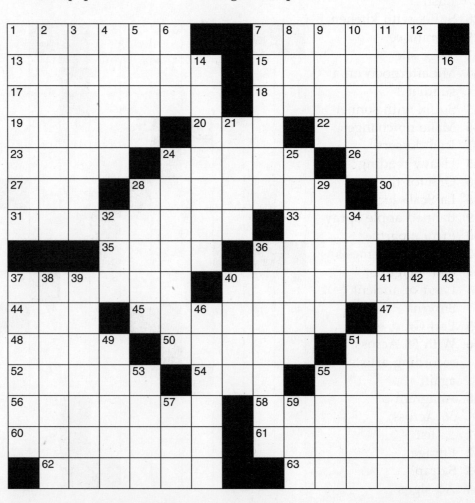

ACROSS

1 Espresso
7 Pocketbook material, maybe
14 Opens
16 Make too many eggs?
17 More than dull
18 Juicy morsels
19 Cabbies
20 Valuable deposits
22 Gymnast's need
23 Ticks off
24 Tea type
25 Deft
26 Zip
27 Point count bidding pioneer
28 Amaze
29 Flips out
31 Undiluted
33 Cycle starter
34 Crowd noise
35 Squirrels' sustenance
38 Game fad of the 50's
42 Shade of white
43 Pull strings
45 Preschooler
46 Standard
47 Religious devotion
48 "Star Trek" Klingon
49 Sphere opening
50 "Hans Brinker" author
51 "Madonna With Saints" artist
52 Comic Dick
54 Parasite
56 Activist actor
57 Clothing, informally
58 Lineups
59 Idi Amin, e.g.

DOWN

1 Former Boston cardinal Richard
2 Least great Great Lake
3 Spot for Howdy Dowdy
4 Y's
5 Crimson rivals
6 Expansion wing
7 They're up for discussion
8 Just like ewe?
9 Bolsheviks
10 Ball
11 Invitation to ride
12 Piece of junk mail
13 Kind of bar
15 Stern
21 ___ out (just manage)
24 Visit unexpectedly
25 Islands welcome
27 Game-show host Moore
28 Blunt
30 Gale of "Oh! Susanna"
32 Cartoon crime-fighter
35 It surrounds a pit
36 Popular cigars
37 Eight-footers
38 Most adorable
39 Makeshift
40 One cursed by Farragut
41 Initially
42 "Well, ___!"
44 Stocking stuffer
47 Logroller, in a way
48 Cellar contents
50 Unit of force
51 Wives' tales
53 Clock-resetting abbr.
55 Degree of distinction

ACROSS

1 He wrote "The Bronx? No, thonx!"
5 Cramped Mother Goose dwelling
9 Renaissance beauty Isabella __
14 Anent
15 Follow the game
16 Send packing
17 "Dark Lady" singer
18 Tallinn native
19 Actor Keach
20 Hollywood palmist?
23 Make cherished
24 Ump's purview
25 Roget's entry: Abbr.
27 Percussion at a powwow
31 Actor Davis
35 Well-oiled grp.
38 New Rochelle college
39 Hollywood quack?
42 For takeout
43 Ex of 17-Across
44 He wrote "The Proper Bostonians"
45 Available for
47 West Point subject
49 Yield slightly
52 Sports jacket
57 Hollywood's leading undertaker?
60 Originated
61 The last Mrs. Chaplin
62 Member of 35-Across
63 In accord (with)
64 Skidded
65 Scottish tongue
66 Heavy of old comedies
67 Location
68 M-G-M co-founder Marcus

DOWN

1 Mother-of-pearl
2 Pale-faced
3 Bed frame
4 Genghis Khan's mass
5 Jerez product
6 Silence
7 Ready if needed
8 Word on old gas pumps
9 Mississippi discoverer
10 Ultra credo
11 Minor dispute
12 Georgia __
13 TV Tarzan Ron
21 Canvas prop
22 Do guard duty
26 Say __ (refuse)
28 Kansas pooch
29 "__ about . . ."
30 Lots and lots
31 Tetra × 2
32 The Old Curiosity, e.g.
33 Nestor
34 Unyielding
36 Review a flop
37 Adequate, way back
40 Domicile
41 Confederate general Jubal
46 Dempsey's nemesis
48 Scrape
50 Luster
51 Carlo Levi's "Christ Stopped at __"
53 Swiss diarist Henri Frédéric __
54 Man in a mask
55 Get rid of
56 Freshen
57 "__ smile be . . ."
58 Borodin's prince
59 Singleton
60 "Phooey!"

ACROSS

1 Dries (off)
7 The color of honey
12 Wining and dining place
13 Bob of reggae
15 The "thee" of "Of Thee I Sing"
16 Teases
18 __ soda
19 Napoli night
21 Least big
22 Football no-no
24 Prefix equivalent to -ish
26 Way on or off
27 He told a hare racing story
29 Outlets
31 Hemingway novel setting
32 Furniture trim
34 Property restriction
36 Site of a Lewis and Clark stop, 1804
38 Inevitable
41 Up, in a way
44 Glaciate
45 Arises (from)
47 "It's __ never"
49 "Stuffed Shirts" author
51 Blithe
53 Find, with "out"
54 Wassail flavor enhancer
56 Penicillin target, for short
58 Sermon subject
59 Semisoft Danish cheese
61 Approved
63 Modern phone option
64 Dürer and others
65 Oboelike in sound
66 Rest-less, perhaps

DOWN

1 Wrapped food
2 Giant stele
3 Disturber of the peace
4 Hibernia
5 Rimsky-Korsakov opera opener
6 Park art
7 Definitely not a know-it-all
8 Fannie __
9 Steep
10 Venerable one
11 Legal O.K.
12 Abettor of Brutus
14 Rubber stamps
17 March honoree (with an aptly numbered clue)
20 Free of duties
23 Balance
25 "__ the bag!"
28 Fussbudgets
30 "Dragonwyck" author
33 Nail's companion
35 "Discus Thrower" sculptor of ancient Greece
37 With worry
38 Rip off
39 Eyepiece, in jargon
40 Bounce back
42 Ballroom dance
43 Nylons
46 Toots
48 Pulls apart
50 Get around
52 Streisand title role
55 Detroit River's destination
57 Runners try to pick it up
60 Just a bit
62 Amigo of Fidel

100 *by Manny Nosowsky*

ACROSS

1 Book of the Apocrypha
7 Apse setting
15 Catchall phrase
16 Esthete
17 Uncompromising
18 Swain song
19 Doctrinal holding
20 French assembly
21 Teachers' grp.
22 They have namesakes: Abbr.
23 Grammy-winning country group
25 Results of conks
26 Farm building
30 Guarding mobilely
34 Its fruit is monkey bread
36 It's played at the 7-Down
38 Rose's home
39 Without concern for the future
40 Baron in "Der Rosenkavalier"
41 Wistful one
42 Epcot neighbor
44 Computer add-on?
47 G. & S. princess
50 Embarrass
51 Strauss's "Ariadne auf __"
53 Transportation Secretary Pena
55 Theater's Willy, Linda, Happy and Biff
56 St. Louis arch designer
57 Charlotte __ Virgin Islands
58 Printed, as a quote
59 Way with words?

DOWN

1 One-liners
2 Complete
3 Fills in a hole
4 Tennis hothead
5 XXX activity
6 Derby
7 36-Across's site
8 Circus locales
9 Sportscaster Hank
10 "__ song go . . ."
11 Mr. Chaney
12 A Karamazov
13 Part with
14 Purlieu
20 Southernmost U.S. point
24 Michaels of "Saturday Night Live"
26 __ speak (as it were)
27 Footnote abbr.
28 Literally, superior one
29 Be loyal to
30 Knowing
31 Pusher's nemesis
32 Chief god of Memphis
33 Afflicts
34 Howled
35 Copernican concern
37 Lustrous velvet
41 Kind of mining
42 Umpire for the duel in "Hamlet"
43 Zoo critter
44 Rate highly
45 Artist Delaunay
46 Car of the 20's
47 Conditional words
48 College leader
49 Month after Shevat
52 "__ for All Seasons"
54 Prior to
55 Scale notes

101 *by Peter Gordon*

ACROSS

1 Like Ike
5 Like most colleges today
9 One 39 Across
13 "I cannot tell —"
14 Heraldic band
15 Sandbags, maybe
16 Holds up
17 Café additive
18 Chemically nonreactive
19 Chiffonier
21 One 39 Across
23 One 39 Across
25 Verboten: Var.
26 Cantankerous
32 Rep.'s rival
35 "— be a cold day in Hell . . ."
38 Ancient region of Asia Minor
39 Each of eight in this puzzle
43 Like measles
44 Elliptical
45 Compass dir.
46 Home to Denali National Park
48 Teases
51 One 39 Across
56 One 39 Across
60 Stay informed
62 Island group near Fiji
63 Periodical of haute couture
65 Small dog breed, for short
66 One 39 Across
67 Plaintiff
68 Get ready
69 Fusses
70 Orly birds?
71 Lighten up

DOWN

1 Fishhook part
2 One way to read
3 Sign of autumn's beginning
4 Go AWOL
5 One 39 Across
6 — pro nobis
7 Statesman Root
8 Coup —
9 Transportation Secretary Federico —
10 Penultimate fairy tale word
11 Wonk, maybe
12 Pocket
15 Actress Ullmann
20 One–time link
22 Symbol for density
24 Expenditure
27 Singer Ocasek of the Cars
28 Classic drama of Japan
29 Seth's son
30 Ocho —, Jamaica
31 One 39 Across
32 1982 movie thriller
33 Iniquitous
34 Pianist Hess
36 Broadway comedy of 1964
37 Live's partner
40 — Palmas (Canary Islands seaport)
41 Benevolent guy
42 Macs
47 King Kong, e.g.
49 Quilt-making gathering
50 Treeless plain
52 Like the Boston-accented pronunciation of many words
53 Card catalogue abbr.
54 Where the fat lady sings
55 Zaps
56 Ask to produce proof of age
57 Melville novel
58 Participates in a regatta, perhaps
59 One of the Bobbsey twins
61 — Le Pew
62 Loan-granting Fed. agcy.
64 Fill a flat?

ACROSS

1 Gore's "__ in the Balance"
6 One who's "agin" it
10 Train unit
13 "__ Without Windows" ('64 song)
14 Supermarket meat label
15 Territory
16 Major Bowes updated?
18 Fat
19 Home on the range
20 Kind of signal
21 Part of SEATO
22 Mail HQ
23 Breakfast order
25 Lift up
29 Woodworker's choice
32 Belgian airline
34 Bests
38 Hemingway opus
41 Dub again
42 Took ten
43 Ingenious
45 Shows remorse
46 Up
50 Marinaro and others
52 Slough
53 Reckon
56 Bosom companions
60 "Remember the neediest," e.g.
61 Olympia Dukakis film
63 Fast time
64 Capri, for one
65 Misrepresent
66 Pupil's place
67 African lake
68 Volvo worker

DOWN

1 Bridge seat
2 Comic Johnson
3 Imitation morocco
4 Civil wrong
5 __ Pinafore
6 Cottonwoods
7 Grammy-winning pianist
8 Yacht heading
9 Person of will
10 1929 event
11 High nest
12 "M*A*S*H" character
15 "Too bad"
17 Parapsychology study
22 Authentic
24 Singing sisters
25 D.C. zone
26 Comic Bert
27 Have __ in one's bonnet
28 Probe
30 Flat sign?

31 Vienna is its cap.
33 In opposition to one another
35 River to the Seine
36 Town near Padua
37 Osmose
39 Melmackian of TV
40 60's org.
44 Craved
46 With room to spare
47 "Little Orphant Annie" poet
48 Goodnight girl
49 Pants part
51 __ Plaines
54 Deluxe
55 Southeast Kansas town
56 Witch's __
57 Golden, e.g.
58 Tart

59 __ Ball (arcade game)
62 Kitchen meas.

ACROSS

1 Former Mississippi Senator Cochran
5 Nutty
9 Gangbusters at the box office
14 River to the Rhine
15 Lena of recent films
16 Like the skies in "Ulalume"
17 Sorts
18 Carty of baseball
19 Oh, so many moons
20 Go astray
23 Stack-blowing feeling
24 Countdown start
25 Tak's opposite
26 Alphabetical run
27 As a whole
31 Bit
33 Mezzo-soprano Marilyn
34 Santa Fe Trail town
35 Pickle
38 Red of firefighting fame
39 Words of wonderment
40 With respect to
41 "Whip It" rock group
42 Drawing card
43 The Divine Miss M
44 Play the siren
46 Smelt, e.g.
47 Aquarium oddity
49 Cry of delight
50 It has its point
51 Harvest goddess
52 Not yet in full bloom
58 Tubby the Tuba creator Paul
60 Reed of note
61 Light-footed
62 Hint
63 An order of the court
64 W.W. I German admiral
65 Pond covering
66 Silent O.K.'s
67 With defects and all

DOWN

1 Shadow
2 Christmas play prop
3 Synagogue cabinets
4 Not dose
5 World's third-largest island
6 '79 sci-fi thriller
7 Muscle spasms
8 Bird that summers in the Arctic
9 Agree
10 Sugary suffix
11 Many skiers use these when they (see diagonal)
12 Writers Jean and Walter
13 Assault
21 Mink's relative
22 Pretension
27 '64 musical "__ a Ball"
28 Leaf's starting point
29 Getting across
30 Stew ingredient
31 Skier Phil
32 Original Jed Clampett
34 Score for Barry Sanders
36 Observe
37 Great Scott of 1857
40 Sound as __
42 Animal that sleeps with its eyes open
45 Noodle topper
46 Candy
47 Must, slangily
48 Part of an Argentine autumn
50 Steer clear of
53 River of Spain
54 Greek peak
55 Third addendum to a letter
56 "... __ saw Elba"
57 Shoemakers' bottles
59 Trevino's org.

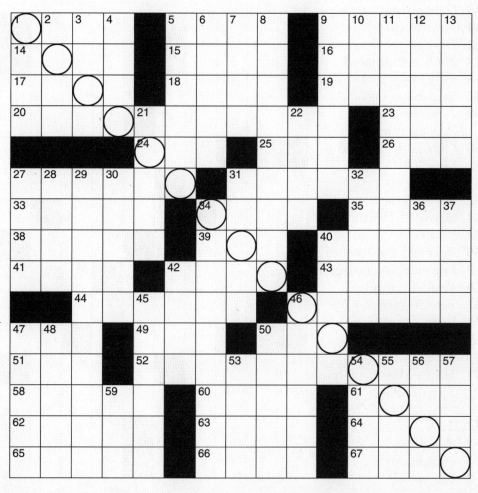

ACROSS

1 Dog star
5 Gull's cousin
9 Eyeball bender
14 Ground grain
15 Mini revelation
16 Red-eyed bird
17 Haitian despot
20 Cordwood measure
21 Israeli dance
22 Out's opposite
23 Vidal's Breckinridge
25 Actor Young of TV's 67 Across
27 Is grief-stricken
30 Book subtitled "His Songs and His Sayings"
35 Supped
36 Relative of a Bap. or Presb.
37 Balkan capital
38 Gabor sister
40 Thimbleful
42 Dryden work
43 Help get situated
45 Plugs of a sort
47 Saturn's wife
48 1956 Rosalind Russell role
50 "For __ us a child is born"
51 Headlight?
52 Survey chart
54 Seaweed product
57 __ fixe
59 Reached the total of
63 Popular psychologist
66 Paul Anka hit
67 See 25 Across
68 Deep blue
69 Throat malady
70 Achy
71 James Mason sci-fi role of 1954

DOWN

1 Rock band equipment
2 Usher
3 Mend, in a way
4 Alternatives to The Club
5 Round stopper
6 Delights
7 Change the décor
8 Kind of network
9 Roman breakfast?
10 Light beers
11 "Jewel Song," e.g.
12 Mariner's peril
13 Raced
18 She played Grace Van Owen on "L.A. Law"
19 Passepartout, to Phileas Fogg
24 Strongly scented plant
26 Stellar Ram
27 Fiji neighbor
28 City in northern Japan
29 Set in motion
31 Dinnerware
32 Building contractor
33 Not suitable
34 Final authority
36 Madness
39 Oust
41 Nurse, maybe
44 Directed toward a goal
46 Hair fixative
49 Office connections?
50 Donny Osmond, e.g.
53 Record-holding N.F.L. receiver __ Monk
54 Postfixes
55 Sandpaper surface
56 Opened a crack
58 Catalonian river
60 Hawaiian hen
61 In shape
62 Kon-Tiki Museum site
64 Shrill bark
65 Lyric poem

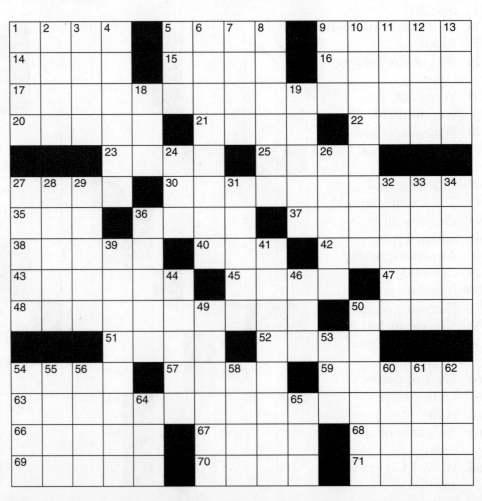

ACROSS

1 Crocus bulb
5 "Son of the Sun"
9 Set-to
14 Pastiche
15 Score in pinochle
16 "A house is not __"
17 Restaurant request
18 Vessel for Jill
19 "Anticipation" singer
20 Song by 11 Down
23 Vinegary
24 Scottish hillside
25 Westernmost Aleutian
27 A clef
32 Unsettle?
35 Scruff
38 "Aeneid" locale
39 Musical or song by 11 Down
42 Nobelist Wiesel
43 Rows before P
44 Gorky's "The __ Depths"
45 Had a hunch
47 Carol
49 Daffy Duck talk
52 Bedtime annoyances
56 Song by 11 Down
61 Mercutio's friend
62 Cigar's end
63 Prefix with China
64 An acid
65 Alert
66 Ending with gang or mob
67 Guided a raft
68 Kane's Rosebud
69 Libel, e.g.

DOWN

1 Pause sign
2 Relating to $C_{18}H_{34}O_2$
3 Dyeing instruction
4 Some handlebars
5 Collision
6 Circa
7 Mountaineer
8 Psychiatrist Alfred
9 Tennessee Senator Jim
10 I.O.U.
11 Late, great composer
12 Mine: Fr.
13 "State of Grace" star
21 Thurber's Walter
22 Informal goodbye
26 Word on a coin
28 Student of animal behavior
29 Make coffee
30 Knowledge
31 Spectator
32 Farm mothers
33 Base
34 "The doctor __"
36 Barley beard
37 Exploited worker
40 It may be golden

41 Actress Verdugo
46 Friend of Harvey the rabbit
48 Belgian port
50 Mergansers' kin
51 Perfumery bit
53 Showed allegiance, in a way
54 Downy bird
55 Stable sound
56 Envelop
57 Our genus
58 Biographer Ludwig
59 Hawaiian honker
60 To be, to Henri

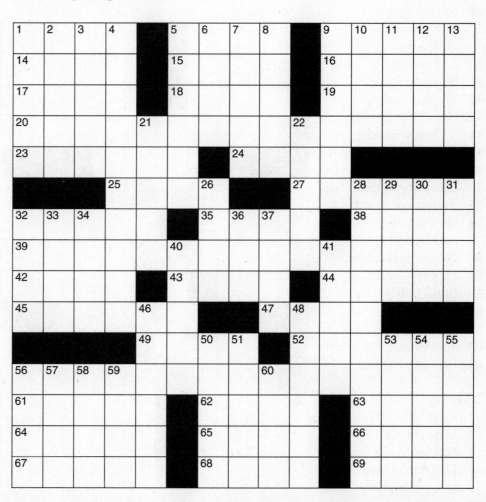

ACROSS

1 Outlet center?
5 Wheat __ (crackers)
10 Stick around
14 The last Mrs. Chaplin
15 Storyteller of old Greece
16 Opening for a sweat bead
17 Ballerina's skirt
18 Strainer
19 Novelist Murdoch
20 Colonist's command
23 "Piggies"
24 Have a hunch
25 Like crazy
28 Waikiki dances
31 Dungeons & Dragons beast
32 Row, e.g.
34 School grp.
37 Judy Garland's command
40 Embroider
41 Bowling lanes
42 The hunted
43 Feeds the flame
44 __ Haute, Ind.
45 Thursday's eponym
47 In a mo
49 February command
55 Invitation word
56 Heretofore mentioned
57 House nickname
59 __ even keel
60 Basic belief
61 Ballooned
62 Took off
63 Shorthand, for short
64 Fair to middlin'

DOWN

1 Kitty
2 Musical forte?
3 Golden Rule word
4 Knight's glove
5 Discrimination
6 Will-reading attendees
7 "Um-hmm"
8 Award-winning scienc show
9 Expedited
10 Places for titles
11 "The Velvet Fog"
12 "The Little Mermaid"
13 Sandburg's "The People, __"
21 1982 Pryor film, with "The"
22 Best __
25 May honorees
26 "Let Us Now Praise Famous Men" author
27 Columnist Pearson
28 Sharpens
29 __ daisy
30 O.K.'s
32 Athlete from Tres Coracoes, Brazil
33 Brooklet
34 Good engine sound
35 Level
36 "__ sow . . ."
38 TV host Povich
39 Job vacancies
43 Incite
44 Candidate for day care
45 Butcher's cut
46 Rambo, e.g.
47 Early evening
48 __ a customer
50 Winery fixtures
51 Drive the get-away car, maybe
52 Sole
53 Claudius's adopted son
54 Sheepcote matriarchs
55 Intimidate
58 Brace

ACROSS

1 Noodlehead
5 Dagger handles
10 Silver-tongued
14 Eminently draftable
15 He has "99 beautiful names"
16 San __, Italy
17 "Murder in the Cathedral" setting
19 Faux pas follower
20 Auto part
21 Abe's "The Woman in the __"
22 Bohea, e.g.
25 Caddies carry them
27 In fairness
28 Boulevard
30 Genteel
32 Aquarium fish
33 Humble toiler
34 Pick
37 Training-room complaint
38 Robbery
39 National Enquirer rival
40 66, e.g.: Abbr.
41 Like "Hee Haw" humor
42 Italian Renaissance poet
43 Two-time A.L. M.V.P
45 Lecture
46 Reserve supply
48 Promise word
50 Beat one's gums
51 Brook
52 Writer Angelou
54 Eaglelike, perhaps
55 Perambulates
61 Plains Indian
62 Regarding
63 Xenia's home
64 First-rate
65 Violet relative
66 Arctic native

DOWN

1 Baseball's Gooden
2 __ roll
3 Actor Cariou
4 "So long"
5 Yamaha rival
6 Noted absurdist
7 Kind of shot
8 Tobacco figure
9 Like a wallflower
10 Ptarmigan
11 Assassin's victim, 8/20/40
12 Spur
13 Imperious
18 Lagniappe
21 Con
22 Golden Horde member
23 Upright
24 Miss Marple film "Murder __"
26 Upholstery concern
27 Stun
29 Up to
31 Cheerful
33 Persian sprite
35 Fettuccelle, e.g.
36 Scout group
38 __ de combat
39 "They called her frivolous __"
41 Tobacco wad
42 Singer Tucker
44 Deteriorates
45 Nice and warm
46 Work shoe
47 "Symposium" man
49 Sibyl subjects
53 Baseless?
55 Kind of dance
56 Cultural collection
57 Writer Auletta
58 "Great idea!"
59 Sass
60 Keystone fellow

ACROSS

1 Snake with a nasty bite
4 Snide
9 Doggone pest?
13 Rung
15 Sap sucker
16 Galley propellers
17 Tight closure
18 Bulls and Bears, e.g.
19 Abdul-Jabbar's alma mater
20 Slippery
21 "Cubist" Rubik
22 Nixon's infamous '72 org.
23 Aftershock
25 Poisonous Asian snake
27 Some General Motors cars
29 Flower named for a Swedish botanist
33 Freighters' delays
37 Sea bird
38 Friendship
39 Disencumber
40 Oncoming
41 Well-off
42 "And *then*..." stories
44 "Light" ammunition?
46 "... bombs bursting __"
47 __ a million
49 Nag
53 Easily split rock
56 Eye
58 Unsavory bar
59 It can be a stretch
60 Witch's home
61 First name in cookies
62 Astronaut Shepard
63 Radio hostess Hansen
64 Harness fitting
65 Award for "Kiss of the Spider Woman"
66 Hen, perhaps
67 Just in

DOWN

1 Figure in black?
2 Guide
3 Painter Charles Willson __
4 Party provider
5 Mimic
6 November 25, some years
7 Indonesian island
8 Football gains: Abbr.
9 Date for 6 Down
10 Doily material
11 First name in detective fiction
12 Immediately
14 Site of the first 6 Down
22 O.S.S. successor
24 Grand Ole __
26 Plugs, of a sort
28 Hog fat
30 Lecherous look
31 "Dies __"
32 No ifs, __...
33 Bull's-eye hitter
34 Abu Dhabi V.I.P.
35 Isinglass
36 Churchill successor
40 End in __ (draw)
42 "We __ not amused"
43 Officer in charge of the king's table linen
45 Wind dir.
48 Ancient land on the Aegean
50 "__ of Athens"
51 Bring out
52 Fix stitching
53 Louver
54 Hawaiian port
55 "That's one small step for __..."
57 Solitary
60 Building wing

109 *by Richard Silvestri*

ACROSS

1 Iron-pumper's pride
5 Washerful
9 Make pigtails
14 Columbia athlete
15 Oppositionist
16 Diploma word
17 Rattles
19 Comatose
20 Came upon the maharajah?
22 F or G, for example, but not H
23 "__ Cane" (1963 movie)
24 Lead ore
27 Forming opinions
31 Hugo or Tony
32 Neighbor of Chad
34 Easter preceder
35 Gives no stars
36 Got a new address
37 Sneaky guy?
38 Scratch (out)
39 High numbers?
40 Oscar-winning film of 1955
41 Dislike to the max
43 Puts in the scrapbook
44 An Astaire
46 Destiny
47 Intrepid Eric?
54 Form-related
55 Double-crossers
56 Muscat resident
57 Point at the table
58 Mountain sign abbr.
59 Star's small role
60 Slaughter in Cooperstown
61 Decline

DOWN

1 Deep purple
2 German article
3 Overhead
4 Gym shoes
5 One of the Jacksons
6 One's partner
7 First-stringers
8 Ousts
9 Stupid error
10 Hit-or-miss
11 Autobahn auto
12 Creative input
13 "Jurassic Park" actress
18 The way things are going
21 "You're All __ to Get By"
24 Goggled
25 Up and about
26 Strike locations
28 Still
29 Night, in Napoli
30 Lady Jane and Zane
32 Long short story
33 "__ Got My Eyes on You"
36 Silas Marner, e.g.
37 Hobbies
39 Beethoven opera
40 Aucklander, maybe
42 16th-century dance
43 China, perhaps
45 Word maven Newman
47 Coll. hotshot
48 It's on the Tevere
49 "Paradise Lost" character
50 Stereo precursor
51 Dudley Do-Right's love
52 ". . . __ saw Elba"
53 Invitation letters

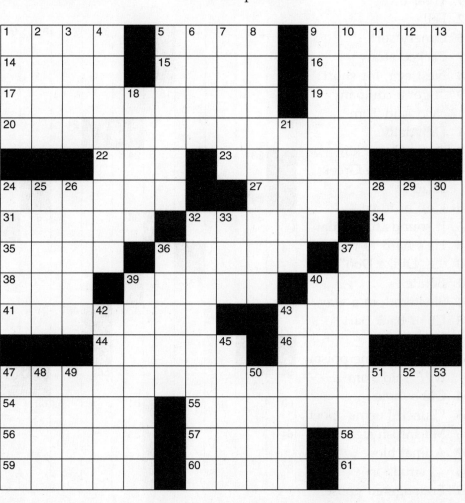

110 *by Lois Sidway*

ACROSS

1 Old actress Anna May
5 Kiwi soldier
10 It follows the Gospels
14 On __ with
15 Goddess of fate
16 Miss Loughlin of "Full House"
17 "I'm off to bed," said Tom __
19 Live wire
20 Obliterate
21 Disillusioned by
23 Takes in
26 Desert of dinosaur finds
27 Vicuña relative
29 Wear away
32 Fella
35 Ornery sort
37 Packed straw
38 Nest egg, for short
39 "I get a company car," said Tom __
41 Dillydally
42 Peace Corps kin
44 Chunks in a Greek salad
45 Unit of force
46 It sounds like B flat
48 He's hard to find
50 "__ Dinka Doo"
51 Berate
54 Sheltered, in a way
58 Chair-back part
60 Impulse
61 "I sat in some poison ivy," said Tom __
64 Cubbyhole
65 "Lunch Poems" poet
66 Macintosh sign
67 A final blow
68 __ situation
69 Endangered goose

DOWN

1 Forks and spoons
2 "Lakmé," e.g.
3 Horoscope-related
4 You can chew on this awhile
5 Jack Horner's last words
6 Parisian vote
7 Sidesteps
8 Mr. Guthrie
9 An Iroquois
10 Search for the unknown?
11 "I'll have a curaçao," said Tom __
12 The Bee Gees, e.g.
13 Speak with one's hands
18 Film short
22 Actor Benson
24 Tear
25 Blue fellow
28 Cockeyed
30 1934 baseball M.V.P.
31 Advantage
32 Met #1?
33 "The Haj" author
34 "Gotta run," said Tom __
36 Lute's kin
39 Skiwear
40 Carol syllables
43 Fruit created circa 1904
45 Aquarium star
47 __ Weems
49 Harrow blade
52 Author Walker
53 Avian preening aid
54 Twain hero
55 'Hood
56 Mimic
57 Gunslinger's command
59 One of the Dalys
62 Jackie's second
63 Famous Amy

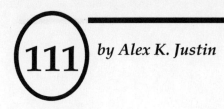
ACROSS

1 David Bowie's model wife
5 Famed Dublin theater
10 Terrier of fiction
14 Canceled
15 Pen
16 Paul of "CBS This Morning"
17 Burgeon
18 "Read my lips" declaration
20 Never
22 Actress Graff of "Mr. Belvedere"
23 It's forbidden
24 It may be blind
26 Veteran sailor
29 Polite refusal
33 Montreal street sign
34 Indian craft
35 Suffix with diet or planet
36 Bush Attorney General William
37 Become misty
38 Computer symbol
39 "How was — know?"
40 Buy a round
41 Cultural: Prefix
42 1987 Costner thriller
44 Carried on
45 PC operator
46 Country ballroom?
47 Alamogordo's county
50 "Jack Sprat could —"
54 Straight from the shoulder
57 Bear up?
58 Kuwaiti ruler
59 Get — of one's own medicine
60 Go smoothly
61 Actress Thompson
62 Kind of situation
63 Noted Ferrara family

DOWN

1 Swenson of "Benson"
2 Satirist Sahl
3 Attic contest
4 "I'm not surprised!"
5 Storefront sight
6 Headache easer, for short
7 Twining stem
8 Riviera season
9 Material for archers' bows
10 Rhododendron
11 —-Coburg (former duchy)
12 "— He Kissed Me" (1963 hit)
13 Addie's husband in "As I Lay Dying"
19 Church gift
21 Drinking binge
24 Dunking item
25 Over
26 Polio fighter
27 Lyrist of myth
28 "This way" sign
29 Complain relentlessly to
30 Strauss's "Eine — in Venedig"
31 Jockey Julie
32 Religious council
34 — d'Alene, Idaho
37 Splitting tool
38 "I can't go on!"
40 Spinks defeater, 1988
41 Deserve
43 Roman Eos
44 Mediterranean vessel
46 Ezio Pinza and others
47 Singles
48 Tony Musante TV series
49 Novelist Bagnold
50 Sufficient, once
51 Lippo Lippi et al.
52 Didion's "Play It — Lays"
53 Chaucer piece
55 Antonio or Juan
56 Conductor de Waart

112 *by Sidney L. Robbins*

ACROSS
1. Brazilian dance
6. Teen woe
10. Loot
14. "The Tempest" sprite
15. Avoid
16. Sherwood Anderson's "Winesburg, —"
17. Letter turner
19. Home for some crocodiles
20. Crimson foes
21. Ones who brood
22. Sees socially
23. Artist Magritte
24. Measured (out)
25. Sir Isaac
29. Teeter
31. Singer Merman
32. Beauty's companion
33. Oklahoma city
36. Comedian Jerry
38. Neck artery
40. Tit for —
41. Destroy for fun
43. Tip over
44. Storied Plaza girl
46. Alarms
47. Square, e.g.
48. Help in mischief
50. Makes a mess
51. Off base, maybe
52. Use a letter opener
56. Papal name
57. "Perils of Pauline" star
59. Otherwise
60. First name in mysteries
61. Movado rival
62. Not natural
63. Olympian's quest
64. You'll get a rise out of this

DOWN
1. Pack rat's motto
2. Asia's — Sea
3. 60's fashion
4. Writer Hecht and others
5. Pie — mode
6. Wan
7. One-fifth of humankind
8. Goofy
9. Opposite WSW
10. "Moonlight," e.g.
11. Arkansas location
12. Felt below par
13. "Here —!"
18. Invitation info
22. Ruin
23. Stylish desks
24. Tableland
25. Egg container
26. Ms. Kett of old comics
27. Executive branch
28. Part of ITT: Abbr.
30. Per
32. Women's support group?
34. Eat well
35. Puts two and two together
37. Admiral Perry victory site
39. W.W. II agcy.
42. Beach protector
45. Like an unpaid policy
46. Wall Street order
47. In a foxy way
49. Yawning?
50. Raced
51. Space prefix
52. Tree locale
53. Valentino co-star — Lee
54. Residents: Suffix
55. Not pictures
57. "— o' My Heart"
58. Kind of humor

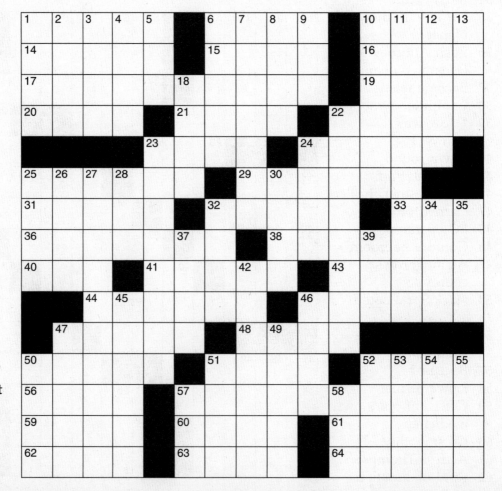

ACROSS

1 Battle of 1836
6 Snoozes
10 Read, as bar codes
14 Actress Linda
15 Song for one
16 Tropical food plant
17 "Great!"
18 Shaker contents
19 __-European
20 Rarely
23 Zero
24 They use lassos
25 Product with Ammonia-D
29 Ineptly
31 Counterpart of Mars
32 Jai __
33 Kind of cow, dog or horse
36 Hercule Poirot's pride
41 Feminizing suffix
42 The last word?
43 Seamstress Betsy
44 Cons
45 TV secretary
47 New York's __ Island
50 Wide's partner
51 Surrenders
58 Double-reed woodwind
59 "The Wind in the Willows" character
60 Something to fall back on?
61 Stir up
62 Toledo's lake
63 Heavy reading
64 Lump
65 Auction off
66 Baker's need

DOWN

1 In addition
2 White House area
3 With: Fr.
4 Roger Bannister's distance
5 Connected to the information superhighway
6 Twang type
7 Show horse
8 Tablet
9 Sinatra's "__ Night"
10 Part of a 90's TV duo
11 Transport for Hiawatha
12 Zeal
13 Middays
21 Overrule
22 Windblown
25 Cloth texture
26 Showy flower
27 Snares
28 Summer hrs.
29 Owls' hangouts
30 Pub draught
33 __ gin fizz
34 Otherwise
35 Like some profs.
37 Intertwines
38 Flows forth
39 Small wonder
40 Blunder
44 Addison contemporary Richard
45 Plopped (down)
46 Peace maker
47 Like some enemies
48 No-no
49 Eschew
50 Cuba's Castro
52 Had on
53 "__, Caesar!"
54 Ice chunk
55 South American capital
56 "Honest" one and namesakes
57 Essence

114 *by Sidney L. Robbins*

ACROSS

1 Extreme point in an orbit
6 "Hogan's Heroes" extra
10 Cole __
14 Hayes's predecessor
15 Arabian sultanate
16 __ colada
17 Cecil B. DeMille epic with "The"
20 Prohibition oasis?
21 Pilgrim John
22 What a ring lacks
23 "Finally!"
24 On ship
28 Plate scrapings
29 In a moment
30 Peculiar
32 Fast plane
35 English-French conflict beginning 1337
39 Greek vowel
40 Bay window
41 Prefix with pilot
42 "Scram!"
43 Went in a hurry
45 South American plains
48 Shock
50 __ acid
51 Jerk
56 What 17 Across had
58 Tooth pain
59 Los Angeles 11
60 Skater's figure
61 "The __ the limit"
62 Relative of the heckelphone
63 Teacher's charge

DOWN

1 10-percenters: Abbr.
2 Get ready, informally
3 Of sound mind
4 Native Peruvian
5 "Dracula" author Bram
6 Wanderer
7 Gather
8 Wacky
9 Neither Rep. nor Dem.
10 Takes part in a bee
11 One of the McCartneys
12 Opening bets
13 Jimmy Dorsey's "__ It You?"
18 Repair
19 Make a difference
23 Sills song
24 Late tennis V.I.P.
25 Title __
26 Mrs. Chaplin
27 Also
28 Pitcher Hershiser
30 Revise copy
31 Potato feature
32 Done laps
33 Surfeit
34 Trampled
36 Florid
37 Times to write about
38 __ Paulo, Brazil
42 Treats with malice
43 Bantu people
44 "Just a moment . . ."
45 Drug-yielding plants
46 "Alas and __"
47 Netted
48 Sad sack
49 The ones over there
51 Knife
52 Drop in a letter box
53 Actress Swenson
54 Old English letters
55 Beach-storming vessels: Abbr.
57 To and __

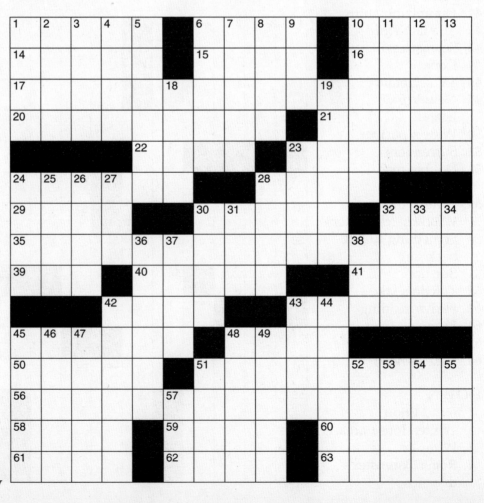

ACROSS

1 Greatly impressed
5 Chairman __
8 Poet Mandelstam
12 Charming
15 Viper
16 Moore of "A Few Good Men"
17 Sagan's "__ Brain"
18 40 Across's beloved 11
20 Shifty shoe?
22 African nation since 1993
23 Danger
25 Reps.
26 Close, as friends
29 Musician's job
31 Composer of "Socrate"
34 National park in Maine
36 Shem's father
38 Getting on
39 Indian writer Santha Rama __
40 Theme of this puzzle
42 End up ahead
43 Frank Baum's initial initial
44 Angel's headgear
45 California's motto
47 Hebrew master
49 Dutch airline
51 Spinners, e.g.
52 Brain tests, for short
54 Essentials
56 Common speech
59 Bureau
63 Locale of 40 Across
65 Mourn
66 Prolific "author"
67 __ pro nobis
68 Plains Indians
69 Items in a code
70 __ Luthor
71 Boss Tweed lampooner

DOWN

1 Liturgical robes
2 Eroded
3 Bacchanalian cry
4 Crab, e.g.
5 Small rug
6 Late tennis great
7 It may be seria or buffa
8 Single-named folk singer
9 40 Across landmark
10 Hungary's Nagy
11 Galileo's home
13 40 Across's eastern border
14 Belgian river
19 Feature of 40 Across, according to Sandburg
21 Get-up
24 1860 nominee in 40 Across
26 Less cluttered
27 Florida city
28 1976 Nobel Prize winner from 40 Across
30 Indian district
32 "__ Ike" (50's slogan)
33 Millay and Ferber
35 Cry of discovery
37 Ripen
41 Kind
46 Type of roulette
48 Sets sail
50 Avg.
53 Pub perch
55 Therefore
56 Perfume holder
57 Humerus neighbor
58 Mary Robinson's land
60 Nintendo rival
61 Impending times
62 "Give it a __"
64 Wailing instrument

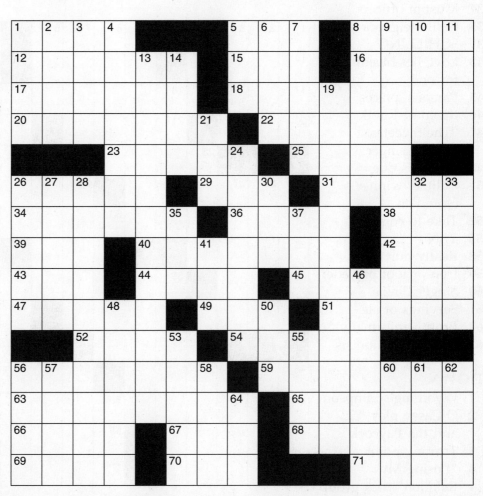

116 *by Janet R. Bender*

ACROSS

1 Not fully shut
5 Penalty
9 Ragu competitor
14 Richness
15 Irish Rose lover
16 Prepared potatoes, in a way
17 POUND
20 Denials
21 Computer insert
22 Discharges
23 Earring site
24 "Ain't She Sweet?" composer
25 Guarantee
28 Scottish Highlander
32 RAND
34 Knock the socks off
35 Away from the wind
36 Sorority character
37 Muslim officers
38 Calif. neighbor
39 SCHILLING
43 Love-lies-bleeding, for one
45 Parsons' places
46 Inventor Rubik
47 "The Sweetest Taboo" singer
48 Timmy's dog
51 Pulitzer winner Quindlen
52 Take to court
55 YEN
58 Really hurt
59 Iron or foot preceder
60 Singer Pinza
61 Servings of ale
62 Profits, informally
63 Antiprohibitionists

DOWN

1 Wyoming's Simpson
2 O'Casey play "___ and the Paycock"
3 Turning point
4 "Losing My Religion" rock group
5 Bullet size
6 More than flabby
7 Swim's alternative
8 Gumshoe
9 Offspring
10 Stairway parts
11 Old French coins
12 Goldfinger portrayer Frobe
13 Lyric poems
18 Think the world of
19 Permitted
23 Time co-founder
24 To whom a caliph prays
25 Turkish city
26 Western capital
27 1983 Indy winner Tom
28 Work behind the plate
29 Biblical gift bearer
30 Cognizant
31 Hornets' homes
33 Fistfight
37 Bad marks?
39 Rinds
40 English novelist Hammond ___
41 Flow forth
42 Detection device
44 Take offense at
47 Move stealthily
48 Speech impediment
49 Prefix with skid
50 Throw for a loop
51 Jean Auel heroine
52 Capacity
53 Military group
54 Selves
56 Newt
57 Unused

117 *by Joan Yanofsky*

ACROSS

1 Petite or jumbo
5 Gobs
9 Final Four rounds
14 Composer Satie
15 __ avail
16 Gather into folds
17 Fashionable African land?
19 Chain of hills
20 Till compartment
21 Tartarus captive, in myth
22 Military encounter
25 __ projection (map system)
27 Escargots
28 Embarrassment
30 Accede (to)
31 Places of refuge
32 Neither's partner
34 "The Twilight of the __"
35 Unites
36 Deal (out)
37 __ Lanka
38 Birdie beater
39 "Give My Regards to Broadway" composer
40 Meeting musts
42 "Canterbury Tales" inn
43 Gabriel, e.g.
44 Curmudgeon-like
45 Composer Duparc
47 Courts
48 "__ Cowboy"
49 Fashionable state?
54 Enact
55 Zone
56 Arched recess
57 "Flowers for Algernon" author Daniel
58 "... leave no __ unstoned"
59 Haydn's "Nelson," for one

DOWN

1 Wine description
2 George's lyricist brother
3 Address part
4 __ out a living
5 Some temps
6 "Two Women" Oscar winner
7 Remnants
8 Tale of __
9 Naiads' homes
10 Donizetti's "The __ of Love"
11 Fashionable Canadian city?
12 "Othello" villain
13 Actress Anna
18 Curtain fabric
22 Silky-haired cat
23 Fashionable Welsh body of water?
24 Bonds
25 Scold
26 Rest on one's __
27 Is weary
28 Summons
29 Person with a seal
31 Kind of tender
33 Rip
35 1977 Wimbledon champ
36 Crowds around
38 Turbojet and others
39 Movement
41 Infuriate
42 Paris or Hector
44 Cringe
45 Corn covering
46 Russian-born designer
47 "__ off to see ..."
49 King Cole
50 Computer capacity, for short
51 Site of rejuvenation
52 Double twist
53 "You bet!"

118 *by Christopher Hurt*

ACROSS

1 Author Bret
6 Oberon's imp
10 Not vivid
14 "Goodbye, mon ami"
15 King Harald's capital
16 Cameo stone
17 "__ to Belong to You" (1939 song)
18 McKern and Carroll
19 "Auld Lang __"
20 Tough toy
21 Apollo, Aphrodite, etc.
23 Without exception
25 Scrap
26 Interstate haulers
27 What's sweet about parting
31 Discouraging word
34 Burden
35 "Behold!"
36 Massachusetts vacation spot
38 Brandy cocktail
40 Loose
41 Bruce or Laura
42 Elephant's org.
43 Offering vistas
45 Long tales
47 High note
48 Site of 36 Across and 22 Down
51 Accept, after negotiation
55 Like a mouse
57 Kind of arch
58 1986 #1 hit by Starship
59 "La Gioconda," e.g.
60 Taximeter reading
61 In __ (stuck)
62 Alate
63 Tennis score
64 Seven Hills site
65 What roll calls count

DOWN

1 Reagan pal Al
2 Extemporize
3 Spanish wine
4 Domingo and others
5 1936 Literature Nobelist
6 Victim of Hamlet
7 Vain
8 Become tiresome
9 Greek universe
10 Physics particle
11 Author Seton
12 Actress Redgrave
13 Alimony getters
22 __ Players (theater group)
24 Atlanta sports site, with "The"
28 Diana of "The Avengers"
29 Ersatz butter
30 Twist
31 So
32 Lip-__
33 Model Moss
37 Sophomore's age, maybe
38 Divide
39 Stumble
41 Propriety
44 Onetime chief of 64 Across
46 Opponent of Hannibal
49 Foreshadowings
50 Lament for the dead
51 It can hide a bed
52 "Oh, my!"
53 Garr of "Tootsie"
54 Casino game
56 Calendar pages

ACROSS

1 Horoscope
6 Pachacuti was one
10 Safety specifications
14 Personal care workers
15 Dickensian orphan
16 Stormy greeting?
17 Fat City dwelling?
20 Loudness unit
21 Jots
22 Actor Davis
23 Gatsby portrayer, with 36 Across
25 Just those of Juan things?
27 Outwit, in Fat City?
33 Was a busybody
34 Gibbons
35 Common Market money
36 See 23 Across
37 Warp
39 Parts of matches
40 Unstop, poetically
41 Germany's __ Mountains
42 Munchkins
43 Fat City office attire?
47 Bearing
48 Inspector
49 Sphere, e.g.
52 Paraphernalia
54 Final words
58 Be insincere, in Fat City?
61 Crow's-nest cry
62 "Little Sheba" playwright
63 Yellow-fever mosquito
64 "Ladders" in hose
65 Turned gray
66 Take by force

DOWN

1 1983 Tony musical
2 "Farmer in the Dell" syllables
3 Arabian Peninsula port
4 Prepared leftovers
5 General on Chinese menus
6 Bonkers
7 Requisite
8 Zoom-lens shots
9 Actor-director Kjellin
10 Ballroom glide
11 Boating couple
12 Actress Conn of "Benson"
13 Besides
18 Bountiful's state
19 Despoils
24 Old Ford
26 Printer's mark
27 Plot mathematically
28 Place to get down from
29 Fabric akin to felt
30 Chaucer pilgrim
31 Eightsome
32 Ado
33 Novelist's concern
37 Race's end
38 Using extortion
39 Barely mention
41 Johanna Spyri classic
42 Canton finish
44 Dickinson and Brontë
45 Halted
46 Rochester's beloved
49 Practice à la Marciano
50 Kauai neighbor
51 Where the Rhone meets the Saône
53 Sidle
55 Remain
56 Finishes the cake
57 Examine
59 __ mater (brain membrane)
60 Like sashimi

ACROSS

1 Luggage
5 Sneaking suspicion
9 Waist material
13 Broadway aunt
15 "The Old Curiosity Shop" heroine
16 Words of enlightenment
17 Everybody's opposite
18 Brickbat
19 Bear head, once
20 Sgt. Friday's comment at the office equipment store?
23 Check-cashing needs
24 Insubstantial
25 Biblical initials
26 Lend a hand
27 Tour grp.
28 "Mighty __ a Rose"
31 Big salmon order for a security firm?
36 Unvarnished
38 "Don't tell me!"
39 Goes it alone
41 __-European
42 __ the iceberg
44 Part of the cost of floor covering?
46 __ Canals
47 Comic Philips
49 High dudgeon
50 "__ tell"
52 Clock part
54 Emulate
57 Musical instrument that throws Troy Aikman for a loss?
60 "__ never fly"
61 Nobel chemist Harold
62 Championship
63 Clock part
64 Clears (of)
65 Have the helm
66 Grand Ole __

67 Crime battler of 60's TV
68 Once, once

DOWN

1 Movie pooch
2 Not sotto voce
3 Shine
4 Wired
5 Actress Stevens
6 More than ennoble
7 Exile site
8 Writer de Tocqueville
9 Eastern lute
10 Bushwhacker
11 Where ends meet
12 That ship
14 Kind of price
21 Squirrels away
22 Alphabet quartet

26 Peek ending
27 Wife, to Caesar
29 Verdi's slave girl
30 Landon's running mate, 1936
31 Pointillist's marks
32 Wheeling's river
33 Out of style
34 Bats
35 Suffix with pay
37 Lo-cal
40 Star in Virgo
43 Misgiving
45 Pitches, in a way
48 1989 Nancy Reagan book
51 Comeback
52 Bandleader Waring et al.
53 Gaping hole

54 Sunflower, in furniture decoration
55 Loses color
56 Wield
57 Ear spear
58 Albany-to-Buffalo route
59 Tom of golf
60 Words before a kiss?

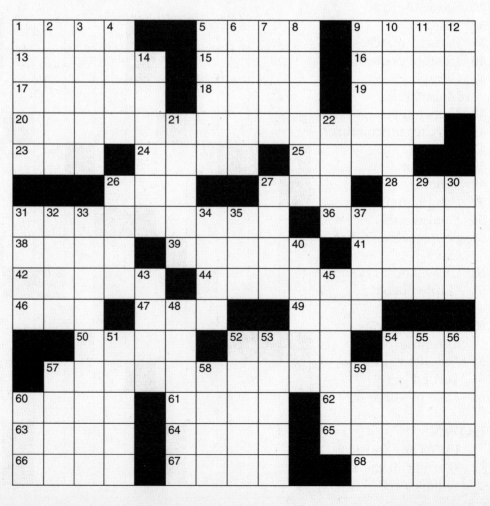

121 *by Bryant White*

ACROSS

1 Beelike
6 Longtime record label
9 Funny Anne
14 Popovich or Gagarin, e.g.
16 Michaelmas daisy
17 Sandwich devotees?
19 Greek vowels
20 Expressed wonder
21 Singapore's Kuan Yew __
22 Cube with 21 spots
23 Passeport info
25 Du Maurier's "Jamaica __"
26 Year in the reign of Pius I
28 Perfect
31 Sum of one's virtues, to the Greeks
33 Palmer of "Twin Peaks"
35 Stravinsky and others
36 Sandwich fit for royalty?
38 British P.M., 1970–74
39 "Aminta" poet
40 Is left undecided
41 Hemingway moniker
42 In __ (following)
45 Shaver
46 One vote
48 Grosbeak's beak
50 Fred Astaire's daughter
51 Laundromat appliance
55 To __
56 Chicken sandwich?
60 Mounted lancer
61 Synthetic rubber
62 Hypothesize
63 Lion's __
64 They're more than rare

DOWN

1 Hurt
2 Graceful, in a way
3 Acre's acres?
4 Freeman Gosden radio role
5 "Move it!"
6 __ avis
7 Astrological point
8 Villa Albani statue in Rome
9 Plan
10 It's psychic
11 Painting locales
12 Sublets
13 Lupin of detective fiction
15 Eggy quaff
18 Familiar vow
24 Balthazar, e.g.
27 Work translated by Chapman
28 The "H" of W. H. Auden
29 Spanish Main cargo
30 Issue of 1993
32 Obedient helper
34 Nervous
35 Ingrid in "Casablanca"
36 Actresses Kay and Suzy
37 Shako, for one
38 Final throw
40 Emphasize
41 Diagrammed
43 Punctual
44 Freud, e.g.
47 Relative of Geo. or Chas.
49 Parts of boilermakers
52 Kind of tide
53 Statesman of 3 Down
54 Want ad abbr.
55 Elvis __ Presley
57 My __
58 Minn. neighbor
59 From __ izzard

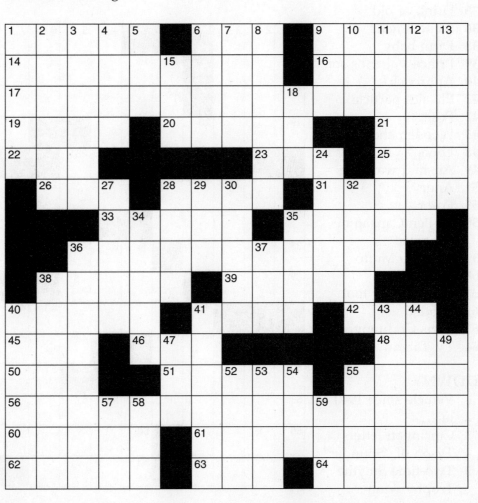

ACROSS

1 Chew the fat
4 Feature of Doyle's "The Adventure of the Dancing Men"
8 Faceup card in faro
12 Fraternal one
13 Region in NW Greece
15 Don Juan's mother
16 Mr. Potato Head accessory
17 Poser
19 Lab tube
21 Busy
22 Lobster claw
24 Kind of acid
25 Poser
30 Golden statuette
31 Jejune
32 Humbug?
35 Drink of old
36 Incite a hen?
38 Farm baby
39 Prince Valiant's son
40 Approach
41 Physics particle
42 Poser
45 Wooden shoe
48 Louis XVI's wife
49 Air-raid warnings
51 Angry
55 Poser
58 __ Ben Canaan of "Exodus"
59 Soprano Moffo
60 Reduces
61 Slate-cutting tool
62 Spotted
63 Boris Godunov, e.g.
64 TV Tarzan

DOWN

1 Vehicle since 1940
2 Jai __
3 Cincinnati letters
4 Tyson of "Sounder"
5 Two-time Smythe Trophy winner

6 Couple in Rome
7 This: Sp.
8 Use a heliograph
9 Best Supporting Actress, 1973
10 Tooth: Prefix
11 Montezuma, e.g.
13 Old Testament book
14 Gunn with a gun
18 Partner of dangerous
20 Outward
23 Coasters for Socrates, e.g.
25 Site for a Cézanne: Abbr.
26 W.W. I battle site
27 Scrutinize
28 El Dorado loot
29 Sauterne, e.g.

32 Ruth's husband
33 Manor head, maybe
34 Actress Sommer
36 Some doctor's reading: Abbr.
37 Empty talk
38 Large-headed match
40 Capone's chief enforcer
41 Counterpanes
42 River in an old spiritual
43 Football's pop
44 Poet Matthew
45 "Heimskringla" et al.
46 Solo
47 European capital
50 Save, with "away"
52 Stupefy

53 Caspian feeder
54 Folklore figure
56 Vetoes
57 __Zulu (South African region)

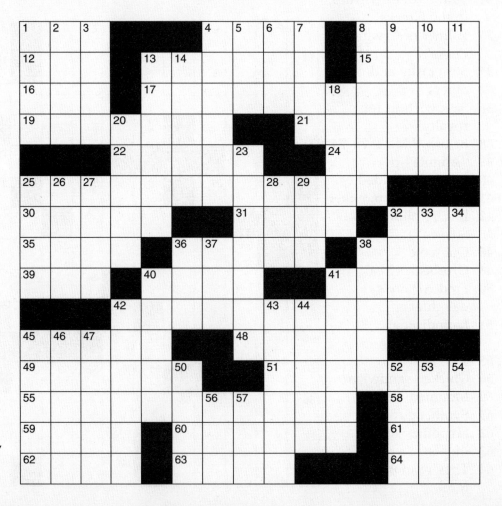

ACROSS

1 He reached his peak in 1806
5 Wahine's welcome
10 Steep
14 "__ close to schedule"
15 Screened over
16 "__ Ever Need Is You"
17 Overpriced insects?
20 "Naughty, naughty!"
21 Three minutes in the ring
22 Kosher
23 O.R.'s locale
24 Party cheese
26 __ oneself (go)
29 Aussie's hello
30 Mortgage agcy.
33 Skylit courts
34 Hoodlum
35 Oscar role in "The Killing Fields"
36 Where to buy Maid Marian mums?
39 Goes out with
40 Filthy lucre
41 "I Love Trouble" star
42 Pre-Columbian
43 Like falling off a log
44 Climbed up
45 40's White House name
46 Fraud
47 March honoree, for short
50 Express alternative
52 Kicker
55 Scans departure screens?
58 Science magazine
59 "Cookery is become __": Burton
60 Film
61 Look
62 Looks at
63 Tabloid topics

DOWN

1 Spender, for one
2 "New Sensation" rock group
3 Crackpot
4 Go wrong
5 Tuneful
6 Abate
7 "The Plague" setting
8 Relinquished, as a football
9 Farm critter
10 Western capital
11 First name in fashion
12 Jai __
13 Star-__ tuna
18 Rather rival
19 Castigate
23 Components of locks
25 Part of Boone's signature
26 He sings low
27 Mrs. Mertz
28 Cornered
29 Devout
30 Something extra
31 Expeditiousness
32 Chipped in
34 Agrees
35 Tournament type
37 Shade of gray
38 Available for duty
43 Grub
44 Treats treacherously
45 Hindu ascetic
46 Alarm
47 Hog food
48 Considerable volume
49 Corn product
51 Kind of tradition
52 End-of-week exclamation
53 "This can't be!"
54 Vous __ (you are): Fr.
56 Toy merchant Schwarz
57 Emer. locale

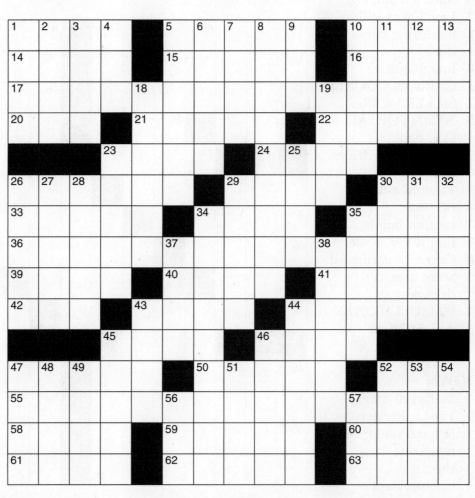

124 *by Randolph Ross*

ACROSS

1 COPPER CHARGES
8 MERCURY WATER SOURCES
15 Furniture piece
16 Glee
17 Competitor
18 "O, where is __?": Shakespeare
19 Hemingway novel setting
20 Bygone auto
21 Quarantine
22 Ship officers
24 Of oneself: Lat.
25 GOLDEN GALE
28 POTASSIUM PORTIONS
33 TIN SOURCE
34 HYDROGEN GAS
35 Auction offering
36 Mauritanian, e.g.
37 Like Oscar Wilde
38 Flintstone pet
39 Zip
40 Imagine that!
41 CARBON COOKER
42 SILVER DEBRIS
45 NEON PORTAL
46 O.T. book
47 Recreational drives
49 Grants
53 Take measures
54 Boz boy
57 Lets, in tennis
58 Bug River locale
60 Current instrument
61 Some new-car drivers
62 HELIUM DRINKS
63 ALUMINUM FISHING GEAR

DOWN

1 Mediocre marks
2 The __ Reader (alternative press magazine)
3 Pro __
4 Cabinet dept.
5 Scented blossom
6 He went to camp in a 1987 movie
7 __ Hall
8 Port opening
9 Back-of-the-book section
10 Rad
11 Latin list extender
12 Actress Kedrova
13 Senator from Mississippi
14 Backwater
22 Bedroom community, for short
23 Kerrigan and company
25 Yoga position
26 Take apart
27 Strive mightily, with "out"
29 U.S. poet laureate __ Dove
30 Former Twin batting champ
31 Largish singing group
32 Attack in a way
34 Bury
37 Recalled
38 Follows hostilely
41 Indispensable
43 __ one's head
44 Slightly tapered
45 Monticello site
48 Comic Poundstone
49 Esau's wife
50 Approach
51 Search
52 Lith. and Lat., once
54 Deck
55 Memo words
56 Dining hall
59 Tempe sch.

125 *by Daniel R. Stark*

ACROSS

1 Kind of sleeve
7 In the cards
15 Symphony written for Napoleon
16 Furniture polish ingredient
17 Spreads the news
18 With no exceptions
19 Poet's contraction
20 One who's squeezed in
22 Mauna __
23 Rough it
25 Seating areas
26 Say truly
27 Up a __
29 Kittenish response
30 Fiery dance
31 Team originally called the Colt .45s
33 Guard
35 Not clerical
37 Split
38 Founder of Detroit
42 Smith of sorts
46 Prince Valiant's wife
47 Fanatic
49 Succinct
50 Scream and shout
51 Traveling aids
53 Business letter encl.
54 Actor Vigoda
55 Quiescent
57 Poison __
58 Nymph changed into a bear
60 Like Don Juan
62 Added up
63 Drill
64 Stonecutter
65 Less muscle-bound

DOWN

1 Daphne du Maurier novel

2 In __ (behind)
3 Bon vivant
4 Year in Claudius's reign
5 Romans preceder
6 Countryish, in a way
7 Made a toast
8 Critic
9 A shaman uses them
10 Dull fellow
11 Jane Fonda farce "__ Wednesday"
12 Library item
13 Family tree
14 __ of Aquitaine
21 Computer capacity, for short

24 Plant growth medium
26 Cloaks
28 Zoo critter
30 Adoxy
32 Part of R.S.V.P.
34 Small number
36 Kitchen container
38 Cat with tufted ears
39 Creek Indian land
40 Unfold
41 Charge
43 Wall hanging
44 Gist
45 Join again
48 Mai __
51 Goddess of the hearth

52 Herbal alcoholic drink
55 Part that's thrown away
56 Catch hold of
59 Him, in Marseilles
61 Inspector Van __ Valk (literary detective)

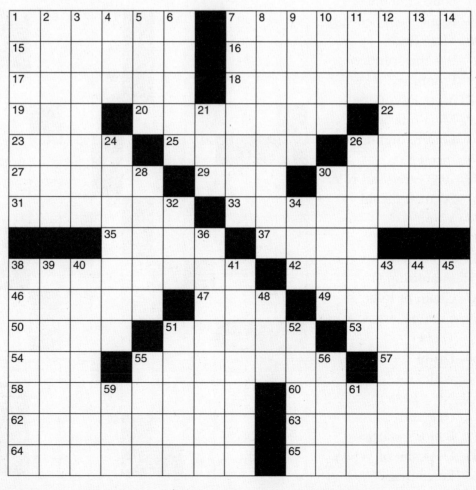

ACROSS

1 Expire, as a membership
6 Show hosts, for short
9 Fill
13 Secretary of State Root
14 Dadaist Hans
15 Like Old King Cole
16 Baseball bigwig Bud
17 Assurance
19 Not brand-name
21 Spring blooms
22 Wildebeest
23 Entomological stage
25 Less original
28 Monks and nuns
32 Apartment sign
33 Lebanese symbol
34 Soup container
35 Immense, poetically
36 Mine find
37 Lift the spirits of
39 From __ Z
40 Most Egyptians
42 Meet official
43 Louvre highlight
45 Insult
46 1983 Streisand role
47 Scottish denial
48 Value
51 Lethargy
55 Prohibition establishment
57 Chain of hills
59 Country music's Tucker
60 Drunk's problem, with "the"
61 Near Eastern chieftain
62 Bettor's starter
63 Opposite of WNW
64 Pores over

DOWN

1 Broadway's "__ Miz"
2 Words after shake or break
3 Mass
4 Roof worker
5 Noted name in puzzling
6 Biblical trio
7 Fancy term for 5 Down and 15 Down
8 Vacation destination
9 Grad-to-be
10 Liberal __
11 Corner
12 Potato features
15 Noted name in puzzling
18 Lasso
20 Capek play
24 Styles
25 It may come in a head
26 Kemo Sabe's companion
27 Crazy as __
29 "__, I saw . . ."
30 Eroded
31 Dummy Mortimer
33 Slide
38 Cable choice
41 Washer cycle
44 "Roger," at sea
45 __ for the books
48 Film dog
49 Breadth
50 Faxed
52 Wall Street abbr.
53 Brainstorm
54 Like some cheeses
56 Suffix added to fruit names
58 Speech stumbles

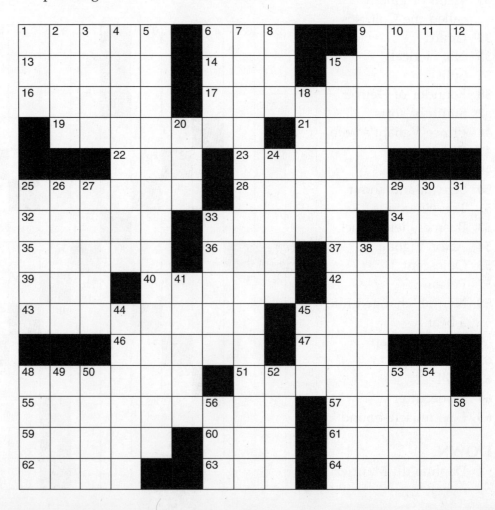

127 *by Ernie Furtado*

ACROSS

1 Play opening
5 Ran
9 Shawl or afghan
14 Forsaken
15 Yellow brick, e.g.
16 Moonshine
17 Unencumbered
19 Composed
20 Follower of 21 Across?
21 Follower of 20 Across?
22 Small: Suffix
23 Ripped
24 Dems. opposition
27 Proverbial distancer
32 Sleepy Hollow schoolmaster
34 Ampersand
35 Firpo of the ring
36 Folk tales
37 Ship's officers
39 __ time (never)
40 Upshots
41 Morning hrs.
42 Waffle topping
43 Kind of disease, facetiously
47 Hook shape
48 Alphabet quartet
49 Unmixed, as a drink
51 Character actor George
54 Starts
58 In the thick of
59 Be afraid to offend
60 Hope of Hollywood
61 Manhattan campus
62 Gamblers' game
63 Boorish
64 Some combos
65 Sharp put-down

DOWN

1 __ Romeo (automobile)
2 Hip
3 De __ (too much)
4 Words before "red" or "running"
5 Literary sister
6 Give some slack
7 Maneuver slowly
8 White House monogram
9 Block
10 Fun and games
11 Kind of beer
12 Eight, in combinations
13 A question of time
18 Singer Lenya
21 Merchandise
23 Manner of speaking
24 Staff leader
25 University of Maine site
26 TV announcer Don
28 1980 DeLuise movie
29 Bizarre
30 "Peanuts" character
31 Stock plans providing worker ownership: Abbr.
33 Young 'uns
37 Horace and Thomas
38 BB's
42 Disreputable
44 Some are spitting
45 World cultural agcy.
46 Flirts
50 Stylish Brits
51 Baby powder
52 Poet Khayyám
53 __ fide
54 Where humuhu-munuku-nukuapuaa might be served
55 Filly or colt
56 Roman marketplaces
57 Quit
59 Abbr. in a mail-order ad

128 *by Robert Zimmerman*

ACROSS

1 Rig
5 Big dos
10 At a distance
14 Ur locale
15 New York's __ Tully Hall
16 Berg opera
17 M
20 Kicker's aid
21 Names in a Saudi phone book
22 Bury
23 Cut and run
24 Yearn
26 Talk radio guest
29 Playwright O'Casey
30 Army rank, for short
33 African lily
34 Brazzaville's river
35 Through
36 H
40 Fabergé objet
41 Collection
42 Candied items
43 1969 Three Dog Night hit
44 Pup's complaints
45 Lively wit
47 Some heirs
48 Time founder
49 "Orlando" author
52 Forum fashion
53 Quarry
56 Y
60 Organ setting
61 Type style
62 Eros
63 Ruptured
64 Tell's target
65 Currycomb target

DOWN

1 Investigate, in a way
2 Tribe whose name means "cat people"
3 Old gray animal?
4 Some ratings
5 Newgate guard
6 1966 Caine role
7 Wagons __
8 German cry
9 Bishop's domain
10 Solo
11 Candid cameraman
12 Der __ (Adenauer)
13 Krupp family home
18 Tall writing?
19 Tiny swimmer
23 Took off
24 Director Marshall
25 "Othello" plotter
26 Literary sketch
27 Collimate
28 Moose, e.g.
29 Divans
30 Opera prop
31 Pioneer atom splitter
32 Kingfisher's coif
34 __ de ballet
37 Opposite of hire
38 St. Patrick's home
39 Publicity
45 Conductor Ormandy
46 Analyze verse
47 Skier's site
48 Dietary
49 __ Point
50 "__ victory!"
51 Stink
52 Substitute
53 Cougar
54 Caddie's offering
55 Home of Jezebel
57 __-la-la
58 School dance
59 Scottish cap

129 *by D. J. Listort*

ACROSS

1 Break down grammatically
6 Items in a still life
11 Braincase
13 "__ Fables"
15 Considers bond values again
16 Reduce to ashes
18 Fred's sister
19 __ Speedwagon
20 Not give __
21 Mediocre
22 Argued
24 Loudonville, N.Y., campus
25 Classical name in medicine
27 Sprinted
28 "__ Believer" (Monkees hit)
31 Barn topper
32 Football squad
36 Court ruling
37 Hint to solving the eight italicized clues
39 __ Jima
40 Ignite
42 Plane or dynamic preceder
43 Actress Ryan
44 Deteriorate
45 Curses
47 Sprockets linker
50 Reps. counterparts
51 Riding whip
55 Natural gait
56 Emily, to Charlotte
57 Madrid attraction
58 Kind of lot
60 Zebralike
62 March laboriously
63 Paired nuclides
64 Catch suddenly
65 Harvests

DOWN

1 *Trims*
2 Kind of recording
3 Passage ceremony
4 Cash's "A Boy Named __"
5 Printers' widths
6 Set the standard for
7 Architect Saarinen
8 Chemical suffix
9 Lettuce variety
10 *Bowling score*
11 Tomorrow: Lat.
12 Try again
14 Laurel or Musial
17 Wetlands watchdog
19 Deserters
22 Venus, for one
23 River to the Laptev Sea
24 Game fish
26 50's singer Frankie
27 Supplies with better weapons
28 Kind
29 __ tai (cocktail)
30 Cereal bristle
33 Robust energy
34 Pronoun in a cote?
35 Norfolk ale
38 20 quires
41 Evaporated
46 Act niggardly
47 Actor Gulager
48 Emcee
49 *Copycats*
50 More extreme
52 *Mustard plants*
53 Baltic Sea feeder
54 Pea places
56 Long account
57 Swift sailing boat
59 B–F connection
60 Salutation for Edmund Hillary
61 Half a fly

ACROSS

1 Actress Winger
6 Park, in Monopoly
11 "Honest" fellow
14 Where Gauguin visited van Gogh
15 Funnyman O'Brien
16 Bloodshot
17 "Cheers!" in Cherbourg?
19 Chang's Siamese twin
20 Brand of lemon-flavored drink
21 Daydream
23 Koch and Wynn
24 Pampering, for short
26 It's heard in a herd
27 Garibaldi in Genoa?
33 Pickle
36 Paparazzi prey
37 Avaricious one
38 October gem
40 Beam fastener
42 1963 Oscar winner
43 Arose
45 Danger
47 Hang in the breeze
48 Madrid's equivalent of a Texas university?
50 Performance
51 Had lunch
52 Montana and Moon, in brief
55 Gladstone rival
60 Real
62 "Poppycock!"
63 Pre-photo pronouncement in Geneva?
65 Some
66 Skirmish
67 "Dallas" Miss
68 Simonize
69 Classic theater name
70 4 Down again

DOWN

1 Peri opera
2 Made a boner
3 Post-sneeze word
4 Take money for a spare room
5 Loner
6 Agt.'s share
7 Creator of Lorelei Lee
8 Med. subj.
9 Winter melon
10 Competitor
11 Vicinity
12 Early German carmaker
13 Barely beat, with "out"
18 Woman's top
22 Cartoonist Wilson
25 Islamic leader
28 Crowbar
29 Portugal and its neighbor
30 Barely managed, with "out"
31 Raise
32 Alternative to Charles de Gaulle
33 Clinton's runs
34 Each
35 First name in spying
39 Moon-based
41 Alternative to Certs
44 "Desmoiselles d'Avignon" artist
46 Bloodletting practitioner
49 Potted
52 Put down
53 Count in music
54 Winter weather
55 Extract
56 New Rochelle college
57 Charon's domain
58 Kind of beer
59 Relationship words
61 Prefix with play or scope
64 Favorite relative in politics?

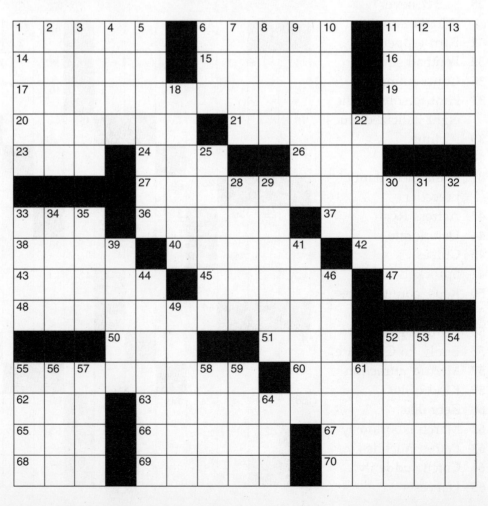

ACROSS

1 Twelve __ ("G.W.T.W." home)
5 Cousin of the cobra
8 Pelt
12 Insomnia causes
14 Sausage, e.g.
16 Having no deferments
17 "__ akbar" (Arab cry)
18 The Sphinx and the Parthenon?
20 Available
22 Speech problem
23 Until
24 Author Murdoch
26 Took the most credit
28 Socks and Millie?
32 Popular Dutch export
33 Zero-shaped
34 Mr. Hulot's portrayer
36 Gossip-column snippet
38 Poe story setting
39 Piers 19 and 20?
41 Tony-winner Caldwell
43 Ending for tip or team
45 The Untouchables
46 Russian sea
47 Goneril's father
49 Two-spot and six-spot?
51 Helter __
54 Problem for Superman
55 Unsafe, in a way
56 1982 Stein/Plimpton biography
58 Subject of Freudian study
61 20 cents?
64 Obloquy
66 Blueprint
67 Bald head

68 Cry from the sick ward
69 Barks
70 Town on Long Island Sound
71 Unclothe

DOWN

1 Seraglio room
2 Singer Guthrie
3 Potter's need
4 Kind of sense
5 Concert hall equipment
6 Bewhiskered animal
7 City of Light
8 __ polloi
9 Light entertainments
10 Farm-gear pioneer
11 Sugar-coated
13 Nattily clad

15 Kind of test
19 Floral spike
21 Attraction at St. Peter's
25 Show alarm
27 Squeal
28 Top 40 music
29 Budget rival
30 Jalopy
31 Notary public's need
35 Exemplar
37 Lows
39 Jabbered
40 "No right __"
42 Turgenev's "On the __"
44 Conger
46 Made sense
48 Gave a room a face lift
50 Hall-of-Fame Brave

51 Excessively sentimental
52 __ Lumpur
53 Inflexibility
57 Prize since 1948
59 River through Leeds
60 Chew (on)
62 Years in 7 Down
63 Date
65 Country singer McDaniel

ACROSS

1 G. E. subsidiary
4 Mob member
8 Robotic rock group of the 80's
12 Emphasized, in a way
15 Gov. Bayh of Indiana
16 Mercury
18 "Ich bin __ Berliner"
19 Uses a scope
20 Lipton competitor
21 Snap request?
22 Spread
23 Mars
30 "Pardon me"
31 Successes
32 Hubbub
33 Strings of yore
34 Prevailing mood
36 Stash the bags
37 Jersey call
38 Sea east of the Caspian
39 Down to the __
40 Saturn
45 Stack part
46 "Now __ me down . . ."
47 Knowing
50 Fair-to-middling
51 Ashen
54 Pluto
57 Woody's kid
58 Hidalgo highway
59 Ancient Mexican
60 Parcel (out)
61 Guinness Book suffix

DOWN

1 Nostalgic soft-drink brand
2 "Très __!"
3 Gridiron pos.
4 Three-horse sleigh

5 "U Can't Touch This" rap singer
6 Western Indians
7 "__ a life!"
8 With dexterity
9 Kind of eye
10 Singer Jerry
11 One and __
12 Numbered rd.
13 High-tech memos
14 Diplomats' quest
17 Interprets
21 TV correspondent Brit
22 Wound
23 Majorca seaport
24 "__ Beautiful Doll"
25 Nafta opposer
26 Kind of dog

27 Hand-dyed fabric
28 Love to death
29 Galley drudge
34 Double __ (puzzle type)
35 Etna locations
36 Influence
38 Change
41 "__ customer"
42 "I __ Like That" (60's hit)
43 Comic Bossler
44 Hot cereal name
47 Did the crawl
48 Irene of "Fame"
49 Unfavorably
50 "Don't tread __"
51 Trials
52 One __ (ball game)

53 Flyer's org.
55 Actor Waterston
56 Tram contents

ACROSS

1 "The Nazarene" writer
5 "Elephant Boy" boy
9 ___ night
12 Cheer noisily
14 "Am ___ Love?"
15 1990 Best Supporting Actress
17 Juárez river
18 Newswoman Compton
19 Twiggy willows
21 Singer James
23 Nurse a drink
25 Conductor Dorati
26 Poverty
27 "Waterlilies" artist
29 ___ Z
30 Partying with Eddie Cantor?
34 René or Renée
35 Toymaker
36 Noisy bird
43 Scale notes
44 Lambaste
45 Composition
48 Road from Dawson Creek
51 Kind of hill or lion
52 Feast
53 Canned-tomato style
55 Truckers' watchdog
57 Any ship
58 Nothing to shout about
62 "Xanadu" rock group
63 Noisy festivity
64 Manuel's intro
65 One of a trio in Scandinavian myth
66 Pursue

DOWN

1 ". . . ___ Christmas"
2 ___ up (film genre)
3 Bill's partner
4 "May I?" step
5 Hires
6 Act of contrition
7 Biblical month
8 Hairstyle that needs hairpins
9 Coordinate
10 Listen in on
11 Unappreciative one
13 Airline to Karachi
15 Songbird
16 Scouting org.
20 Kind of gin
22 Town in a W.W. II novel
24 Notre Dame bench
27 Copycat
28 Heat unit
31 Keystone officer
32 Rock ___ (jukebox brand)
33 Land ___ (night locale)
36 Package
37 Hair products maker Curtis and others
38 Warring Seminole chief
39 Brady bill opposer
40 Father
41 Become popular
42 Occurrence
46 Loose a bra
47 Filter
49 ___ Parker, 1904 candidate for President
50 Mint
54 How the answer to this goes
56 Ceiling
59 Greek letter
60 Typewriting abbr.
61 Start of a bray

ACROSS

1 Honeydew kin
7 Fatherless fellow
11 Crow's feat?
14 Slurred over a syllable
15 Ring happening
16 Part of a flick?
17 College study
19 NNW antithesis
20 Gerund maker
21 It's sold in bars
22 Wrangle
23 Screech, for one
25 Bit for Fermi
26 Stories connector
27 Bring in the crops
29 In an evil way
31 Stealthily
33 Flying Peter
34 Carry
35 Type of tiger
38 Religious sch.
39 Reflected on
41 Abandoned
45 Penny or Lois
46 See eye to eye
47 Hertz alternative
48 Lose (to)
49 Way out
50 Slow down from a run
51 Start of the St. Ives riddle
53 Fleur-de-__
54 Trinidad and Tobago's capital
58 Exaggerator's suffix
59 Philharmonic instrument
60 Monopoly card
61 Hog haven
62 Obscene
63 Perfumed, in a way

DOWN

1 Animation frame
2 "Thrilla in Manila" victor
3 Ssspeak like thisss
4 Arabian Sea gulf
5 Glacier Bay sight
6 Orthodontist's org.
7 Seafood order
8 Scale opening
9 Jam ingredient
10 Short range?
11 One of the Magi
12 Lambaste
13 Light rowboat
18 Skin softener
22 Baseball's Old Professor
23 El Dorado treasure
24 Travel
25 "__ Goes By"
26 Kiosk
28 Piece of eight
30 Loses one's balance?
32 Annapolis freshman
35 Fish like a mackerel
36 Spirited steeds
37 Letterman rival
39 Swiveled
40 Drops in the morning
41 Soup scoops
42 Self-centered sort
43 Snowman of song
44 Cultivating tool
50 Option for Hamlet
51 "Off the Court" author
52 Stretch over
54 D.C. figure
55 TV watchdog
56 Rocks in a glass
57 Actor Beatty

ACROSS

1 Section under the mezz.
5 Scuttlebutt
9 Send by parachute
13 Yarborough, et al.
15 Middle name of "The King"
16 One abroad
17 "Utopia" author
19 Earring locale
20 It sounds right
22 Aggrieve
23 Role for Shirley in '63
24 Transport, in a way
25 Christian monogram
26 They dog AWOL's
27 Campaign name of '52
29 ___ loss
31 See 26 Down
32 Half and half
33 Jonson's "Sweet Swan of ___!"
34 It sounds right
39 Couple's pronoun
40 Make a doily
41 Antonym: Abbr.
42 Contorted
43 ___ favor (please)
44 Baden-Powell offshoot org.
45 CNN parent company
48 Start of many a tale
50 Boldly attempt
52 Air
53 It sounds right
56 "Take ___"
57 Exactly
58 Bear in the sky
59 Be full
60 Kewpie doll, perhaps
61 Leave in
62 Bo Derek film before "10"
63 "Greystoke" extras

DOWN

1 Sushi bar selection
2 Peppy
3 New Mexico city noted for archaeological finds
4 Cut off from escape
5 Circus people
6 Woolf's "___ of One's Own"
7 Verdun's region
8 Socialized with
9 Street in old TV
10 Wayne–Martin western of 1959
11 Remote control feature
12 Milord
14 Kerouac's Paradise
18 Don
21 Treat a sprain
26 Cocktail, with 31 Across
28 Shale oil product
30 Whatever
31 Troy Aikman stats
32 Calendar abbr.
33 Roadie equipment
34 Bowl over
35 Economic association since 1957
36 Newborn attendant
37 Person who makes beds?
38 Clean air org.
43 Grade school ammo
44 Rodeo mount
45 ___ greens
46 Proceed easily
47 Accept a proposal
49 Sole attachment
51 Montezuma II, for one
52 Marketplace
53 Currency for 35 Down
54 Emerald City visitor
55 Forbidden City occupant: Abbr.

ACROSS

1 Suit
6 Bit of smoke
10 __ scratch
14 Town near Bangor
15 "The __!" (hmmph!)
16 Good enough to eat
17 One __
19 Gray's subj.
20 Disprove
21 Go all-out
23 Washington story, maybe
25 Remembrance of things past
26 Easier to count
29 Turn-of-century Secretary of State
31 Fleece
33 Hurrays
34 U.C.L.A. rival
35 Knocked, in a way
37 She raised Cain
38 One side in an 1862 battle
40 1951 Johnnie Ray hit
41 Disk spinner
43 Exception word?
44 Deliberate
45 Vending machine part
46 Stewed
47 Firedamps
48 Name in robotry
50 "Once __ a midnight . . ."
52 Dinner alfresco
55 Fancy-coiffed bird
59 Nobelist __ von Behring
60 Two __ (dilemma)
62 The L of L-dopa
63 Scads
64 __ up (relented)
65 From the top
66 Popular source of quotes, for short
67 Sans élan

DOWN

1 Beethoven's birthplace
2 Spooky waterway?
3 80-day traveler
4 Gulps
5 Rock
6 Dorothy Parker, e.g.
7 G. & S. princess and others
8 Door stopper?
9 Army chaplain
10 Box label
11 Three __
12 Type of glass
13 Dish (out)
18 Main
22 Worrier's risk, so they say
24 Turkish for "ruler"
26 Oscar-winning film director Zinnemann
27 Runoff site
28 Four __
30 Convenient story
32 In itself
34 Not 100% open
35 Make a memo of
36 Aids in disguises
38 Photo choice
39 Balletic put-on
42 Mr. Average
44 Sports legend of 1920
46 With trumpets ablare
47 Spurred on
49 Symbol of vastness
51 Reward for yrs. of study
52 Gymnastics coach Karolyi
53 "I agree!"
54 Inflatable items
56 Bouquet
57 Heavily damaged city of W.W. II
58 Swirl
61 Somme summer

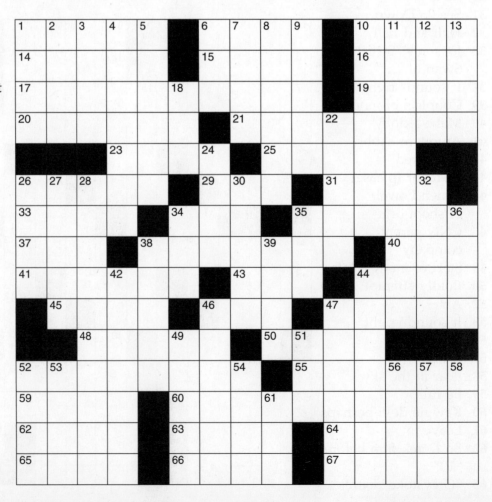

137 by Bernice Gordon

ACROSS

1 Like some eagles or tires
5 Poker Flat chronicler
10 Price
14 "Now __ me down . . ."
15 Dillies
16 Patron saint of physicians
17 In need
19 "Miss __ Regrets"
20 Former Washington nine
21 Journalists Joseph and Stewart
23 Bog
24 Dutch painter Jan
25 Actor Peter
28 Fleet cats
31 Comic Costello
32 __ incognita
34 Psalms word
35 "Bon" words
37 Appears
39 Flintstones pet
40 Bit of clowning
42 Soup ingredients
44 Cattle call
45 Newborns
47 Shortly
49 End of a tunnel, proverbially
50 Came in horizontally
51 Manhandler
53 Fellow crew member
57 Have an itch for
58 "Fantastic!"
60 1949 hit "__ in Love With Amy"
61 Sky-hued flower
62 Shoe support
63 Glassmaker's oven
64 Broadcasts
65 Asserts

DOWN

1 Invitations
2 A lily
3 Mowing site
4 Ball of fire
5 Feted ones
6 Tennis's Agassi
7 Collectors' cars
8 Robert Morse stage role
9 Subject of a will
10 Shut up
11 In a tenuous position
12 Leave hastily
13 1994 film "Guarding __"
18 Like Pisa's tower
22 Sediment
24 Humiliate
25 Broadway tune "__ River"
26 Ten-__ odds
27 Not with it
28 Northern Indians
29 Vietnam's capital
30 "Darn it!"
33 Rent out again
36 Presaging trouble
38 One-way transporters
41 Zoo fixture
43 Cuts
46 Pulses
48 Owns up to
50 Protected, as the feet
51 Subject to court-martial, maybe
52 Curse
53 Bedaze
54 Taj Mahal site
55 "__ also serve who . . ."
56 Hot times on the Riviera
59 Little: Suffix

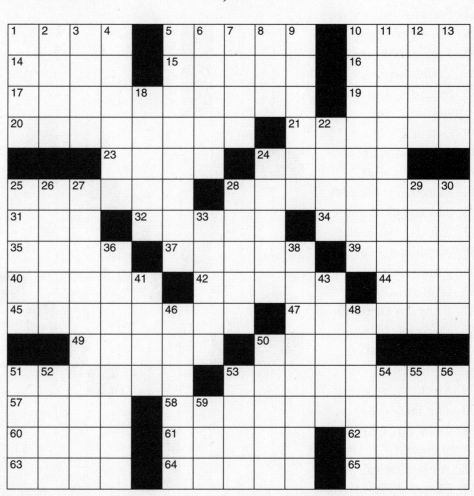

138 *by Robert Zimmerman*

ACROSS

1 Gregory Hines specialty
4 Take for granted
10 Colorless
14 Actress Gardner
15 Stay-at-home
16 Roof overhang
17 House member: Abbr.
18 Interior decorator's hiree
20 Wields the gavel
22 Swear (to)
23 Pinker inside
24 Opponent
25 Greek geometer
27 Premolar
31 Pallid
32 Secrete
33 Poi ingredient
34 Fed. power agcy.
35 Diffidence
38 Sword's superior, in saying
39 Craving
41 Ends' partner
42 More than fat
44 Stereo components
46 32-card card game
47 Effect a makeover
48 Napoleon's cavalry commander
49 Slow, in music
52 Bring an issue home
55 Pet rock, maybe
57 Hair application
58 Formerly
59 Mother —
60 The 90's, e.g.
61 Goes out with regularly
62 Archeological finds
63 Director Howard

DOWN

1 Canvas cover
2 Declare positively
3 Houseman TV series, with "The"
4 Two are often prescribed
5 Under the elms
6 "Great!"
7 Salt Lake City team
8 Russian for "peace"
9 Makes more valuable
10 Person who's feeling down in the mouth?
11 Fad
12 Lexington and Madison: Abbr.
13 Lahr or Parks
19 One of the Aleutians
21 Shopper's lure
24 Adjutants
25 Noblemen
26 Exhaust
27 Ties
28 Toothless threat
29 "— my case"
30 Gift recipient
32 Kind of power
36 Barn dances
37 Legendary hemlock drinker
40 Sidewinder lock-ons
43 False god
45 Actor Dullea
46 A form of 46-Across
48 Tycoon
49 Primates
50 Madonna's "Truth or __"
51 Church area
52 Lo-cal
53 Mr. Mostel
54 Flair
56 Chow down

139 *by Raymond Hamel*

ACROSS
1 Room between rooms
5 Handouts
9 Farm building
13 Opera solos
15 West Virginia resource
16 Sack starter
17 1970 Tommy Roe hit
20 Spain's locale
21 Leslie Caron role
22 Hesitation sounds
23 Writer Bombeck
25 Swindle
26 Sweet treat
30 "Fiddler on the Roof" fellow
35 Literary collection
36 Weep loudly
37 Arctic, for one
38 Recurring theme
41 French denial
43 Lisboa's sister city
44 1985 Kate Nelligan title role
45 Big shot
47 Calendar ender: Abbr.
48 Anglo's partner
49 Tentacled sea creature
52 Ostrich's cousin
54 Author Bellow
55 Lemon drink
58 Meadow bird
60 Drinkers' toasts
64 "Black Bottom Stomp" performer
67 Came down
68 Christmas centerpiece
69 The elder Judd
70 Critic Rex
71 Cruising
72 Tiff

DOWN
1 Pilgrim to Mecca
2 Pilgrim to Mecca
3 Citrus flavor
4 Emblem of victory
5 Item up the sleeve
6 Take it easy
7 Slander
8 With cunning
9 Visit Vail, perhaps
10 "Come Back, Little Sheba" playwright
11 Cowardly Lion portrayer
12 Chooses
14 Helical
18 Doorway parts
19 Perfect
24 Long, long time
26 Caan or Cagney
27 — Gay
28 Type of rubber
29 Superior to
31 Author Umberto
32 "Rigoletto" composer
33 Film director Peter
34 Tennyson's "— Arden"
39 Odysseus's rescuer, in myth
40 Exquisitely
42 Guitarist Lofgren
46 Ecto or proto ending
49 Panel of 12
50 Alaskan river
51 Groups of indigenous plants
53 "I Remember Mama" mama
55 Partly open
56 Take out of print
57 Nobelist Wiesel
59 "Red Balloon" painter
61 On
62 — Linda, Calif.
63 Fit of anger
65 Former Ford
66 — & Perrins

140 *by Roger H. Courtney*

ACROSS

1 Cremona violinmaker
6 Henri's squeeze
10 Tennis units
14 Quarrel
15 Stadium protests
16 Wynken, Blynken and Nod, e.g.
17 Criticize a prizefight?
19 Small brook
20 Transgression
21 Blackmailed
22 Cold stick
24 Le Sage's "Gil __"
25 One way to run
26 Instruments for Rostropovich
29 Economic hostility
33 Poet T. S.
34 Trumpeter Al
35 __ morgana (mirage)
36 Highway caution
37 Skater Sonja
38 Late king of Norway
39 "I __ Got Nobody" (20's hit)
40 Mare's feed
41 Jacques, in song
42 Rings loudly
44 Bell's signal
45 Itineraries: Abbr.
46 Handed-down stories
47 Expensive
50 Bit
51 Word with date or process
54 Imitator Little
55 Boxing commission?
58 Medicinal plant
59 Killer whale
60 "Happy Birthday" medium
61 Cravings
62 Shade of blue
63 Cup of thé

DOWN

1 Clumsy boats
2 Actor Paul
3 Ever and __
4 Idiosyncrasy
5 Imagination tester
6 French clergymen
7 "__ Indigo"
8 Chit
9 Guesswork
10 How hard Riddick Bowe can hit?
11 Rock star Clapton
12 Cash drawer
13 Fileted fish
18 "What a pity!"
23 Delivery letters
24 Items used in "light" boxing?
25 "Mrs. __ Goes to Paris"
26 Actor Romero
27 "Dallas" matriarch Miss __
28 Detroit footballers
29 Hues
30 Charles's princedom
31 Old name in game arcades
32 "Nevermore" quoter
34 Call at a coin flip
37 Winnie-the-Pooh receptacle
41 Awhile
43 Shoshonean
44 Humorist Lazlo
46 Not an express
47 Devoutly wish
48 Annoy
49 Religious image
50 Peruvian Indian
51 Speaker's spot
52 Coffee dispensers
53 Fisher's "Postcards From the __"
56 Suffix with fail
57 Wood sorrel

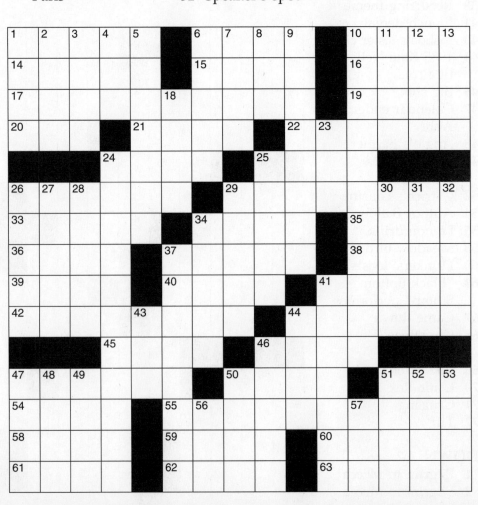

ACROSS

1 Whip end
5 Mystery writer's award
10 Sassy young 'un
14 "___ silly question . . ."
15 Painter Andrea del ___
16 Portnoy's creator
17 Hmm?
20 ___ Dame
21 Packwood, for one
22 Curse
25 Purse fastener
26 Jeweler's weight
28 Some of the Brady bunch
31 Eat like a chicken
34 Blend
36 Utah's Hatch
37 D.D.E.'s command
38 Hmm . . .
40 Volga tributary
41 Writer Terkel
43 Requisite
44 Porch adjunct
45 Arab capital
46 Ignoramus
48 South African statesman Jan
51 Gospel singer Jackson
55 Many TV shows
57 Cathedral displays
58 Hmm!
61 Mitch Miller's instrument
62 Mountain nymph
63 Electricity carrier
64 District
65 Don Knotts won five
66 Actress Young

DOWN

1 Suburban greenery
2 Seeing ___ (since)
3 Do figure eights
4 Where to hang your chapeau
5 Biblical verb ending
6 "Zip-a-Dee-Doo-___"
7 Alum
8 Relics collect here
9 The "R' " in H.R.H.
10 Pugilistic muscleman
11 Famous debater
12 Rat chaser?
13 Talese's "Honor ___ Father"
18 Word repeated after "Que"
19 Speaker
23 In a line
24 Eagle's nail
27 Like Neptune's trident
29 Adidas rival
30 Break sharply
31 Annoyance
32 Famous last words
33 Camp V.I.P.
35 Concert hall
38 Debate subjects
39 Irish novelist O'Brien
42 Like a golf ball
44 Manatees
47 Word sung twice before "cheree"
49 Lake near Carson City
50 Drang's partner
52 DeVito's "Taxi" role
53 Venous opening
54 Gray
55 Ms. McEntire
56 Cherry leftover
58 "Far out!"
59 Spring time
60 Lots of ft.

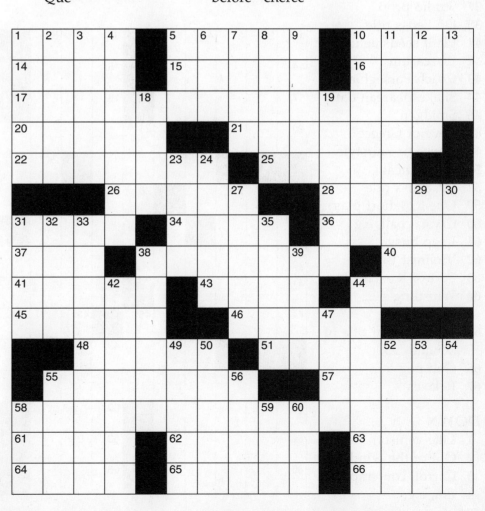

ACROSS

1 Masquerades
6 "Fe, fi, fo, ___!"
9 Batman foe, with "The"
14 Native Alaskan
15 Prince Hirobumi
16 Sheeplike
17 Irving's "A Prayer for Owen ___"
18 The lambada, once
19 Grand mountain
20 Dr. Seuss title
23 Actress Skye
24 Ho Chi ___
25 Car job
28 ___ Bingle (Crosby)
30 God Almighty
34 A year in Mexico
35 Put to the grindstone
37 Studio prop
38 Dr. Seuss title
41 Plant seeds again
42 ___-scarum
43 Coach Parseghian
44 Shakespearean oath
46 Smidgen
47 Love of Greece?
48 Dance or hairstyle
50 Calf's meat
52 Dr. Seuss title
59 One-___ (short play)
60 Crystal ball, e.g.
61 Keep busy
62 Violinist Isaac
63 Part of R.S.V.P.
64 Wrestling's ___ the Giant
65 Western film title of '75 and '93
66 Golf peg
67 Relaxes

DOWN

1 Like venison
2 Out of the wind
3 Carroll contemporary
4 Em, e.g.
5 Pen, for Pierre
6 About mid-month, with "the"
7 Brigham Young's home
8 Computer-phone link
9 Norse land of giants
10 Make out at a party?
11 Songstress Eartha
12 Organic compound
13 Philosopher Descartes
21 Conclude with
22 Small bird
25 Dens
26 Hungry
27 Idaho city
29 Betty Ford program
31 1991 Stallone comedy
32 Brain surgeon's prefix
33 Columnist Maxwell et al.
35 Author from Salem, Mass.
36 Inferable
39 Dinner chickens
40 More like Shirley Temple
45 ___ Solo of "Star Wars"
47 Sir Galahad's mother
49 Popular word game
51 "___ Is Born"
52 Fastener
53 VIII, to Virgil
54 Blvds. and rds.
55 Toledo's vista
56 Hitches
57 William of "The Doctor"
58 Unlocks, in a sonnet

ACROSS

1 Rustic lodging, informally
6 The Fighting Tigers: Abbr.
9 Bust
14 Make _ out of (contradict)
15 Rustic lodging
16 "... partridge in _ tree"
17 "Alone" composer Brown
18 To catch a thief
19 Yo-Yo string?
20 With 53-Across, 1940 Reagan film
23 Reagan TV series
27 Singer Tucker and others
28 Language suffix
29 On the Baltic
30 Opposite of nord
31 Courage
33 Ultrasound is one
34 Part of NASA: Abbr.
35 _ homo
38 Part of The Shadow's attire
41 Yellowish red
43 Old hand
46 Colorado Indians
47 TV frequency
48 Used a blender
50 Much-maligned Reagan flick
53 See 20-Across
54 Contradict
56 Certain savings, for short
57 Oil-well capper Red _
60 With no letup
61 French seasoning
62 One of the Fab Four
63 Piece of pie
64 N.F.L. scores
65 _ Hall (South Orange school)

DOWN

1 Prohibit
2 _ carte
3 _ Nora Charles ("Thin Man" pair)
4 Delicate
5 Uproar
6 Start of a tax form
7 Angry dog
8 Dim the spirits of
9 Exuding kitsch
10 Scheduling break
11 Dismissal
12 "My gal"
13 Spanish gold
21 Family room piece
22 Middling mark
23 Drunk's affliction
24 _ Claire, Wis.
25 Affirmation
26 Took a load off
32 Scientific charlatan
34 A little bird
36 Isle of song
37 Pullman units
38 _ games (Reagan announcing job)
39 Lunched
40 Biked
42 Put up for sale
43 Kind of race
44 _-de-chaussée
45 Prefix with meter
47 Thurman of "Johnny Be Good"
49 Tour assistant
51 _ France
52 Some exams
54 Arc
55 Opposite of WSW
58 Goodman's "When _ A-Dreamin' "
59 Diminutive Reagan

144 *by Jim Page*

ACROSS

1 Hang up one's jersey
7 Roll of bills
10 Chi. time zone
13 It ties the score
14 Palatine Hill site
15 Pi follower
16 Less messy
17 Actor Estrada
18 __-hoo
19 Old bandleader Edmundo
20 Keeled over
22 Library censures
24 Eats at the beach
26 They follow morns
27 Common suntanning locale
29 Eager to leave the picnic?
30 Atlanta Hawks arena, with "The"
31 Bites ineffectually
33 "Blech!"
34 Olympics skiing champion Alberto
36 "Car 54, Where Are You?" creator Hiken
37 Tiny mark
40 Nope's opposite
41 Was friends with
43 "My People" author
44 Xerox copy, for short
46 Equestrian competition
48 Director Kazan
49 Plains Indian
51 Woman's bio word
52 Jackie's hats
54 Turndowns
56 Prince Edward, e.g.: Abbr.
57 Sailor's direction
58 Rambo types
61 Classical start
62 Iodine source
63 To whom the Parthenon was dedicated
64 Vane direction
65 Speech pauses
66 Prepare fruit for eating

DOWN

1 Stimpy's pal
2 Adam's apple?
3 Little Anthony and the Imperials hit
4 "__ the Night," 1985 film
5 __ Peanut Butter Cups
6 Drop the ball
7 Not so good
8 Wrong
9 Hockey fake
10 1970 Vincent Price film
11 Huzzahs
12 Foot, in slang
14 Poker-table phrase
20 Nowheresville
21 Hangs like an earring
22 It can be soft or blind
23 __ sapiens
25 18-wheeler
28 Rush Limbaugh target
29 "__ Wiedersehen"
32 Backs
35 G.I.'s address
38 Tweety's home
39 Bender, of a sort
42 Very early
44 Fixes diapers
45 Molière miss and namesakes
47 Group of 100
49 Gondola guide
50 Nancy Kerrigan jumps
53 Shirr
55 Publishing notable Adolph
58 Like the woman of Chaillot
59 "A Chorus Line" showstopper
60 Rueful

145 *by Rich Norris*

ACROSS

1 Fitzgerald's forte
5 Inter __
9 W.W. I battle site
14 Science fiction's __ Award
15 Persuade cagily
16 Prime
17 Bon Ami rival
18 Dog command
19 Robert Louis Stevenson home
20 NO RUNS
23 Conservatory site?
24 Prepare to shoot
25 Have a few
28 Takes away (from)
33 Very, to Vivaldi
34 Muscovite, e.g.
35 Ring around the collar
36 NO HITS
40 Actor Wallach
41 1962 Met __ Chacon
42 Backspace, on a computer
43 Lorenz Hart, for one
46 Razzed
47 Music hall tune
48 Linkletter subjects
49 NO ERRORS
57 Reddish equines
58 Baker
59 Vitamin D source
60 "... the better __ you with"
61 Memphis's locale
62 __ vera
63 Flag features
64 Without much thought
65 TV's "__ Blue"

DOWN

1 Ayatollah preceder
2 King work
3 Mideast potentates
4 E.P.A. concern
5 Mount up
6 Slack
7 Sonnet part
8 Kerrigan feat
9 "You bet!"
10 Sci-fi energy source
11 The Apostle of the Franks
12 Coll. course
13 Buck
21 Be pushy
22 Corrode
25 Drive
26 Tart-tongued writer __ Ivins
27 Washington's __ House
28 One, for one
29 Cavern phenomenon
30 Exonerate
31 Coquette
32 Fathered
34 Thickness units
37 Be lordly
38 Beginnings
39 Pledge, probably
44 One whose work is decreasing?
45 Reasons why
46 Bus
48 Sound at sundown
49 Some are liberal
50 Geezer
51 __ Grande, Ariz.
52 Grammy winner Braxton
53 More than willing
54 Too glib
55 Sit (down)
56 Managed, with "out"

ACROSS

1 Swit co-star
5 Record label abbr.
8 __ E. Coyote
12 Foreman
14 Superdome and Silverdome, e.g.
16 Nursery rhyme listeners
18 Dig it!
19 Puzzlement
20 Kind of badge
22 "The Counterfeiters" author
23 __ hound
24 Mail client
27 Model Carol
28 Corn chip topping
30 Lacoste and others
32 Karl Malone's team
34 Pleases
36 Large number
37 Pave over
39 Heroic story
41 Actress Farrow
42 More retiring
44 Outshines
46 "... __ saw Elba"
47 Eniwetok, e.g.
48 Brooklyn Bridge designer
52 Early TV's Denise
53 Pretty Maid's nursery rhyme declaration
58 Former Philly mayor Wilson et al.
59 Fiddle-faddle
60 Toshiba rival
61 Band's booking
62 Campaign

DOWN

1 Just dandy
2 Year in Nero's reign
3 Reading room
4 Zeals
5 Certain firearms
6 Actress Ryan
7 Modern site of ancient Kish
8 1962 Dion hit, with "The"
9 "The very __!"
10 Line to the Hamptons, for short
11 "Don't overdo it"
13 Subway __
14 Conservative
15 Like grade-A meat
17 Lively tots
20 Soda jerk's drink
21 Property
23 "Ironside" actress Elizabeth
24 Basketry twig
25 Kind of paint
26 Another round
29 Coasting at Lillehammer
31 Union and others: Abbr.
33 Opposite of 8-Down
35 Thievery
38 1970 Ossie Davis musical
40 Lauds
43 Holds one's horses?
45 First-rate joke
48 Fixes
49 Novel set on Tahiti
50 Designer von Furstenberg
51 The Daltons, e.g.
54 Miss Piggy word
55 __ flash
56 Wash. advisory grp.
57 Command to a plow horse

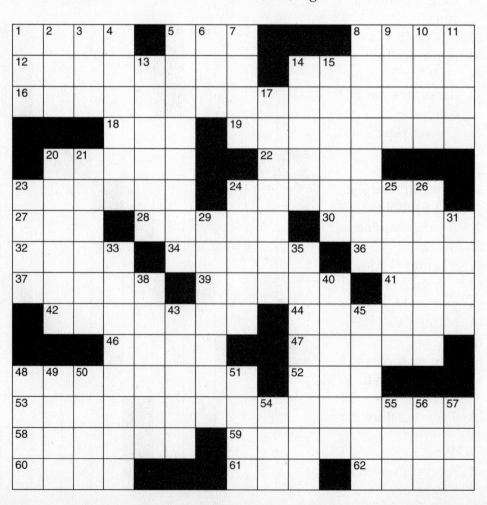

ACROSS

1 Rear
6 Edible rodent
10 Address abbr.
13 Historic earldom
14 Jambalaya locale
15 Perrier, par exemple
16 Smog?
18 More than aloofness
19 Yves's eve
20 Write off
22 Belly laugh
25 Like Desmond Tutu
28 Synge's "__ Island"
29 Fred Harman's comics cowboy
32 Of ecological stages
34 Athlete's foot
35 Hack
36 Ownership
37 U.N. arm
38 Firms (up)
40 Bambi's aunt
41 Rings
43 Mountain capital
44 Freedom
46 Head overseas
47 Showed indecision
50 Sound of a live wire
51 Belle and others
53 Appear ahead
55 Comics interjection
56 How a young lady succeeds?
62 Sign
63 Goodbye
64 __ Fountain
65 Dance step
66 Almost up
67 Indians whose name means "lovers of sexual pleasure"

DOWN

1 Actor Stephen
2 "Do __ say!"
3 Medit. nation
4 At some times of the year
5 Fair
6 Something to be up to
7 One vote
8 Tell secretly
9 Overlords
10 Inaugural balls?
11 Confront
12 "Parigi, o cara," in "La Traviata"
14 Old dance site
17 Airline to Karachi
21 Bit of light
22 Low-priced lodging
23 __ million
24 Results of deer hunting?
26 Cross-examiner
27 Jay and family
30 Uses force
31 Has a second meeting with
33 Ed Sullivan Theater host
34 Cañon feature
39 Hornswoggle
42 Diamond call
45 Comparative suffix
48 Tennyson's "doves in immemorial __"
49 __ good turn
51 She at sea
52 One of the Sinatras
54 Aware of
57 MNO, on a phone
58 Tippler
59 Storm producer
60 Time before
61 Family member

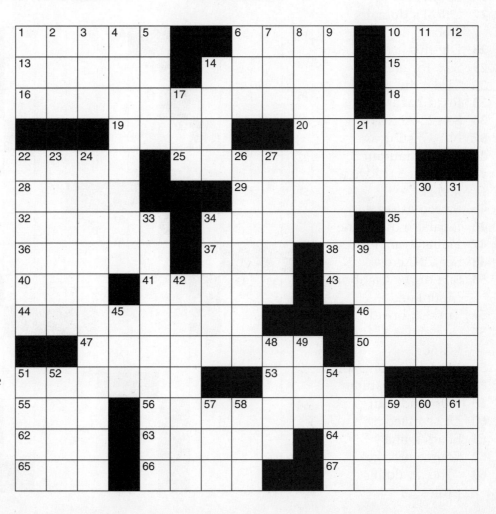

148 *by Timothy S. Lewis*

ACROSS

1 Lowly homes
5 One of the Simpsons
9 Abundantly supplied
13 Dairy section purchase
14 Overly sentimental
15 60's singer Sands
16 Knitting loop
17 Crude transportation?
18 House cat
19 House shader
20 Baseball's Canseco
21 "On Golden Pond" Oscar winner
22 With 34-Across and 48-Across, Wordsworth lines on Lucy
26 Fur type
27 Otto I's domain: Abbr.
28 Dig this
29 Sax, for one
30 "Take the __"
33 Road hazard
34 See 22-Across
37 N.Y.C. subway
40 "__ Restaurant"
41 "Amo, __, I love a lass . . ."
45 Sweep at sea
46 Japanese discipline
47 Pennsylvania folks
48 See 22-Across
53 Site of the Cambrian Mountains
54 Turkish bread
55 __ Palmas, Canary Islands
56 Model Macpherson
57 Equatorial capital
59 Huff and puff
60 Dissembled
61 Shark's line
62 Source of sake
63 "The __ doth protest . . ."

64 High point
65 German border river

DOWN

1 Desire
2 Wail
3 It can eat you out of house and home
4 La preceder
5 Verdi's "__ Miller"
6 Jersey and Guernsey
7 "__ walks in beauty . . ."
8 Burns's birthplace
9 Cut again
10 Rowena's inamorato
11 Grate expectations?
12 Six-carbon molecules
14 Farm sounds
20 Bump
21 Diva Mirella

23 Make over
24 Banquo, e.g.
25 Astronomical butter
30 "Anthony Adverse" author
31 Making bows
32 Transportation for Sinbad
35 Nuremberg defendants
36 Aforementioned
37 Dr. Johnson's biographer
38 First name in gospel
39 Warbled
42 Lost
43 Obliquely
44 Not one to trust
47 Sleuth's cry
49 Strapped
50 Home of the Trojans

51 KNO_3
52 Home of the Trojans
57 Sine __ non
58 Home of the Trojans
59 Old hand

ACROSS

1 Ezio Pinza, e.g.
6 Leak
10 Mention publicly
14 Mythological figure
15 It's found on the end of a string
16 Hogarth depiction
17 Texas A & M student
18 Untimely arrival
20 National anthem?
22 907 kilograms
23 Sip
27 Houston, for one
28 "To __" (with 44 Across, tune to which U.S. anthem was set)
31 Belli's bailiwick
34 Gold Cup Day site
36 "Holy cow!"
37 Cross to bear
39 Not by a long shot
40 Lay by
41 Straight prefix
42 Yemeni's neighbor
43 Took the van
44 See 28-Across
46 Pourboire
49 Direct
50 Obsolescent occupation
53 National anthem?
58 Whoop it up
61 Nick of "Cape Fear"
62 Impersonator
63 Hold overseas
64 Grenoble's river
65 Shadows
66 More than cheerfulness
67 Relinquished

DOWN

1 Whilom airline inits.
2 About 1% of the atmosphere
3 Transition
4 Louis and Paul, e.g.
5 Folk singer from Birmingham
6 Most populous N.Y.C. boro
7 Former Irish Prime Minister Cosgrave
8 Alaskan wildlife refuge site
9 Killer __
10 Gains
11 Beat it
12 Maui strings
13 Neighbor of Pol.
19 U.S. Pres., militarily
21 Peter I, II or III
24 Splendid
25 Italian white wine
26 Ran its course
28 Israelite stoned for stealing at Jericho
29 Twelve
30 Moving jerkily
31 Bulgarian king, 1918–43
32 As to
33 Pleated trimming
35 A number of
38 Four-time Super Bowl champs
45 Ancient Syria
47 Peaceful
48 Hirsute
50 Distinctive manner
51 In bundles
52 Among: Fr.
54 Burglar
55 Rigorous test
56 Cleaving tool
57 Actual performance
58 Touched
59 Mail abbr.
60 Tapster's unit

ACROSS

1 __ temple
8 Grippers
14 Like the White Rabbit
15 Unrefined metal
16 Hawk's home
17 Benedictine, e.g.
18 Bar servings
19 December 31 event
21 Biblical writing on the wall
22 Seasons
23 Diamond girl
24 Uru. neighbor
25 __ Lama
26 Supports
28 Cable alternative
31 "Double Fantasy" singer
32 Bit of reproof
33 Tabloid topics
40 Throw for __
41 1980 fadmaker
42 Cutup
44 Pop hit "Da __ Ron Ron"
45 Nice nights
46 Crystalline rock
47 Diamond point
50 Coast
51 Version
52 Not a run-of-the-mill entertainer
54 Milk-curdling agents
55 Dock
56 Awards for P. D. James
57 Letterman lists

DOWN

1 Effluvium
2 Pollen bearers
3 The original Miss Saigon
4 Speak to the Senate
5 They have their orders
6 Practitioner's suffix
7 "12 Tribes" painter
8 TV transmitter in space
9 Cause of gray hair
10 Extension
11 Camden Yards ennead
12 Against
13 Tackle box items
15 N.B.A. Hall of Famer Bob
20 Kyrgyz range
22 Permanent place?
25 Patron saint of France
26 "Wanna buy __?" (old radio comedy line)
27 Snack
29 Robin Williams film
30 Notions holders
33 Overwhelmed
34 On the horizon
35 Sounds of strain
36 Prove acceptable to
37 Bow to bow, perhaps
38 Comeback
39 Polish, with "up"
40 Stick
43 Acts foppish
45 Vegas equipment
46 Top
48 Lab vessel
49 Landing
50 Red's signification
53 Sorority letter

151 *by Thomas W. Schier*

ACROSS

1 Canyon sound
5 Cross-legged exercises
9 August forecast
14 Bumbler
15 50-50
16 Mohawk Valley city
17 Kitchen fat
18 Shea Stadium nine
19 Pressed one's luck
20 Big-eared animal
21 Vacation locale
23 In __ (ready for release)
25 Sign of summer
26 Cordage
29 It will be printed tomorrow
34 Gerald Ford's birthplace
36 Banned apple spray
38 By way of
39 Vacation locale
42 Declare
43 Speaker Gingrich
44 Solemn procedures
45 "__ forget"
47 1959 Fiestas song
49 Comic Charlotte
51 Outcome
54 Vacation locale
60 Have a tab
61 Like gold
62 On-the-cob treat
63 Ilsa of "Casablanca"
64 Wrist movement
65 Tale starter
66 Pre-owned
67 Army vehicles (You're welcome)
68 Blue-green
69 Jolly, to the British

DOWN

1 Brilliance
2 Sharply disagree
3 Monmouth Park events
4 __ man out
5 Sana native
6 "Back to you"
7 Fetches
8 Photographer Adams
9 Rock of Hollywood
10 Jazz locale
11 Muralist Joan
12 Cake decorator
13 Janet Reno's home county
21 Lacquer
22 Pine
24 Associate
27 Put the finger on
28 Is brilliant
30 Painter's mishaps
31 Russian parliament building
32 Sea swooper
33 "Broom Hilda" creator Myers
34 Whitish gem
35 Military command?
37 "Wheels"
40 Late-late show hour
41 Vacation events
46 Violent downfalls
48 Tornado part
50 Orlando attraction
52 Shareholder
53 Sleepwear item
54 __-Hartley Act
55 Hip-shaking in Kauai
56 Actress Moran
57 Rube
58 TV knob
59 Whale of a movie
63 Broadway hit of 1964–65

152 *by Randolph Ross*

ACROSS

1 Like Job
8 Bob or beehive
14 Leisurely musical pieces
15 Decrees
17 Pentagon advocate?
19 Parlor piece
20 Ex-Knick coach Jackson
21 Author of "Life in London"
22 Heart of France
24 Part
25 Visit Robert Reich?
31 Medical apprentice
32 Ease
37 Blue "Yellow Submarine" characters
38 Revised
40 Ancient beginning
41 Off course
42 Foggy Bottom boat?
46 Narc's collar
50 "Since __ Have You"
51 Not for
52 Juan's uncle
53 Pescadores neighbor
59 Reno's piano practice?
62 Tympanic membrane
63 Guides, in a way
64 Brews tea
65 Menu listings

DOWN

1 Falsifies accounts
2 Chick ender
3 White House heavyweight
4 Beach Boys' __ Around"

5 "__ kleine Nachtmusik"
6 Titan tip
7 Poetic monogram
8 Spa installation
9 Maestro Toscanini
10 Words often exchanged
11 Twice as unlikely
12 Down Under dog
13 "Love Story" star
16 January 1 song ending
18 Riding the waves
23 Bullfight cries
25 Walk with difficulty
26 Unwanted classification, once
27 Printing style: Abbr.

28 Hawaiian state bird
29 Kingston and others
30 Fee schedule
33 Friend of Ernie
34 Sills solo
35 Caterpillar construction
36 Advantage
38 Calling company
39 Intersection maneuver
43 Asks for a loan
44 They trip up foreigners
45 Magician's sound effect
46 First or home, e.g.
47 Last of the Mohicans
48 Genesis

49 Spanish squiggle
54 __ were (so to speak)
55 Ovid's way
56 Oenologist's interest
57 Entr'__
58 Costner character
60 Prior, to Prior
61 G.I. __

ACROSS

1 Rolling stone's deficiency
5 Anchor position
10 Complain
14 Aleutian island
15 __ Loa
16 Literally "high wood"
17 Obstinate
20 Royal spouses
21 Be on the brink
22 Professional bean counters
23 Designer Christian
24 Hardy's pal
27 Describe
28 Org. founded in 1948
31 Bandleader Shaw
32 Imparted
33 Sondheim's "__ the Woods"
34 Elusive
37 Branch Davidians, e.g.
38 Speaker's platform
39 Worker's wish
40 Off __ tangent
41 Curb, with "in"
42 Daredevil acts
43 Actor Sean
44 Lady in an apron
45 "Yessir," e.g.
48 Moon of Jupiter
52 In the altogether
54 Final notice
55 Teach one-on-one
56 Lion's den
57 Like 52 Across
58 Atlanta university
59 Thompson of "Howards End"

DOWN

1 Opposite of fem.
2 Mr. Preminger
3 Daze
4 Like the 2 in B_2
5 Not knowing right from wrong
6 Small pies
7 Hosiery snags
8 Actress Claire
9 Diversions
10 Future star
11 Border on
12 Actor's part
13 Look with squinty eyes
18 Sheepish lass
19 A long time
23 Prima donnas
24 Rope a dogie
25 Senator Specter
26 City east of Syracuse
27 Store up
28 __ a million
29 Alamogordo event, 7/16/45
30 Shoe bottoms
32 Rye or corn
33 Silent, or almost so
35 Toothless
36 With pretentiousness
41 Tear
42 Compensation
43 Pro golfer Calvin
44 TV's "__ Dad"
45 Presently
46 "Elephant Boy" star, 1937
47 Have brake problems
48 Roman statesman and censor
49 Thailand, once
50 Adjust the sails
51 Polish border river
53 Add

154 *by Ronald C. Hirschfeld*

ACROSS

1 They're plucked
6 Busy as __
10 Lake formed by Hoover Dam
14 Bye
15 Druid, e.g.
16 Presque __, Me.
17 Close behind
20 Chair plan
21 Setter or retriever
22 "Fables in Slang" author
24 Part of a bridal bio
25 Words after "The last time I saw Paris"
34 Buck follower
35 Muddies the water
36 "The Company"
37 Bara and Negri
39 Years in Paris
40 Mole
42 Native: Suffix
43 Comedienne Fields
45 Hebrides language
46 Completely unperturbed
50 Olympian: Abbr.
51 Knock-knock joke, e.g.
52 Sounds the hour
56 1967–70 war site
61 Discourage
63 Japanese aboriginal
64 Assassinate
65 Put up
66 Cuff
67 Cod relative
68 Drinks with straws

DOWN

1 It's a laugh
2 1985 film "My Life as __"
3 __ of passage
4 Drudge
5 Dairy bar order
6 Otto's "oh!"
7 English channel, with "the"
8 Like many textbook publishers
9 Adjective for Rome
10 Cellar growth
11 Old gas brand
12 Sleep like __
13 Excellent, in slang
18 Cry of achievement
19 Ancient capital of Macedonian kings
23 Corrigenda
25 June in Hollywood
26 Sister of Thalia
27 Alfa __
28 Sock __
29 Quinine water
30 Smarten
31 Lip-puckering
32 Hair-coloring solution
33 __ et Magistra (1961 encyclical)
38 It causes sparks
41 Lapidarist's object of study
44 City on Lake Winnebago
47 Tar
48 Actor Gooding
49 Glues
52 Earth
53 Bluefin
54 Scat cat
55 It's north of Neb.
57 Flying: Prefix
58 TV exec Friendly
59 Cape __ (westernmost point in continental Europe)
60 Colonists
61 __ de deux
62 Fork

155 *by Joel Davajan*

ACROSS

1 College digs
5 Haggadah-reading time
10 Coarse hominy
14 Piedmont city
15 Cuisine type
16 The Magi, e.g.
17 Railbird's passion
20 Certain wind
21 Check
22 Opposite of "yippee!"
23 Buyer caveat
24 Bottoms
27 Darlings
28 Railroad abbr.
31 Old toy company
32 Trim
33 It's not a dime a dozen
34 Bettor's bible
37 Grocery buy
38 Sword of sport
39 Archaic "prior"
40 Political abbr.
41 Cutting reminder
42 Didn't quite rain
43 Broadcasts
44 Baptism, e.g.
45 Corner piece?
48 Some legal documents
52 Across-the-board bet
54 Mont. neighbor
55 Mercantilism
56 Mrs. Chaplin
57 Curaçao ingredient
58 Downy duck
59 Snoopy

DOWN

1 Desert dessert
2 Agcy. founded in 1970
3 Hwys.
4 Results of some errors
5 Summer wear
6 Some House of Lords members
7 Word before free or calls
8 Ike's command, for short
9 Double-check the seat belts
10 Muddles
11 "Judith" composer
12 Cold-war fighters
13 Starting gate
18 Like some gates
19 A Kringle
23 Penthouse home?
24 Pheasant broods
25 Words to live by
26 Stoop
27 Race-track runner
28 Snob
29 Notre planète
30 1947 Horse of the Year
32 "__ Got a Brand New Bag"
33 Track hiatus time
35 Have fun
36 Like trotters, e.g.
41 Dust collector?
42 Actor Martin
43 Dismay
44 "The Cloister and the Hearth" author
45 Switch
46 Roofing item
47 Chip in
48 Interpret
49 "Git!"
50 Geologists' times
51 Waffle
53 Dernier __

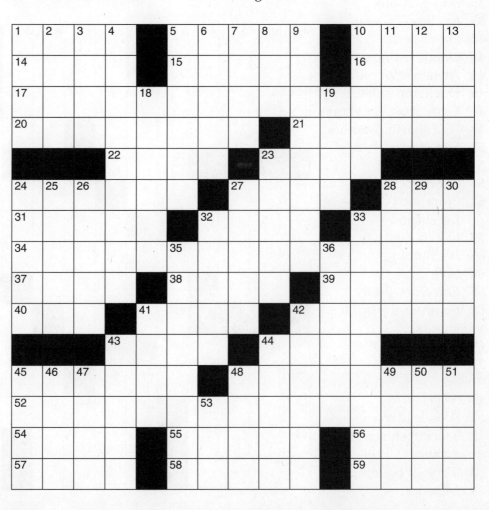

156 *by Fred Piscop*

ACROSS

1 Like Caspar Milquetoast
6 Yodeling locale
10 Quantities: Abbr.
14 City south of Gainesville
15 Chip's partner
16 Attack of the flu
17 Hook's flag
19 Florence's river
20 Like some shopping
21 Just say no?
23 Grp. founded in 1960
25 Present, for one
26 Antiknock number
30 __ and hounds
33 Calhoun of "The Texan"
34 Swiss mathematician
35 Son–gun link
38 Dr. Seuss classic
42 Da or ja
43 Onetime pupa
44 Austen's Woodhouse
45 Duchamp subject
46 Gym class, for short
48 "Siddhartha" author
52 Stat starter
54 Craftsperson
57 Short vocal solo
62 "Jurassic Park" beast, for short
63 Ocean denizen
65 It's nothing
66 Split __
67 Ottoman: Prefix
68 South-of-the-border shouts
69 Catch some Z's
70 Torpedoes

DOWN

1 Axis leader
2 Macintosh screen symbol
3 Type of bonding?
4 Miseries
5 Wright brothers' home
6 See 18 Down
7 Jet follower
8 No contest, e.g.
9 Belgrade resident
10 Cut down
11 Notorious Bugs
12 City near the ruins of Carthage
13 "JFK" director
18 With 6 Down, Ali maneuver
22 "Private Parts" author
24 Locomotive, perhaps
26 Overindulgence
27 Roy Innis's org.
28 Very, in Versailles
29 Parliament vote
31 What's more
32 Davidson's "The Crying Game" costar
34 "Holy cow!"
35 Resistance figures
36 Celebrity
37 Make __ dash for
39 Dress to the __
40 Cassowary kin
41 Susan of "L.A. Law"
46 Saucy
47 Block and tackle et al.
48 Little Iodine creator
49 "My Wicked, Wicked Ways" author Flynn
50 Eydie's partner
51 Boxcars
53 Medieval guild
55 Like some cheeses
56 El __ (ocean current)
58 Lateral lead-in
59 Go sour
60 __ off (anger)
61 Commotions
64 Cooper's tool

ACROSS

1 Smelling things?
6 Howard and Brown
10 Hill-climber of rhyme
14 Well-nigh
15 Hand-cream additive
16 Writer Wiesel
17 "__ Davis Eyes"
18 1982 Beineix thriller
19 Flat amount?
20 Subject of this puzzle
22 Designer Gernreich
23 Opulence
24 __ Islands
26 Hamilton of the Carter White House
30 "Topper" pooch
31 Tom Joad, e.g.
32 Bond
35 Fixed-up building
39 Accord signer of '78
41 G.I. address
42 Tool for bending cold metal
43 Laugher?
44 Bumper blemish
46 Noted name in lithography
47 TV palomino
49 Maintain
51 Promised Land
54 Bumpkin
56 Barbra's costar in '68
57 Noted performers on 20 Across's show
63 Falling-out
64 "__ Man" (Estevez flick)
65 Kind of cannon
66 Opposed
67 Geometry datum
68 Wipe out
69 It may generate interest
70 Clobber
71 Jinni

DOWN

1 Kemo __
2 Sacked out
3 A good deal
4 1984 Nobelist
5 "__ by Starlight"
6 Base of a number system
7 "Thimble Theater" name
8 Smoked salmon
9 Rap session?
10 Performer on 20 Across's debut show
11 Alimentary canal part
12 Yorba __
13 Admit
21 Bronchiole locale
25 Snobbery
26 Playwright Logan
27 Rubber-stamp
28 The Cyclone, e.g.
29 Performer on 20 Across's debut show
30 Light gas
33 Alan or Cheryl
34 News org. founded in 1958
36 Wealthy person
37 Ripening agent
38 Insurance writer A.M. __
40 Georgia home
45 Mr. Kaplan
48 Draw in
50 Used wax, perhaps
51 __ Sea (W.W. II site)
52 __ acid
53 Gore/Perot debate topic
54 Beat the offense
55 Lusitania sinker
58 "You are __"
59 Ran like mad
60 Rich soil
61 Former Sinclair competitor
62 Examined

158 *by Richard Silvestri*

ACROSS

1 Obsolete
6 Serpent song
10 Up to snuff
14 Type type
15 Put a stake on the table
16 Mr. Kadiddlehopper
17 Campaign-poster word
18 Night light
19 Litter littlest
20 Marquis de Sade's favorite side dish?
23 Before, to bards
24 Grandiose poetry
25 Wound reminder
28 Lingerie buy
31 Undiminished
35 Start of M-G-M's motto
36 Pop singer Abdul
38 Seven-time N.L. homer champ
39 Marquis de Sade's favorite entree?
42 Start of the año
43 Begin, as winds
44 Morn's opposite
45 Wanted-poster word
47 Snitch
48 Shelley output
49 Lab bottle
51 Former Mideast monogram
53 Marquis de Sade's favorite vegetable?
60 Ambition
61 At the summit of
62 More than manly
63 Move like the Blob
64 A little
65 Cultural characteristics
66 Ran in the laundry
67 Had no doubt
68 Ocean areas

DOWN

1 Regard
2 __ breve (2/2 time)
3 Dad's Day gifts
4 Whistler was one
5 Dissuade
6 Fastening device
7 '85 film, "__ the Night"
8 Washington, e.g.
9 Ranchero's wrap
10 Verse with a message?
11 In a funk
12 Brownie's eye?
13 CPR specialist
21 Interdict
22 Hanoi's region
25 Fencing weapon
26 Brom Bones's prey
27 In __ (agitated)
29 Has misgivings about
30 Birch kin
32 Readied the press
33 Christopher of the screen
34 Crossword birds
36 "Will it play in __?"
37 Official records
40 Made a basketball boo-boo
41 Ask for a loan
46 Upholstery fabric
48 Baroque
50 Admit
52 Aligned the cross hairs
53 Air-conditioned
54 Bulldoze
55 Igloo shape
56 Gush forth
57 Need a backrub
58 Karate motion
59 Ponderosa name
60 Lump

ACROSS

1 Ace depository
7 Peter Lorre typecast
13 In no hurry to buy
15 Inexpensive
16 Table spread
17 Humiliate
18 Twice-told
19 Fairy tale kid
22 Hoodwink
26 Mosaic piece
28 —-per-view
29 University of Maine town
31 Jazz star, with 36 Down
34 Dialing for dollars?
37 Slums Mother
38 Heavy bundles
39 Einstein's birthplace
40 Indy 500 occurrence
44 Humdrum
46 Vodka cocktail
49 Coach Holtz of Notre Dame
50 "All systems —"
52 Survey
53 Spying on who's buying?
59 Alternatives to malls
60 "Marriage is —": Cervantes
61 Saint-Tropez is one

DOWN

1 Makes confetti
2 Company trademark
3 Clean water agcy.
4 Prefix with glottis or gram
5 Pinot ou Chardonnay
6 Downstairs: Fr.
7 For beginners
8 Armored god
9 Like many football stadiums
10 Scheduled
11 Reception site
12 N.Y. summer time
13 Chambre
14 Kotter of 70's TV
15 Start, as a computer
19 Start of a toast
20 Spray, perhaps
21 Grandma
23 Knowing about
24 Bit of distress
25 Goggle
27 Fish entree
30 Sun or moon
31 Bear riot
32 "This is only —"
33 Not discounted
34 — off (scold)
35 Anecdotal Bombeck
36 See 31 Across
37 Butter container
41 Writer at Orchard House
42 Guffaws
43 — out (ignore)
45 "It — Be You" (Kahn-Jones hit)
46 Romance or sci-fi, e.g.
47 Pop music's — Pop
48 Drive
51 Bravo and Grande
52 Ending with spin or speed
53 Art deg.
54 Golfer Woosnam
55 Sgt., for one
56 Color
57 U.F.O. occupants
58 —-mo (replay technique)

ACROSS

1 Beckoned
5 Arroyo
9 Edith Evans, e.g.
13 Travel writer Thollander
14 Arrangement containers
15 Enthralled
16 Start of a quip
19 "__ was saying . . ."
20 "Women Who Run With the Wolves" author
21 Appearance
22 Stipple
23 Rent out
24 Quip, part 2
33 Punts, e.g.
34 Out of place
35 "Bleak House" girl
36 Moons
37 TV adjusters
38 Court score
39 1959 Kingston Trio hit
40 __ nous
41 In reserve
42 Quip, part 3
45 Stable particle
46 Super Bowl QB Dawson
47 "Kenilworth" novelist
50 "Luck and Pluck" writer
53 As well
56 End of the quip
59 A Guthrie
60 Marshal
61 Other
62 Jim Morrison, e.g.
63 Nanny, perhaps
64 Home bodies?

DOWN

1 Kind of star
2 Comments to a doctor
3 Half of sechs
4 High ways?
5 Bulb measure
6 Court V.I.P. Arthur
7 Tunisian rulers, once
8 Theory
9 Lennon's last home, with "The"
10 Exchange premium
11 One of Chaucer's travelers
12 Hash-house order
14 Horizon, maybe
17 Persian cries
18 Bright-eyed and bushy-tailed
22 Silent-spring causers
23 More than snips
24 Frightful force
25 It comes from the heart
26 Capital on the Bou Regreg river
27 Reach in total
28 Vast, in the past
29 Name on a pencil
30 Point of greatest despair
31 Order
32 Decreases
37 Puzzle
38 Betimes
40 Woman with a lyre
41 "Siegfried," e.g.
43 Lusting after
44 Thomas Gray piece
47 A herring
48 Mackerellike fish
49 Ibsen's home
50 Farming prefix
51 Turkish money
52 Backbiter?
53 Prefix with port or play
54 Drying oven
55 Hugo works
57 Piano tune
58 Up on

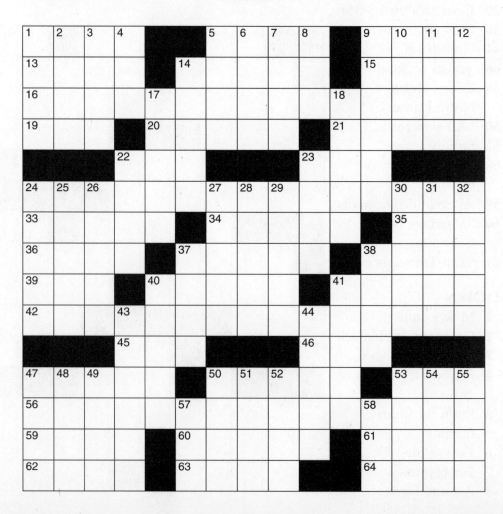

ACROSS

1. Food critic Sheraton
5. In the van
10. __ law (rule of electricity)
14. Green acres?
15. Brendan Byrne, e.g.
16. Muumuu accessories
17. Tilt
18. Jabbered
19. Alternative word
20. Massachusetts musical ensemble
23. Othello's nemesis
24. Louvre annex architect
25. Soviet space station
27. Brussels __
31. Fill driveway holes
33. In back
35. Somme summers
36. Parental substitutes, emotionally
40. Swamp
41. Hairsplitter
42. Wore away
45. Chapel next to St. Peter's
48. It's often seen ringside
49. Carpet down
51. Get __ the ground floor
52. Harvestman
57. French novelist Pierre
58. Skiing mecca
59. Grammatical subject
61. Sponsorship
62. Shiny fur
63. Mrs. Dithers
64. Yiddish writer Sholem __
65. Western "justice"
66. Genesis locale

DOWN

1. Actor Brooks
2. Eye malady
3. Bad luck
4. Kind of circuit
5. Vegas game
6. Retirement nest eggs
7. Flat payment
8. Person with a big nose?
9. "The Resurrection of Lazarus" painter
10. Backdrop for a TV scene
11. Spouse
12. Letters
13. Compass dir.
21. Salvation Army founder
22. Eskimo __
26. Latin thing
28. Suffix with press or moist
29. Maryland athlete
30. They're sometimes cracked
32. Aptness
34. "__ Pagliaccio"
36. Andirons
37. Sweet-smelling
38. Fill-up filler
39. "__ Tomorrow" (Sammy Kaye hit)
40. Columnist Greenfield
43. Windup
44. Wright-Patterson base site
46. Worthless
47. Nail down
50. Greek Academy founder
53. Gossip
54. "__ be in England . . ."
55. Turndowns
56. "Sommersby" star
57. __ & Perrins
60. Bert Bobbsey's twin

162 *by Sidney L. Robbins*

ACROSS

1 Day in Hollywood
6 Like a V.P.
10 Hula hoops, mood rings, etc.
14 Live
15 Talk drunkenly
16 Revise
17 Like Macaulay Culkin, in a 1990 movie
19 Mr. Mostel
20 Diner signs
21 The Boston __
23 Sense of self
24 __ Moines
26 One of the Greats
28 Loathed
33 Zilch
34 Egyptian deity
35 Jeanne d'Arc and others: Abbr.
37 Asp
41 Straddler's spot
44 Ordinary talk
45 Roman "fiddler"
46 Composer Thomas
47 Western Indian
49 Hair curls
51 Cheerleader's prop
54 Kind of nut or brain
55 Live
56 Verne captain
59 Cut in a hurry
63 Poses
65 Intersection concern
68 Mound
69 Tickled-pink feeling
70 Declaim
71 Confederate
72 Paradise
73 Big books

DOWN

1 N.J. neighbor
2 Plow pullers
3 Abundant
4 Ratio words
5 Bleachers
6 Mary Kay of cosmetics
7 Hog filler?
8 Certain wrestler
9 Boring tool
10 Turk topper
11 Run like __
12 Somber tune
13 Remained firm
18 Trypanosome carrier
22 Divide the pie
25 __ fire (ignite)
27 Certain wallpaper design
28 Dewy
29 Eastern V.I.P.
30 Fuss
31 Finishes
32 Postpone
36 Not a one-panel cartoon
38 Yawn inducer
39 Go into hysterics
40 Soft drinks
42 Pretend
43 "I'm telling the truth!"
48 Appear
50 Awkward bloke
51 Bygone title
52 Bay window
53 Kind of detector
57 Fine, temperaturewise
58 Convex/concave molding
60 Dated hairdo
61 Did laps in the pool
62 Abhor
64 Mata Hari, e.g.
66 Hatcher
67 Favorable vote

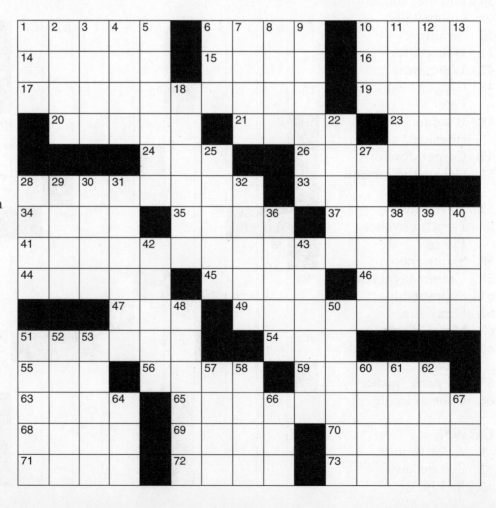

163 *by Sidney L. Robbins*

ACROSS

1 High rung on the evolutionary ladder
6 Alternative to a shower
10 Quatrain rhyme scheme
14 Like __ from the blue
15 Environs
16 Wise guy
17 Popular chocolate snack
19 On the level
20 River through Florence
21 Mother __
22 Help in crime
23 Quad number
24 Lock
25 Torah readers
29 Forgiving one
32 Oscar, e.g.
33 Prefix with cycle
34 Draft org.
37 March events?
40 Lolita
42 Phony prefix
43 Fond du __, Wis.
44 New Zealand native
45 Where Spain and Portugal are
48 Seasoning
49 Afterward
51 Kind of show
53 Singer Minnelli
54 Kick locale
56 Dumb __
60 Paid promotion: Abbr.
61 Give up hard drink?
63 Vegetarian's no-no
64 Sheltered
65 Similar
66 Wan
67 Lease
68 Little ones

DOWN

1 It's a laugh
2 "Deutschland __ Alles"
3 Daybreak
4 What's more
5 To the __ degree
6 Louisiana waterway
7 Bowers
8 Socials
9 Tortoise's competitor
10 Glaring
11 Place to have one's head examined
12 Bouts of chills
13 Borscht ingredients
18 Selves
23 Hoedown musician
24 Shortened
25 Criticizes
26 Not at home
27 Coming-of-age event
28 Cross-one's-heart garment
30 Play on words
31 Some
35 Dried
36 Agitate
38 Unit of corn
39 Phys. or chem.
41 Baby food
46 "Reds" star
47 Out of bed
48 Bygone
49 Andean animal
50 Gofers
52 Commencement
54 Box lightly
55 Patriot Nathan
56 It's full of baloney
57 Final notice
58 Roué
59 War deity
62 Hardly an underperformer

164 *by Wayne Robert Williams*

ACROSS

1 Impudent youngster
6 Salesmen, briefly
10 Impudent talk
14 Cheapskate
15 Beasts of burden
16 Baseball's __ brothers
17 1994 film role for Jim Carrey
19 Movers' trucks
20 More like winter sidewalks
21 Singer Estefan
23 Inge play
26 Closet spook
28 Nabokov novel
29 Clique
31 Norse deity
32 Film maker Wertmuller
34 Window surrounding
36 Fiery gems
41 Photographer's instruction
44 Rob
45 Neophyte
46 Paradise
47 Wedding vow
49 Soak (up)
51 Actor Tognazzi
52 By airmail from France
57 Dealer in cloth
59 "__ Twist"
60 England's Scilly __
62 Call to the phone
63 Happy camper?
68 Kuwaiti honcho
69 Nile queen, for short
70 Neutral shade
71 Does lawnwork
72 Bakery bite
73 Of the eyes

DOWN

1 New Deal grp.
2 Sot's interjection
3 Just manage, with "out"
4 Writer Ira of "Sliver"
5 Concise summary
6 Old-fashioned learning method
7 Long-distance commuter's home
8 For each
9 Full of obstacles
10 "Stompin' at the __"
11 Wake-up noise
12 Actress Braga
13 "Black-eyed" girl
18 Most hospitable
22 "Vive __!" (old Parisian cry)
23 Becomes tiresome
24 Ninny
25 Tippy transportation
27 Those not mentioned
30 Arm art
33 Letters before an alias
35 Not outgoing
37 Leading prefix
38 Make sense
39 Feudal lord
40 Man of the casa
42 __ and kicking
43 Bribe money
48 Straightforward
50 Magician's word
52 Vatican leaders
53 Texas shrine
54 Strict
55 Declares
56 Neighbor of Chad
58 Songwriters' grp.
61 Tab's target
64 Pie __ mode
65 No longer chic
66 Wire service
67 Old-time gumshoe

165

by Jonathan Schmalzbach

ACROSS

1 Son of Abraham
6 RR stops
10 Ill-considered
14 Hajj destination
15 Justice Black
16 "...and to ___ good night"
17 Whittles down
18 The sun, to the skin
19 Hera's husband
20 Noted baseball announcer
22 Give the boot to
23 Actor Ray
24 Lustily robust
26 Cervantes's ___ Panza
30 Improvise
32 Mountain of central Russia
33 Defense acronym
35 Actress Christine
39 Fixed shoes
41 Emancipates
43 Borgnine's "From Here to Eternity" role
44 Pronounced
46 Abstract artist Paul
47 Clear, as a tape
49 Loco
51 Quarterback, often
54 Misplace
56 Compassion
57 All worked up
62 Concept
63 Tastes
64 "___ of Athens"
66 First name in casino ownership
67 Option word
68 Gentry
69 Educator Sullivan
70 Noticed
71 Acted grandmotherly

DOWN

1 Mischief-maker
2 Cook quickly
3 Caldwell's "God's Little ___"
4 Scored on a serve
5 Algiers quarter
6 Archeologist's fragment
7 Harbor helper
8 Author James
9 Horse color
10 Clinton's home team
11 Certain Alaskan
12 Kind of fund
13 Cursory
21 By oneself
25 Is sickly
26 Malibu sight
27 Neighborhood
28 Cartoonist Thomas
29 Near miss
31 Celebrated Freud case
34 Hubbubs
36 Dance performed in a grass skirt
37 High schooler
38 Sinking-in phrase
40 Knowledge
42 "Aeneid" queen
45 Setback
48 Gets up
50 Cleared
51 Jazz trumpeter Louis
52 "The Age of Anxiety" poet
53 Shock jock Howard
55 Novelist Tillie
58 Cairo's river
59 Hawaiian seaport
60 Spew forth
61 Dull routine
65 Pulp penman Buntline

166 *by Arthur S. Verdesca*

ACROSS
1 Yin's partner
5 Toy gun ammo
9 Rift
14 __ patriae (patriotism)
15 Together, in music
16 "It __ Be You"
17 Parisian entree
18 Vatican City monetary unit
19 Down Under soldier
20 1954 Hitchcock hit
23 Bonny one
24 Singer Acuff
25 Beautify
28 Barley bristle
30 Buddy
34 Spanish wave
35 Passage
37 Cain's nephew
38 Behave
42 Clam supper
43 Sacred song
44 Onetime medicinal herb
45 German donkey
46 Élan
47 Charitable foundations, e.g.
49 Chinese ideal
51 Part of a wagon train
52 Merit award
59 Use
60 Candy brand
61 Paint unskillfully
62 Mesa __ National Park
63 Felipe, Jesus or Matty
64 Former Mormon chief __ Taft Benson
65 Shipping amount
66 Desires
67 __ Bien Phu (1954 battle site)

DOWN
1 Croquet locale
2 French call for help
3 __ cloud in the sky
4 Edsel feature
5 Soft leather
6 Farewell
7 Result of tummy rubbing?
8 Ore layer
9 Maria Rosario Pilar Martinez
10 Jacks-of-all-trades
11 Wood trimmer
12 Weekly World News rival
13 Beaded shoe, for short
21 Chinese-Portuguese enclave
22 Coffee server
25 Ice cream mold
26 Biblical prophet
27 Thanks, in Thüringen
28 Journalist Joseph
29 Grieved
31 "My Dinner With __"
32 Brimless hat
33 Test car maneuvers
36 18-wheeler
39 Iron pumper's pride
40 Diligent
41 Lagoon former
46 Actress Caldwell
48 Lacked
50 Locale in van Gogh paintings
51 Breakfast fruit
52 At any time
53 Betting game
54 Kind of vision
55 Fiddlers' king
56 "Schindler's List" extra
57 Fix
58 Israeli diplomat
59 Dow Jones fig.

167 *by Gregory E. Paul*

ACROSS

1 First name in Solidarity
5 Festive
9 Philatelist's item
14 Jai __
15 Mideast gulf
16 Eunomia, Dike and Irene
17 Partner of pieces
18 Schindler's request
19 Kind of orange
20 Feminine suffix
21 1928 A.L. batting champ
23 Correspondence
25 "It's a sin to tell __"
26 Alias of Romain de Tirtoff
27 Substitutes
31 Tupelo's favorite son
33 Impersonators
34 Nosh
35 Fizzles out
36 "__ Jacques"
37 Carol syllables
38 Ex-governor Richards
39 Kind of table, informally
40 She played Lady L in "Lady L"
41 Singer Jim and others
43 Novi Sad native
44 "Diary of __ Housewife"
45 Parched
48 CNN newsman
52 Thou, today
53 Poet's almost
54 Frown
55 Bulkhead
56 Terrify
57 Folk follower
58 Hazzard County officer, on TV
59 Risk
60 Butterine
61 1169 erupter

DOWN

1 Stick-on
2 Molière girl
3 "Peace Train" singer
4 Towel word
5 Aplenty
6 Felipe's farewell
7 Minus
8 U.C.-Irvine's nickname
9 Easy winners
10 Type of salad
11 Uzbekistan's __ Sea
12 Crèche figures
13 Hammer part
21 "Smoke __ in Your Eyes"
22 Tinted windows prevent it
24 Cleveland's Speaker
27 Scharnhorst commander et al.
28 Crimson Tide coach
29 Buckley's "God and Man at __"
30 Cartoonist Drake
31 Cheese town
32 Part of a fishing trio
33 Sticky-tongued critter
36 Newspaper edition
37 Actress Loughlin
39 Tambourine
40 Comic Lew
42 Expedition in Kenya
43 Mono's successor
45 Sky-blue
46 Athenian statesman
47 Oral Roberts University site
48 Big stinger
49 Formerly
50 Limerick man
51 Wrench, e.g.
55 Tiny

ACROSS

1 By the side
6 In the back
10 Hoarded
14 1936 Leslie Howard role
15 Nose (out)
16 Actress Nazimova
17 Foes at Gaugamela
20 Mythological lineup
21 Whomps
22 __ Claire
23 Loyal
24 Foes at the falls of Reichenbach
31 Topple
32 Leisure
33 Card
35 June honoree, for short
36 Taxable income
38 Philippine island
39 Plaintive
40 Out of business
41 Camera carriage
42 Foes at Troy
46 Fix, artwise
47 "Flying Down to __"
48 Bundle barley
51 Cosmetic items
56 Foes at Tenochtitlán
58 Mayberry moppet
59 Simulacrum
60 Ferber title
61 Level
62 Not stifling
63 Levels off

DOWN

1 Not give __
2 "Damn Yankees" role
3 Sign from on high
4 Barber's call
5 Green light
6 Pilot's vision problem
7 Nirvana
8 Cabinet dept.
9 Group based in Geneva
10 First name in the N.B.A.
11 Literary pseudonym
12 Jack Horner's surprise
13 Itar-__ (news agency)
18 Circa
19 As __ (generally)
23 "Take __!"
24 Tankard's kin
25 Rival of Sally
26 "The Cloister and the Hearth" author
27 N.Y.C. subway line
28 Busybody
29 Reb general Richard
30 Dear pelt
34 Fellows
36 Colonial African land
37 Prefix with Disney
38 Mil. rank
40 Caniff's "__ Canyon"
41 Bishop's bailiwick
43 Oregon's __ Lake
44 Narrow opening
45 "Hey you!" sound
48 Dundee denizen
49 Original Arizonan
50 Gannon University home
51 Marston __ (1644 battle site)
52 Don River's outlet
53 Hayseed
54 Ugandan exile
55 Needs a facelift
57 AT&T alternative

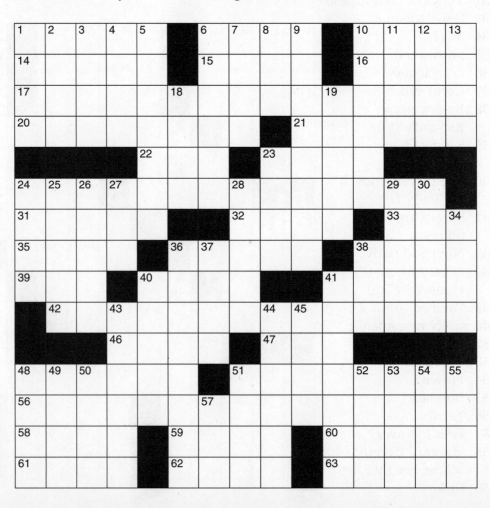

169

by Alfio Micci

ACROSS

1 Be a party to
5 Breakfast strip
10 "__ corny as Kansas . . ."
14 Judd Hirsch sitcom
15 Jagged
16 __ me tangere
17 First place
18 Spry
19 Future flower
20 Start of an old proverb
23 Gran Paradiso, e.g.
25 Mideast export
26 Russian co-op
27 Part 2 of the proverb
32 Ancient city on the Gulf of Aqaba
33 Reduce
34 Muralist José
35 Irritable
37 Give the eye
41 Don Corleone
42 Circa
43 Part 3 of the proverb
47 Birchbark
49 One may be high at 5:00
50 __ Plaines, Ill.
51 End of the proverb
56 __ supra (see above)
57 Understand
58 Mr. Saarinen
61 Graph start
62 École attender
63 Leave shore
64 Apollo craft
65 Playwright Rice
66 Stepped

DOWN

1 Downed
2 Michael Jackson album
3 Archetype
4 A Turner
5 Grin's partner
6 Historic county in Scotland
7 Hairdo
8 Frogner Park locale
9 At no time, to poets
10 Natural
11 Nelson Eddy in "Rose Marie"
12 French avenue
13 Fortuneteller
21 "Goodbye, Columbus" author
22 Lion's pride
23 Iowa university town
24 Singer Lovett
28 Communications conglomerate
29 __ Downs
30 Took a chair
31 Rossini's "Count __"
35 Spasm
36 Ordinal ender
37 Gram. case
38 Firestone rival
39 Darth Vader's son
40 Vacation times abroad
41 Opinion
42 Wise __ owl
43 Garland
44 Loggers' tourneys
45 When some local news is "live"
46 Render impotent
47 Kind of service
48 Stage comment
52 Business exec William
53 Cheerleader's routine
54 Watch part
55 Hatching post?
59 John Wayne's "__ Lobo"
60 Used

170 *by Jonathan Schmalzbach*

ACROSS

1 Symbol of suburbia
5 Author Grey et al.
10 Joyful cries
14 Hand cream additive
15 Sommelier's stock
16 Crow's-nest spot
17 Storage spot in a Brooklyn home
19 Word with sound or dog
20 Jargon suffix
21 Hurry
22 Petrol amount
23 What a Brooklyn guy blames today's problems on
27 It's stuck on Brooklyn theater floors
30 Place that Lot fled
31 Eager
32 What Brooklyn students hate to take
36 Half of Mork's sign-off
37 Serra's title
39 Ages
41 What a Brooklynite catches at J.F.K.
43 Creeper
44 Too-too
46 Where a Brooklynite tipples
47 Body that busted a Brooklyn gangster
52 Anchor position
53 Three, to Gina
54 Job's lot
57 Role for Oland
58 Laundry chore in Brooklyn
62 Annoyed interjection
63 Liver, e.g.
64 Conception
65 Clumsy craft
66 Author Zora ___ Hurston
67 Shore flier

DOWN

1 Forced (to)
2 Pub brews
3 Hoop's locale, perhaps
4 Pastoral spot
5 Austrian-born writer Stefan
6 Anouk et al.
7 Wind dir.
8 Bard's twilight
9 Jet set's jet
10 Sphere of operation
11 Cole Porter's "Katie Went to ___"
12 Type of turf
13 Dutch artist Jan
18 Noah's eldest
22 Hamstrung
23 Unearthed
24 Sleepy ones
25 Fulda feeder
26 Repetition
27 Comic Aykroyd
28 "Heavens!"
29 Missing
33 Little Foys number
34 Newspaper nickname
35 Mens ___ in corpore sano
37 ___ Springs
38 One against
40 Sunday speech: Abbr.
42 Unit of sugar or coal
45 Star-shaped
46 Bunnies' mummies
47 Russian villa
48 Old anesthetic
49 China flaw
50 Sty sounds
51 "Forsyte Saga" heroine
54 Broad
55 Singular person
56 Actor Eddie
58 Slip into
59 Before, to Burns
60 Links grp.
61 Dog command

ACROSS

1 1980 Olympics host
5 Writer __ Louise Huxtable
8 Setting
13 Computer list
14 Outfielders' throws
16 Sleeping problem
17 One-legged ballet pose
19 "Swan Lake" wardrobe
20 Ballet spin
22 Fernando of "The French Connection"
23 __ Grande, Ariz.
24 Café cup
26 Bull in Chihuahua
29 New Mexico artists' town
31 Spots on the face
34 Drinkers' heavens
37 1935 Astaire/Rogers musical
39 "Great Expectations" boy
40 Helpmate of sorts
42 Oil-rich __ Dhabi
43 "In" site, in a phrase
45 Took hold again, as a plant
47 Riga resident
48 Old Syria
50 Latin life
51 "If __ Hammer"
53 Where Cuzco is
56 Took it easy
58 Hopping step, in ballet
61 Plié spots
63 Anna Pavlova, e.g.
66 Accustom
67 Garfield pal
68 Desirous Greek god
69 __ incognita (old map notation)
70 D.C. lawmaker
71 Writer Kantor

DOWN

1 Thurman of "Henry & June"
2 Eccl. talk
3 Lose it
4 Limiting line
5 Lhasa __ (hairy terriers)
6 Pas __ (dance for four)
7 The shivers
8 Contents
9 Computer's heart, for short
10 Ballet leaps
11 Opposite of alte
12 Smooth
15 Begin in earnest
18 Time of importance
21 Sampler
25 Weaken
26 "Fiddler" actor
27 Express a view
28 Ballet coach
30 Ad __ per Aspera (Kansas's motto)
32 Local theaters
33 Old music magazine
35 Cote sound
36 Rub
38 Cortés's quest
41 Series of connected ballet movements
44 Biblical verb ending
46 Artists' lifeworks
49 Stallone role
52 Voyaging
54 Stephen Foster's "__ Bayne"
55 Female ruff
56 Theatrical bit
57 Murray of song
59 Softens
60 Aer Lingus land
62 Be wrong
64 "__ a chance!"
65 Oar wood

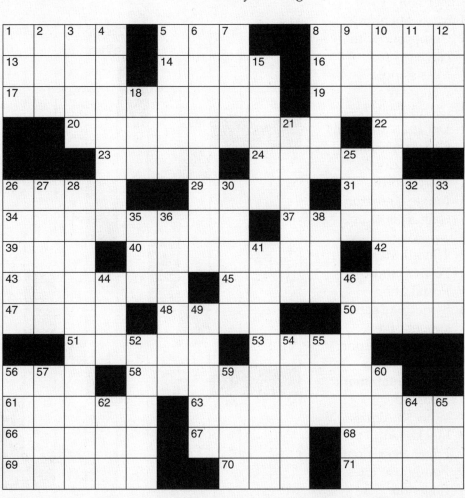

172 *by Manny Nosowsky*

ACROSS
1 Bombay V.I.P.
6 Hacienda part
10 Money grp.
13 With 16 Across, financially O.K.
14 By its very nature
16 See 13 Across
17 Lab containers
18 Hemmed
20 James Murray work: Abbr.
21 Air hero
24 Pro __
25 Kind of violet
29 Hawaiian verandas
31 Cousin of a mlle.
32 Inseparable
33 Lake __ (Mississippi's source)
34 German "I"
35 Musical ending
36 Composer with a clavier
37 Mississippi waterway
39 Gland finale?
40 Der __ (Adenauer)
41 Coll. srs. exam
42 Sophisticated
44 Scare word
45 Jungle squeezers
46 California team
47 Approve
49 The nth degree?
50 Festival time
51 Postal abbr.
52 Soviet workers' cooperative
54 Robin's transport
58 See 63 Across
62 Cost containment measure
63 With 58 Across, blockaded
64 Firecracker's path
65 Fun-house cries
66 Pretender

DOWN
1 Green
2 "The __ Daba Honeymoon"
3 Write a bit
4 Former ova
5 Abélard, e.g.
6 Rushed
7 Balaam's beast
8 See 9 Down
9 With 8 Down, a reply's start
10 Banned chemical compound
11 Had a little lamb
12 Lettuce variety
14 Agenda listing
15 German import
19 See 45 Down
21 Legendary Arabian hero
22 Make a list
23 Doer
25 With a bow, musically
26 Radiator fluid
27 Faster than adagio
28 Least remote
30 Late apartheid opponent
31 Appraises, with "up"
35 Sierra Maestra country
38 Flaherty's "Man of __"
43 Takes the elevator, perhaps
45 With 19 Down, predeparture words
48 Author Bombeck
49 Make ready, informally
52 "Poor pitiful me!"
53 Prefix with type
54 Merit badge grp.
55 Swiss river
56 Hosp. attention
57 Word of disgust
59 Both Begleys
60 "Huh!"
61 Sin

173 *by Edward Early*

ACROSS

1 Gutter site
5 Insomnia cause?
9 Marmon __ (first auto to win the Indy 500)
13 Sick as __
14 Onetime Aegean land
16 Actress Chase
17 Start of a quotation by 9 Down
20 Neighbor of Braz.
21 Popular machine
22 Detroit products
23 Kind of code
25 25, e.g.
28 Runway
30 __ daisy
31 Signal since 1912
34 Indulgent
35 Sister of Selene
36 Straddling
37 Middle of quote
41 All __ (attentive)
42 Zinger
43 Acht, __, zehn
44 1994 U.S. Open golf champion
45 Star of "Mon Oncle"
46 Tidy up
48 Poznan's location
50 Seats, slangily
52 Peacock "eyes"
55 Addition
57 Suffix with insist
58 End of quote
62 "__ boy!"
63 Ruth's mother-in-law
64 Western star Richard
65 Admit, with "up"
66 Girlie show props
67 Certain investor's agreement, for short

DOWN

1 Gobble
2 More than appreciates
3 1985 Tom Hanks comedy
4 Kind of maniac
5 Losing proposition
6 Offspring of 7 Down
7 Rest stop
8 Noisy bird
9 See 17 Across
10 __ Romeo
11 Potato part
12 Mountain route
15 1991 Sondheim show
18 Bag
19 Like a haunted house
24 Hamas adherents
26 San __
27 Savvy about
29 Galatea's sculptor, in myth
31 Salisbury Plain attraction
32 Comic strip reaction
33 Aix-les-Bains, e.g.
36 Chills
37 One of 18
38 Movie computer
39 Bit
40 __, Minn. (1862 Sioux uprising site)
45 Highway robbery?
47 Ballpoint part
48 Guilty and others
49 Stuffed deli delicacy
51 Dictator's aide
52 One of five Norse kings
53 Île de la __
54 Salamanders
56 Ad exec George __
59 Capture
60 Gunk
61 __ Lingus

174 *by Norman S. Wizer*

ACROSS
1 Irrational art
5 One of the Huxtables
10 Summer getaway
14 Not on the level
15 Radio-related
16 __-Altaic (language group)
17 Start of a quote by Will Durant
20 Isaac or Howard
21 Put into difficulties
22 Old spy grp.
24 "On Golden Pond" playwright Thompson
25 Quote continued
31 Prefix with valence
32 Jabir al-Sabah, e.g.
33 Take forcibly
38 Local life
40 Storm heading
41 Pang
42 Mount
43 Pedal pushers?
45 Greek peak
46 Quote continued
49 Shaver
53 Pricing word
54 Touch a chord
57 Racket
61 End of the quote
64 Crosses
65 In heraldry, having small projections in the upper corners
66 Distribute
67 Glamour rival
68 Assemblies
69 Kind of money

DOWN
1 Judo levels
2 Much
3 Fawn
4 Choice of Paris
5 Preserve
6 Blockhead
7 The blue of baby blues
8 Opposite of gormandize
9 Small posy
10 Show rudeness in traffic
11 Glacial formation
12 Shocks of a sort
13 Spy of a sort
18 Split sec.
19 "Groovy"
23 1967 Monkees song
25 Yaks
26 Drop
27 Reed
28 John Ciardi's "__ Man"
29 Curtain fabric
30 Esurience
34 Places for displaying wares
35 Constellation name
36 Optimistic
37 They're sometimes split
39 Arithmetic figure
44 Easy mark
47 Stumped
48 Advanced
49 Babble
50 Kind of eagle
51 Nary __
52 Constrictor
55 Language akin to Shan
56 Site of Galway Bay
58 Noncommittal response
59 Give a bellyful
60 Surveyed
62 Bottom line
63 Mdse.

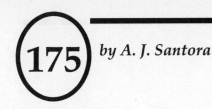

by A. J. Santora

ACROSS

1. 1965 disturbance site
6. Reserved
14. Flog
15. Booker T. Washington, e.g.
16. Fallaci of "If the Sun Dies"
17. Overshadow
18. Half man, half goat of myth
20. Got together
21. Part of 46 Across: Abbr.
22. Rhapsodic
26. Itinerary word
27. Hag's cry
29. Zilch
30. J.F.K. portraitist
34. Spike
35. Eagerly expectant
36. Variety
37. J.F.K. biographer
40. Group shop
41. __ Fail (ancient Irish stone)
42. British actress Bartok
43. Where runs are made
46. "Sweet 16" org.
48. Cow
49. Decking out
53. In the background
57. "G.W.T.W." role
58. Permit
59. Beijing belief
60. Followers
61. Driving hazard

DOWN

1. Guarded
2. Seed covering
3. Drudgery
4. Deli order
5. Bestrides
6. Cold-war forces
7. Conductor de Waart
8. Breadbasket
9. Less hospitable
10. Bar
11. Correlation ratio symbol in statistics
12. Nullifier
13. Trevi coin count
14. __ Alamitos, Calif.
19. One way to get the blame
22. Sinister part?
23. Heads of ancient Rome
24. Designer Simpson
25. Escapade
26. Red-eyed birds
28. J.F.K. Library architect
30. Rodeo yell
31. Marquis Hirobumi __
32. Average name
33. Trial
34. Delineate
38. Anodynes
39. Son of Cedric the Saxon
44. William __ Gladstone
45. Grand
47. Overlays
49. Lime finishes
50. Opponent of Jimmy and Arthur
51. Vespiary
52. Campus facility
53. Actress Hagen
54. Ice cream __
55. Traffic caution
56. Time abroad

ACROSS

1 Insertion mark
6 Rock layers
12 Kojak portrayer
14 It frequently finds itself in hot water
16 Cracker Jack prize
17 Peter Finch movie "Raid on __"
18 Saw
19 Chicken __ king
21 Standing near home, maybe
22 Communion or baptism
23 SALT concern
25 China: Prefix
26 Path for Confucians
27 Language from which "sarong" comes
29 Article in Der Spiegel
30 Hollered
32 Kon-Tiki wood
34 Cool, as coffee
35 Computer unit
36 Idiot box
38 Cash reserves
42 Loan org.
43 Beatty's co-star in "Bonnie and Clyde"
45 Paul's singing partner
46 Watermelon waste
48 To __ mildly
49 Actor John
50 Word with jack or label
52 "I __ You Babe"
53 Prize money
54 Sugar type
56 Gym exercises
58 Enters helter-skelter
59 Works a deal on

60 Least done
61 Founded

DOWN

1 Of the heart
2 Amelia Earhart, e.g.
3 Roundup site
4 Actress Sommer
5 __ kwon do
6 X-rated
7 Countdown beginning
8 Pro follower
9 Aids and __
10 House cats
11 Balkan country
12 Fits' companion
13 Quarterback Ken
15 Divulge
20 Put ammo in

23 Hot-dog
24 Tended tots
27 Became hitched
28 Coopers __ Bumppo
31 Superman symbol
33 Grant opponent
35 Enchant like Samantha
36 Where things vanish
37 Absolutely bland
38 Group with HQ in Brussels
39 Debate stifler
40 Understood
41 Underline
42 Dowdy person
44 Guitarist Ted
47 Spoiler
49 Em and Bee

51 Schnozzola
53 Tilting-tower town
55 Mom's girl
57 Spokes' intersection

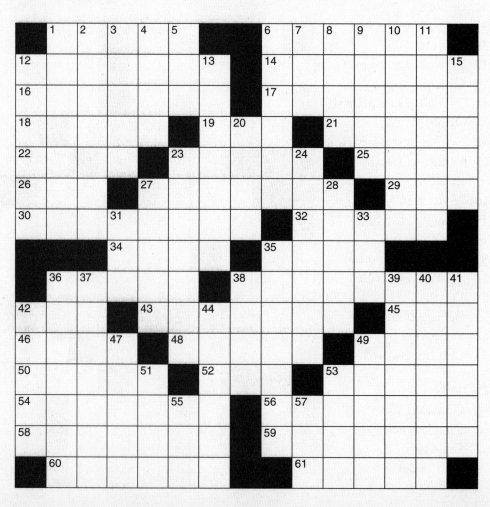

177 *by Sidney L. Robbins*

ACROSS

1 Bakery byproduct
6 Went by plane
10 Copied
14 Arizona features
15 Scottish isle
16 Lemon's partner
17 With 36 Across and 55 Across, a sales pitch disclaimer
20 Baden-Baden and others
21 Shea team
22 Eastern V.I.P.
23 Mr. Caesar
24 Ship to __
25 "Swan Lake," e.g.
29 Tiny bit
31 Not native
32 Printer's employee
33 Printer's measures
36 See 17 Across
39 His wife took a turn for the worse
40 Obsolescent piano key material
41 Bellini opera
42 Hoarder's cry
43 Telescopist's sighting
44 Strength
47 Opponent
48 Xerox competitor
49 "When I was __ . . ."
51 In __ of (instead)
55 See 17 Across
58 Person 'twixt 12 and 20
59 "The King and I" setting
60 Singer Cara
61 Misses the mark
62 Paddles
63 Waco locale

DOWN

1 Concert hall equipment
2 Harvest
3 Greek mountain
4 Wrestlers' needs
5 Type of cobra
6 Shot
7 Artist's pad?
8 Son of Seth
9 Revolutionary, e.g.
10 "Remember the __"
11 Heartbroken swain
12 Leno, for one
13 Bucks and does
18 Give forth
19 Indian noblewoman
23 Feeling
24 Suffix with tip or dump
25 Get-out-of-jail money
26 In addition
27 Bit of fluff
28 Mr. Durocher
29 Harden
30 "Sure, why not?"
32 Borodin's "Prince __"
33 To be, in Paree
34 Secretarial work
35 Burn
37 Confess
38 "__ on your life!"
43 Fashion
44 "60 Minutes" regular
45 Reason out
46 Sentence subjects
47 Country homes
48 Pigeon coop
49 __ da capo
50 Noted James Earl Jones stage role
51 Entice
52 The holm oak
53 Erupter of 1669
54 Applications
56 G.I. entertainers
57 Command to Fido

178 *by Peter (Lefty) Gordon*

ACROSS

1 Spirogyra or frog spit
5 Impression
9 Diamond protector
13 Burpee bit
14 Conclude, as negotiations
16 See 31 Across
17 Lefty, celebrity relative
20 Turkish title
21 Customary practice
22 Strengthens, with "up"
23 Tugs
25 "Babes in Toyland" star, 1960
28 Head of the costume department?
30 Leonard and Charles
31 With 16 Across, former Phillies manager
34 "Queen ___ Day" (old game show)
35 Corporate abbr.
36 Have a hunch
37 Lefty artist
41 Shows one's humanity?
42 Bud
43 ___ Fein
44 Voted
45 Great
46 Overwhelms with humor
48 Catch in a net
50 Pipe type
52 Highest point in Sicily
55 Course for a newcomer to the U.S.: Abbr.
57 Lament
58 Lefty actor
62 French 101 word
63 Copy of a sort
64 Noted rap artist
65 Gloomy
66 Overdecorated
67 Danson, et al.

DOWN

1 Composers' org.
2 Three miles, roughly
3 Lefty President
4 Foofaraw
5 Horus's mother
6 Star in Cygnus
7 Baa maid?
8 Razor-billed bird
9 Kind of sax
10 Publican's offerings
11 Ridicule persistently
12 Is worthwhile
15 Lefty actress
18 Five-year periods
19 Refusals
24 Pontiac Silverdome team

26 Camden Yards team
27 Polaroid inventor
29 Lefty comedian
31 Lefty comedian
32 ECU issuer
33 Lawyer in both "Civil Wars" and "L.A. Law"
36 Student's worry
37 Roman law
38 Before, to Byron
39 Jutlander, e.g.
40 In a despicable way
45 Writer Quindlen
47 Blotto
48 Oldtime knockout
49 Subs
51 Bridge seats
52 Horse that made sense?
53 One of the Jackson 5

54 Tannish color
56 Hot
59 Chaperoned girl
60 Actress Joanne
61 Paroxysm

ACROSS

1 Trounce
8 "My gal" of song
11 Castleberry of "Alice"
14 Have coming
15 Soldier's fare
17 Traveled militarily
18 Catch-22 situation
19 Black and white, e.g.
21 U.S.N. rank
22 Ireland
23 Cosmo and People, e.g.
26 I, to Claudius
27 "__ Lisa"
31 Shower mo.
32 Scruggs of bluegrass
34 Epithet for a tyrant
36 Not a warm welcome
39 Flower child
40 A big blow
41 De Maupassant's "__ Vie"
42 Some of Wordsworth's words
43 Legendary Hollywood monogram
44 Ed of "Daniel Boone"
45 Roller coaster cry
47 "Society's Child" singer Janis __
49 Sang-froid
56 In progress
57 Vegetarian's no-no
59 Alley of "Look Who's Talking"
60 Rodeo ropes
61 Ship's heading
62 Always, poetically
63 Majority's choice

DOWN

1 S. & L. offerings
2 Lover's __
3 Christiania, today
4 Scarlett and others
5 Bear Piccolo
6 Civil rights leader Medgar
7 Change the decor
8 Punic War general
9 Knight's attire
10 Slip-up
11 Fight sight
12 Mislay
13 Washington bills
16 Mai __
20 Like Captain Ahab
23 Like a he-man
24 Sap sucker
25 Bellyache
26 Be off the mark
27 Denver summer time: Abbr.
28 Disgrace
29 Nary a person
30 Saint whose feast day is January 21
32 Biblical judge
33 Word of support
34 Bugs' voice
35 Hairy ancestor
37 Obsolescent disks
38 Engine part
43 Like slim pickings
44 Lacking iron, maybe
45 Essayist E.B.
46 Three-time skating gold medalist
47 Model
48 Novelist Malraux
49 Furnace fuel
50 Getting __ years
51 Bogeyman
52 Pop music's __ Lobos
53 Gardner of mysteries
54 Backside
55 Overindulge
58 Chairman's heart?

ACROSS

1 Zubin with a baton
6 Old streetlight
13 Daley and others
14 Gravel-voiced actress
15 Iron shortage
16 Commit
17 Just the highlights
18 Slammin' Sam
19 Trendy
20 Getting better, as wine: Var.
22 Up to now
24 Size up
26 Paints amateurishly
28 Almost shut
32 Kind of symbol: Abbr.
33 One whom Jesus healed
34 Rodeo rope
35 Dashboard reading, for short
36 Leave the pier
38 Acquire
39 Ask on one's knees
41 Had
42 Short lunch order
43 Belgrade dweller
44 In abeyance
45 Sciences' partner
46 Tooth
48 Comfort
50 Probe
53 Some pads
55 Accident mementos
58 Serves a sentence
60 Byrnes of "77 Sunset Strip"
61 Brown paint, e.g.
62 Six-footer?
63 Resort locale
64 Newspaper section

DOWN

1 Lion's pride?
2 It's hard to miss
3 Respect
4 Nonsense
5 Simile center
6 Comic Kaplan
7 Assuages
8 Picture with its own frame
9 Wheel bolt holder
10 King of comedy
11 Part of a pair
12 Sound of relief
13 Scuff up
14 It's hard to say
18 Fastens with a pop
21 "I have no __!"
23 __ chi ch'uan
24 Tail ends
25 Temptation for Atalanta
27 1991 American Conference champs
29 It's hard
30 Listing
31 Sounds off
33 Digital-watch readout: Abbr.
34 Postal letters
37 Have a hunch
40 1970 Jackson 5 hit
44 Looking while lusting
45 Waylay
47 Time and again
49 In unison
50 Tots up
51 Afternoon TV fare
52 Lifetime achievement Oscar winner Deborah
54 Mingo portrayer
56 Puerto __
57 Play place
59 Take part in a biathlon
60 Kipling novel

ACROSS

1 Give tit for tat
5 Pillow covers
10 Bunco
14 It debuted in Cairo, Dec. 24, 1871
15 Video screen dot
16 So long
17 What's my line: #1
20 Guard
21 They make colorful displays
22 Transcending
23 Have trouble on the ice
24 Gas, in Greenwich
27 Wine casks
28 Cleopatra biter
31 The A in "CAT scan"
32 Cartoonist Peter
33 Utah ski center
34 What's my line: #2
37 Nautical direction
38 Danza of "Who's the Boss?"
39 Refine, as 53 Down
40 Old Ford model
41 Dickey fastener
42 Thinks out loud
43 Level
44 Amatory writing
45 Brutality
48 Ghostly
52 What's my line: #3
54 First name in fashion
55 Prefix with figure or form
56 G.P.A., in slang
57 "Not my __"
58 Intelligence
59 Mr. Culbertson and others

DOWN

1 Easy marks
2 Telegraph
3 Mideast gulf
4 Rural-themed opera
5 Crystalline gemstone
6 Stowaway
7 Leaf angle
8 One of Alcott's Little Women
9 Boy Scout tie
10 Reserved
11 Musical with the song "Memory"
12 __ smasher
13 Viking touchdown site
18 Villa d'Este locale
19 Speaker at Cooperstown
23 Cheerful
24 Of the Vatican
25 Glorify
26 "Dead"
27 Vogue
28 Green-card applicant
29 Hackneyed
30 Cords, e.g.
32 Love, in Le Havre
33 Signature event
35 Goes for
36 Phase
41 Acapulco assent
42 Danish city
43 Bit of color
44 Certain tournaments
45 Difficult position
46 Confederate
47 Philosophical
48 Comics publisher Lee
49 Actor Julia
50 "Go __!"
51 Cleaning agents
53 Ferriferous rock

ACROSS

1 Slates
6 Provinces
11 Part of a footnote abbr.
14 Way of speaking
15 Slacken
16 Paul's "Exodus" role
17 Kind of scout
18 River to the Missouri
19 Charles S. Dutton sitcom
20 Performed a Herculean feat #1
23 Fray
25 Preliminary figure: Abbr.
26 "A Letter for __" (1945 movie)
27 Manipulate
28 Crony
30 Uncle Sam poster words
31 Performed a Herculean feat #2
36 Ile-de-France river
37 Tart apples, informally
38 Performed a Herculean feat #3
44 __ Bornes (classic card game)
45 "Hey, you!"
46 Bravo, e.g.
47 Heraldic band
48 Treaty org. since 1948
50 Painter Hopper
53 Performed a Herculean feat #4
56 List ender
57 Bad, bad Brown of song
58 Appoggiaturas
61 Hilo souvenir
62 Honeymoon follower
63 Pauperized
64 Fast wings, for short
65 Save up
66 Attach an ell

DOWN

1 Become prone
2 TV's Mrs. Morgenstern
3 Aimed
4 Rental sign
5 Suggest, with "of"
6 Baseball's Moises
7 Change "potatoe" to "potato", e.g.
8 Our 50, to Francois
9 Zero
10 Admiral sunk with the Scharnhorst
11 Truck: lorry:: trailer: __
12 Type of board
13 Summons
21 Unseat
22 ". . . consider her ways, and __": Proverbs
23 Baby bloomer?
24 "Do __ say!"
29 Made fun of, in a way
30 Yen
32 Column bases, in architecture
33 Nature outing
34 Mischief-makers
35 More substantial
38 1979 World Series champs
39 Backdoor
40 Results
41 Precision-made
42 Tell the world
43 Staff
44 Mushrooms
48 Concert site
49 Skylit courts
51 Secretary Shalala
52 Wined and dined, perhaps
54 Wagner heroine
55 Regards
59 Tokyo, once
60 Dict. listing

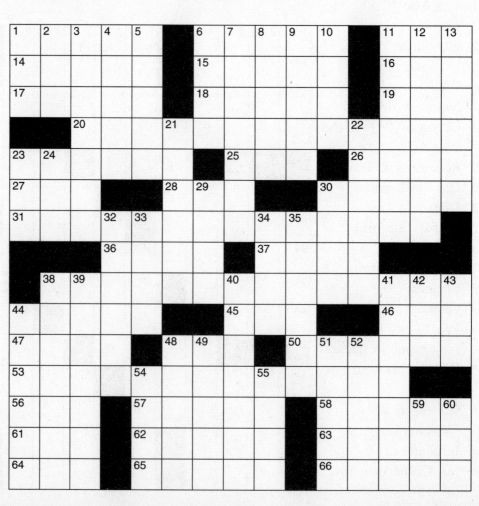

183 *by Manny Nosowsky*

ACROSS

1 Alias of Margaretha Zelle
9 Finish of the 50's
15 Sweet potatoes
16 Trucked
17 Au natural
19 Hoosier humorist
20 With whom Jacob contracted to marry Rachel
21 Cardinal sin
22 One of a vaudeville seven
24 Lip
26 Seven on the Mohs' scale
29 Civil War buffs favorite actress?
34 New news
35 At such a time that
36 At the summit of
37 Summer cooler
38 Two-striper
43 Bar drink, at times
45 Connector of song
46 Sirens
47 Just a bit
48 Golfer Alcott
49 Gulf in 1991 news
53 You can be slapped with these
55 Genes material
58 Just what we need
62 Revisionist?
63 Coffee shop freebies
64 They build up spirits
65 Added as an afterthought

DOWN

1 "The Best Little Whorehouse in Texas" lady
2 Mil. school
3 Receipts
4 Live
5 Kept out of sight
6 Take apart
7 Tabula __
8 Largest of the Galápagos islands
9 They make a difference
10 What "that" ain't
11 Hick
12 Giant chemicals company
13 First name in TV talk
14 Nelson of 30's musicals
18 Tires
22 Fountain order
23 Master Melvin
25 Roman I
26 Mountebank
27 Author Sinclair
28 Dig for squares?
30 Kind of bead
31 Win by __
32 Raider's chief
33 Peter and others
39 Sash
40 Top workers?
41 Lark
42 Most economical in business
43 Word in many tournament names
44 Proceed smoothly
49 Be loyal to
50 Whipped up
51 Solo
52 Meadowlands team
54 This señora
55 Fizzled
56 Poppaea's husband
57 Org.
59 Contrary indication
60 Bother
61 A crowd in Torino?

ACROSS

1 Agcy. vigilant about vittles
4 Make or break, e.g.
8 Two-fisted
13 Abbr. for an old soldier
14 Energy choice
15 Playwright Fugard
16 Gifted
17 Didja ever see a __?
19 "I don't think so"
20 Mine, to Marcel
21 Parenthetical comments
22 Staff
24 Many a hip-hop poet
26 Didja ever see a __?
29 Imprint
33 Jai __
34 Team in an annual all-star game
37 Color
38 Didja ever see a __?
41 Didja ever see a __?
43 Bowl over
44 Thick slice
46 Newsy bit
47 Plight
49 Didja ever see a __?
53 Some like it hot
56 Poet Teasdale
57 They get squirreled away
60 Lenin's police org.
63 Go vroom, vroom
64 Didja ever see a __?
66 Sundial number
67 Antipasto goody
68 Plow man
69 Presidential monogram
70 Devonshire dad
71 Hairdresser, sometimes
72 Grin's stopping point

DOWN

1 Garçon's pourboire
2 Split
3 Where touts tout
4 "Va-va-va-__!"
5 Barcelona bull
6 Project glowingly
7 Buddy
8 Bit of poolroom finesse
9 Garb
10 Nigerian border lake
11 Grind, in a way
12 Ford contemporary
14 __ Na Na
18 Breach
23 Constitutional
25 Child's ammo
27 Wails from baby
28 Bass __
30 Hitch
31 Word on a diploma
32 Drill sergeant's call
35 Black & Decker competitor
36 Famous marshal
38 Certain missile
39 Be in the red
40 Sunscreen ingredient
42 Super Bowl III champs
45 Hogwash
48 Tried hard
50 Simon of fiction
51 French fries brand
52 Cincinnati university
54 Tick off
55 Controversial food additive
57 On
58 Some kind of a nut
59 Last writes?: Abbr.
61 Rumble of contentment
62 French article
65 Tack on

ACROSS

1 __ Islands (Pacific group)
9 Pink end
15 Type of music
16 Generic
17 Whenever
18 VCR user's need
19 Props (up)
20 Faith
22 N.B.A.'s Archibald
23 Kind of crazy
24 Tennis score
25 Perplexed
26 Arch site
27 Complaint
28 Chemical salt
31 Postal abbr.
32 Monte __
35 Marshaled
37 Apollo component
38 Having rectangular cells, as a ceiling
42 Hue and cry
44 Wyoming's Simpson
45 Lose it
49 Early stock speculator Russell
50 Common side order
51 "See you"
52 In __ (doubled up)
54 Serve
56 Moolah
57 Heartfelt
59 Almost any letter in Washington
60 Kind of exam
61 A day ago, dialectally
62 Stopped

DOWN

1 Name in aviation
2 Hello and goodbye
3 VCR user's need
4 Gets stuffed
5 Word repeated before "show"
6 The Beatles' "Yes __"
7 Info on a French passport
8 Big name in small construction
9 On the ocean: Fr.
10 Word with block or test
11 Temper
12 Lori of "Petticoat Junction"
13 Make thin
14 Yielded
21 Singer Coolidge
23 Dipsomaniac
26 Throat problem?
27 Bushed
29 "Up and __!"
30 Govt. investigator
32 Graduates' celebration time
33 Correspondent
34 Conjures up
36 Auden verses
39 Big blow
40 Hugged
41 Eddie Murphy flick
43 Something remembered
46 Floating
47 Forthwith
48 Respired, dog-style
50 Clydesdale outfitter
53 Rock music's Mötley __
54 Some live by them
55 Culture starter
58 Small note

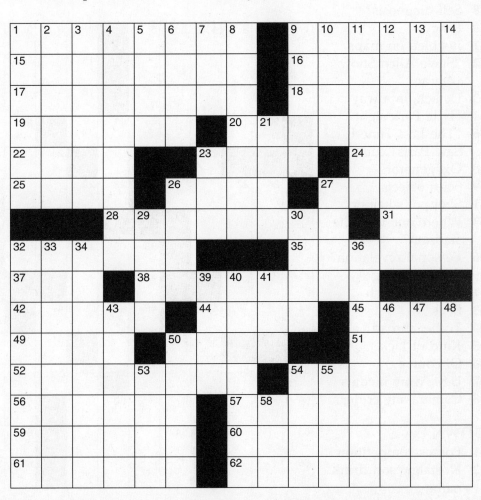

ACROSS

1 Kind of file
7 Dupe
11 Vacation spot
14 Razz
15 Speed
16 Total cost
17 Dear ones
18 Come before
20 Psychiatrist?
22 Mirror image?
23 Pain of a sort
24 Express
25 Cookout fare
28 Bus starter
30 Actor Jannings
34 Canter
35 Re-election runners
36 "__ to Psyche"
37 In a managerial position to
38 Self-diagnosis?
40 Fancy
41 It's bleu on maps
42 "Steve Allen Show" veteran
43 Detach, in a way
44 Hyde Park sight
46 "The Last Time I Saw Paris" composer
48 Oxygenators
49 Sci-fi objects
51 Shopper's helper
53 Where one is in the stadium?
56 Personal revelation?
59 Stove stuffing
61 Land, as a fish
63 Back
64 To be, abroad
65 Kind of kick
66 Of course
67 U.S. Army medals
68 Camera-shy critter?

DOWN

1 Forbes competition
2 Nostalgic soft drink name
3 Boy Scout's act
4 One who makes personal plugs?
5 "__ Restaurant"
6 Condor condos
7 Tangle (with)
8 Ax
9 Demonstrator's doctrine
10 "With Reagan; The Inside Story" author
11 Dateless
12 Orbit
13 Help
19 Urgent
21 Native Nebraskan
24 Sigmund's daughter
25 Tiptoe's opposite
26 Fly like a flying saucer
27 Works
29 Party
31 Display
32 Standard
33 Is attracted
38 Section in a psychological test
39 This puzzle's punning theme
40 Self-defense testifier?
45 Make a proposal
47 Sergeant major: Abbr.
48 "Brighton Rock" novelist
50 Say "I do" again
52 Splatter safeguard
53 Questionable
54 Cassino cash
55 Romance symbol
56 Time in "Julius Caesar"
57 Boola-boola cheerers
58 "__, Pagliaccio"
60 Killer of the deep
62 Formerly

187 *by Sidney L. Robbins*

ACROSS

1 Mosque tops
6 Lone Ranger attire
10 Strike caller
13 Dynamic
14 "I cannot tell __"
15 Mimic
16 Chinese principles
18 Lavish party
19 Tosspot
20 Worships
21 Freshly
22 Life, for one
23 Enlarge
24 Soup dipper
28 Six-stanza poem
31 Lily
32 Does, for example
33 Knot of hair
36 Procrastinator
40 Relative of the
   buttercup
42 Moral no-no
43 Tentmaker of fame
45 Kind of camera focus
46 Modified
49 Mount
50 Sighed (for)
52 Playboy pic
54 Took a taxi
55 Sound choice?
57 Busy person around
   Apr. 15
60 Smidgen that's
   smashed
61 Occasionally
63 Greek letters
64 Kurdish home
65 Throw out
66 N.Y. winter time
67 Trapper's trophy
68 Fires

DOWN

1 TV's "__ of Our
  Lives"
2 Hodgepodge
3 Money maker
4 "Uncle Tom's Cabin"
  girl
5 Spot for 100
6 Giuliani and others
7 Equipped with a
  theft protector
8 Trig function
9 Barrels
10 No longer bedridden
11 Fracas
12 Shrimp
15 Once more
17 Successor to H.S.T.
23 Telegram
24 Lassies' partners
25 Jai __
26 Homeless
27 Conducted
29 Melville novel
   setting
30 Countdown start
34 "Render therefore __
   Caesar . . ."
35 It's a gas
37 Trucker's amount
38 Holy Roman, e.g.:
   Abbr.
39 Squealer
41 Alluring West
44 License extension
47 Considers
48 "The Story of
   Civilization" author
49 Hollow stones
50 Jabber
51 Specks
53 Bear's abode
55 Quick cut
56 Ripped
57 In high style
58 Captain Ahab of film
59 Busy ones
62 Initials of 1933

ACROSS

1 Interlaced
6 Canadian tree
11 Unit of chewing tobacco
14 Idiotic
15 Relieve
16 One of Frank's exes
17 Motion picture award
19 __ Kippur
20 __ ex machina
21 Red Square figure
23 Spacecraft sections
27 Tentative forays
29 Gone from the program
30 Shoulders-to-hips areas
31 "__ Irish Rose"
32 Paper purchases
33 Once existed
36 Guitarist Lofgren
37 See 30-Down
38 __ fide
39 Farm enclosure
40 Crude characters
41 Gershwin hero
42 Jai alai ball
44 "Ode to __ Joe"
45 Votes
47 Hamlet, at times
48 Shrine to remember
49 Spotted
50 Reunion-goers
51 Nature personified
58 First lady
59 "Middlemarch" author
60 Inventor Howe
61 Matched grouping
62 Tears
63 Show shock, e.g.

DOWN

1 Store-bought hair
2 Musician Yoko
3 Actor Kilmer
4 Football lineman
5 Tries to rile
6 John Fowles novel, with "The"
7 "__ Well That Ends Well"
8 Hebron grp.
9 Big, friendly dog, for short
10 Huxley's "__ in Gaza"
11 Teen film hit of 1992
12 To have, to Héloïse
13 Curses
18 Require
22 "Xanadu" musical grp.
23 Signifies
24 Pluto's path
25 Perry's paper
26 Functions
27 Bubble masses
28 Columnist Bombeck
30 With 37-Across, the ground
32 Wild times
34 1973 Rolling Stones hit
35 Word with nay or sooth
37 Bit of poetry
38 Manila machete
40 Early feminist
41 Avant-gardist
43 Slippery __
44 Rabbit's title
45 Hardens, as clay
46 Breathing
47 Borscht ingredients
49 Bullet-riddled
52 Cheer
53 Malleable metal
54 Pale or Newcastle brown
55 Narrow inlet
56 Middle X or O
57 Presidential initials

189 *by Nancy Joline*

ACROSS

1 Tops of wine bottles
6 Wreak havoc upon
12 Gorge
13 Undergoes again, as an experience
14 Fund-raiser
15 Requiring immediate action
16 Postprandial drinks
18 Dessert pastry
19 __ hurrah
20 Actor Jannings
22 Chest rattle
23 Brightened
25 Burghoff role on "M*A*S*H"
27 Columbia, vis-à-vis the ocean
28 Entraps
30 Nullifies
32 Hash house sign
34 Info
35 Reduces
38 Glass ingredient
42 Tex-__ (hot cuisine)
43 DeMille films
45 Exorcist's adversary
46 Elderly
48 Angry to-do
49 Cable TV's C-__
50 Scuttlebutt
52 Take to court
55 Burst inward
57 Aficionado
58 It stretches across a tennis court
59 Bellyached
60 They may be liquid
61 Tried to catch a conger

DOWN

1 Variety of rummy
2 William Tell and others
3 Prevalent
4 Make a sweater
5 Hunting dog
6 Tyrannosaurus __
7 Parted company with a horse
8 Good physical health
9 Nothing special
10 Calms
11 Hold in high regard
12 Stay
13 Sojourned
14 Strike alternatives
17 Muscat is its capital
21 Former capital of Nigeria
24 "__-porridge hot . . ."
26 Word before fire or transit
29 Hitchcock's "The Thirty-Nine __"
31 Hubble, e.g.
33 Cut, as roses
35 Peanuts, e.g.
36 Frees from liability
37 Disfigure
39 Ascribed
40 Like nuts at a chocolatier's
41 French year
42 Boater's haven
44 Plodding person
47 Fellini's "La __ Vita"
51 Cheer (for)
53 Devoid of moisture
54 The dark force
56 O.R. personnel

ACROSS

1 Razor sharpener
6 Health resort
9 More than a mere success
14 Mussolini's notorious son-in-law
15 Assist
16 With uneven gait
17 Mink's poor cousin
18 Ushered
19 Truism
20 Item to cut for dessert
23 Late-night star
24 President Manuel, ousted by Franco
25 TV rooms
26 New Rochelle institution
28 Game show sound
30 Princess Diana's family name
33 Bedecked
37 Mea __
38 Get repeated value from
39 Replaceable shoe parts
42 Agrees
44 Carry on
45 30's and 40's actress Anna
46 Porcine cry
49 Kind of system
51 Weakens
55 Popular poultry entree
58 __ hilt (fully)
59 "Le veau __" ("Faust" aria)
60 Roomy dress cut
61 Chef's attire
62 Consume
63 American statesman Cyrus
64 Oceans, to Longfellow

65 Season on the Riviera
66 Lawn tool

DOWN

1 "Bad mood" look
2 Small obligation
3 Snitch about
4 Entree for a solitary diner
5 Scrutinize, with "over"
6 Marathoner Alberto
7 Michelangelo work
8 Afterthoughts
9 Bridge desideratum
10 Dieter's dish
11 A miss's equivalent
12 Dish's companion in flight
13 Songs of glory

21 Diminish
22 Foray
27 Florida city
29 Like Eric the Red
30 H.S. subject
31 So-called "lowest form of wit"
32 Bygone trains
34 Sally Field TV role
35 Erhard's training
36 __ Plaines, Ill.
40 Prefer follower
41 Latecomer to a theater, maybe
42 Ancient fertility goddess.
43 Suffix with young or old
46 Santa's reindeer, e.g.
47 "__ you're happy!"
48 Potassium salt

50 Summer ermine
52 Geriatric process
53 __ de León
54 Lip curl
56 Understands
57 Pan's opposite

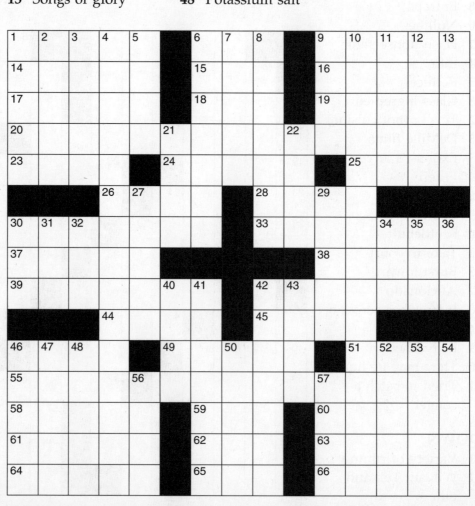

191 *by Betty Jorgensen*

ACROSS

1 Incarcerate
5 Wife, in Madrid
11 U.S./U.K. divider
14 Wearer of an aiguillette
15 Warehouse charge
17 Start of a quip
19 Slippery swimmer
20 Axis end
21 Lift, as ice or oysters
22 Ilk
23 Enormous
26 Stress
29 "McSorley's Bar" painter John
30 Good earth
31 New Zealand native
32 Family V.I.P.'s
35 Middle of the quip
39 Pigpen
40 Brainy group
41 Something to cop
42 Mork's gal
43 Like schlock
45 Extra leaves
48 Ireland's __ Islands
49 Spread for a spread
50 Manchurian border river
51 Sunny day production
54 End of the quip
59 Starlet's hope
60 Lackawanna's partner in railroads
61 Draft agcy.
62 Dallas's __ Plaza
63 Become tiresome

DOWN

1 Rib
2 Yorkshire river
3 Worshiped one
4 Rock's __ Zeppelin
5 Police accompaniment
6 Clown's prop
7 Corn bread
8 Assn.
9 Writer Rohmer
10 Farming: Abbr.
11 "Flow gently, sweet __": Burns
12 Coming-of-age period
13 Shelf
16 Consumed
18 "__ the Roof" (1963 hit)
22 It's good for the long haul
23 Actress Massey
24 Filipino
25 Hotel housekeeper
26 Pauper's cry
27 Old feller
28 Guinea pig
29 Impertinent
31 Obeys
32 House slipper
33 Lincoln and Vigoda
34 Dog command
36 Head of Abu Dhabi
37 Shipped
38 Unguarded, as a receiver
42 Reagan Attorney General
43 Like a curmudgeon
44 Mata __
45 Bridge declaration
46 D.E.A. workers
47 Swizzles
48 Provide divertissement
50 Soviet spy Rudolf
51 Now's partner
52 Siberia's site
53 River of Flanders
55 Proof's ending
56 Half of deux
57 Seventh Greek letter
58 Like a crescent moon

ACROSS

1 Swiss city on the Rhine
6 "Jake's Thing" author
10 Nice shindigs
14 Allan-__ (Robin Hood cohort)
15 Carry on
16 "__ Fire" (Springsteen hit)
17 *Paris site*
18 "__ partridge in a . . ."
19 Kind of fountain
20 Runaway, of a sort
22 Runway, of a sort
24 Book-lined rooms
25 *London site*
27 Cartoonist Bushmiller
29 Twofold
32 Game award, for short
35 Make a pot
36 Skin layer
38 *Rome site*
40 *Amsterdam site*
41 Drop out
42 Seat for two or more
43 "You don't __!"
44 __-tiller
45 They beat deuces
47 *Florence site*
50 Not on land
54 Upset-minded teams
57 Positions
59 Big 10's __ State
60 Letter encl.
62 *Moscow site*
63 Derby
64 Ended
65 Off
66 River to the North Sea
67 Corn bread
68 Having an irregular edge

DOWN

1 With __ breath
2 One of the Astaires
3 Dresden dweller
4 Slip by
5 __ majesty
6 Mr. Parseghian
7 Sea cow
8 Kipling story locale
9 Legendary Packers QB
10 Surgical knife
11 Love, Spanish-style
12 Italian town, site of a 1796 Napoleon victory
13 Fastener
21 N.F.L. standout Lott
23 Not a main route
26 Naldi of silents
28 1964 Four Seasons hit
30 "__ 'n' Andy"
31 Trevi Fountain coin
32 Classic sports cars
33 Turn sharply
34 Somewhat, in music
36 Loss
37 High overhead?
39 Money for Mason
40 "Cheers" role
42 Harold of politics
46 Pianist Gyorgy
48 Noted children's writer
49 An encouraging word
51 Defunct treaty org.
52 Group character
53 Unanimously
54 Nimble
55 Birds Eye product
56 __ over
58 "__ kleine Nachtmusik"
61 Afore

193 *by Thomas W. Schier*

ACROSS

1 Jerk
6 Netman Kriek
11 Peek
12 Even (with)
14 Bristles
15 Symbol of somberness, in poetry
17 Passbook amt.
18 Not a winner
20 Tell (on)
21 Fishes by dangling the bait on the water
23 Meadowlands hockey player
24 Lasso
25 "__ or lose it!"
27 June honoree
28 Farm worker
29 Xerxes ruled here
31 Directional sign
33 Bank burglars
35 Packaging material
36 Informational sign
39 Topped
42 Take __ at
43 Düsseldorf dessert
45 White House resignee of 1988
46 Team finisher
47 Stenos' output
49 Dully colored
50 Author Kesey
51 Indiana town near South Bend
53 French city where Henry IV was born
54 Diane and Ruth
56 Portray, as historical events
58 Outbuilding
59 More __
60 "Following the Equator" author
61 Bridge seats

DOWN

1 Cautionary sign
2 Not in France
3 Theater org.
4 Burn
5 Interfered (with)
6 Spur-of-the moment trips
7 Basketball's Shaquille
8 "Bird on a Wire" actress
9 Meet
10 Cautionary sign
11 Bribe, informally
13 "Grim" one
14 Make sense
16 Forever, to Keats
19 Race track
22 "Yes, sir," in Seville
24 Switched according to plan
26 Packed closely
28 Pluck a uke
30 Muslim honorific
32 __ Schwarz
34 Thinks over
36 Difficult matters
37 Bony
38 Prom night transport
40 Stern and Newton
41 Coming out
44 Juliet's was "sweet"
47 Cuban patriot José
48 Metric measure
51 Yakutsk's river
52 Sigmoid swimmers
55 Go off course
57 End up with

ACROSS

1 __ and hounds (outdoor game)
5 Section of the brain
9 Palindromic name in pop music
13 Mideast carrier
14 Flower part
15 Regrets
16 MANTLE
19 Bars
20 Kind of bed
21 Hubbub
22 Olympus queen
23 RUTH
30 Indian princess
31 Offended
32 Street sign abbr.
33 "Ars Amatoria" author
34 Manages, as for oneself
35 Signaled
36 Command to Rover
37 Absorbed by
38 Prefix with dollars
39 AARON
43 With eyes and ears open
44 Antipollution grp.
45 St. Francis's home
48 Confirming
53 JACKSON
55 British P.M. __ Douglas-Home
56 Jerks' works
57 Westernmost Aleutian
58 Ritzy
59 Word repeated before "1, 2, 3"
60 Nikita's no

DOWN

1 Fab Four flick
2 Controversial orchard spray
3 Zany Martha
4 Dignified
5 Hightailed it
6 __ out (withdraws)
7 Cry from Scrooge
8 Euclid's grand work
9 Ark's terminus
10 Pat baby on the back
11 One of Alcott's little women
12 Sickly, as a complexion
14 "__ a gun!"
17 Color anew
18 Prefix with dollars
22 __ hearing
23 One of a road crew
24 Architect Jones
25 Pioneer of the twist
26 Reach in total
27 __ couture
28 Tinker–Chance link
29 Second draft, informally
30 L.B.J. son-in-law
34 Most passionate
35 __ section
38 Easy catch
40 Jerk
41 Greasy-spoon fare
42 Southwestern formations
45 P.D.Q.
46 One-man band
47 Courts
48 No ifs, __ or buts
49 Command to Tabby
50 __-bitty
51 N.B.A's Thurmond
52 Flood
54 Ebbets Field's Preacher

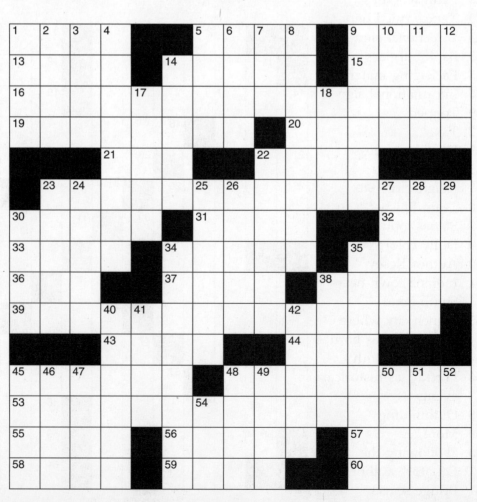

195 *by Bob Lubbers*

ACROSS
1 Monopoly purchase
6 __ of office
10 Singing Beatle
14 Maytag rival
15 German numeral
16 Shade of red
17 Kind of dressing
18 Boccaccio work, with "The"
20 Actress Swenson
21 GLASGOW: __
22 E. B. White piece
24 Put on __
25 Toulouse tams
27 Art __ (master keyboardist)
29 Get up
30 1987 Wimbledon winner
31 Actor Jannings
35 __ Tin Tin
36 From Novi Sad
39 "__ No Hooks"
40 Boat's backbone
42 Geissler tube illuminant
43 Winding paths
45 Fall flower
47 Long-legged shorebird
48 Actress June
50 Memorable shrine
51 MONACO: __
54 Satan's doing
57 LEM driver
58 Ballerina Shearer
59 Spanish province or capital
60 Andrews Sisters, e.g.
61 Shenanigan
62 Quiet street
63 Drains of stamina
64 Ninnies

DOWN
1 Mata __
2 Arabian sultanate
3 TANGIER: __
4 Sheathes
5 __-di-dah
6 Strange to say
7 Kind of rug
8 Gumshoes
9 Son of the West Wind
10 Before kickoff
11 Goldfinger's first name
12 Convoy chaser
13 Boston suburb
19 Waiter's handout
21 Tums target
23 Fr. holy women
25 Sergeant's voice
26 Canal opened in 1825
27 Olden drum
28 "It's __ to tell a lie"
30 Manitoba Indian
32 MOSCOW: __
33 "Oh, that's what you mean!"
34 Paris's Gare de __
37 Contest responders
38 St. Petersburg's river
41 Shotz Brewery worker of 70's TV
44 Gershwin's "__ to Watch Over Me"
46 Utah's state flower
47 Tankard tipple
48 Hebrew prophet
49 Writer Chekhov
50 Detroit output
51 Shopping center
52 __ Delano (F.D.R.'s mother)
53 Witticism
55 Spring flower
56 Teddy material
58 People or GQ

ACROSS

1 Gather
6 Radar gun reading: Abbr.
9 Bend
14 Collector's items
15 France's __ d'Yeu
16 Throng
17 Lewis's Gantry
18 "The Beggar's Opera" author
19 Yeate's __ Theatre
20 Singing sister of old Hollywood
23 American skiing medalist at Lillehammer
27 Cry of disgust
30 Twerp
31 Gross-weight deduction
32 "A miss is as good as __"
34 Toddler
35 Where Zeno taught
36 Filmdom's Sam Spade
38 What's-his-name
40 Annealing oven
41 High school problem
45 In abeyance
46 Over, in Essen
47 __ et quarante (betting game)
49 Posthumous duettist of 1991
50 "The Big Chill" actress
53 "Cheers" star
57 Shortcoming
60 Telephone button
61 Actor Reeves
62 Spy
63 "Gimme __!" (end of a Yale cheer)

64 Patti LuPone role
65 Kind of bag
66 Writer Deighton
67 Attack

DOWN

1 Maintain
2 Venus's home
3 Weaponry
4 Expensive
5 Thinker
6 __ worker
7 Magazine since 1953
8 "Lo!" modern-style
9 Music of the Benedictine monks
10 Noted televangelist
11 Sun, e.g.
12 Hafiz work
13 Pivotal

21 Alas, to Helmut
22 Sideways
24 Sups at home
25 Beethoven's Third
26 Reception china
27 Trite ideas
28 Microscopy subject
29 More costly
33 CNN personality
37 Mongol
39 Cornmeal concoctions
42 Stemware
43 Voyager II subject
44 Animate
48 __ kwon do (Korean karate)
51 Pot
52 Student abroad

54 Café au __
55 Within: Prefix
56 China's dollar
57 Parent
58 Personal pride
59 Importune

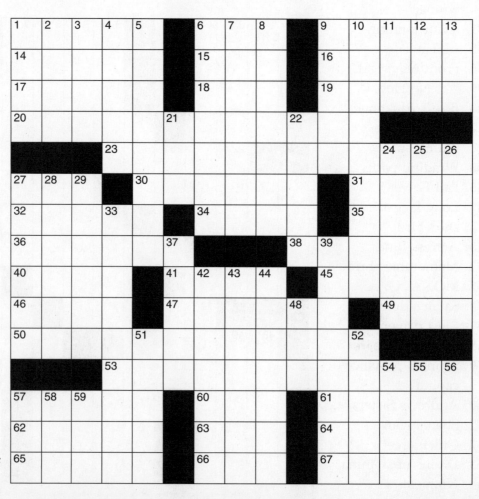

ACROSS

1 Instance
5 Kind of metabolism
10 Loading site
14 ". . . ___ forgive our debtors"
15 Get the lead out?
16 "The Cherry Orchard" miss
17 18th-century poet (whose name shares a feature with 36 and 56 Across)
20 Sweetheart
21 February 14 figure
22 Major-league transaction
23 It may be proper
24 Opera composer Nikolai
26 Highlight
29 Relieved
32 Narrative Byron poem
33 Room to ___
34 Support
36 17th-century dramatist
40 United
41 Navratilova rival
42 Boston athlete
43 Natural habitat
45 "Martha" et al.
47 Isolated
48 TV sheriff Tupper
49 Plus
52 Onetime labor chief
53 Good name for a cook?
56 20th-century writer
60 Old song "___ She Sweet?"
61 Get ___ on
62 Churchill prop
63 Hwys.
64 "John Brown's Body" poet
65 Linemen

DOWN

1 Daisy Mae's drawer
2 "Days of Grace" author
3 "M*A*S*H" actress
4 That's a moray
5 Rough posting for a foreign correspondent
6 Illegal firing
7 Processes lumber
8 Quiet color
9 Dracula actor Christopher
10 Traverse a beat
11 "To Live and Die ___"
12 Looked at
13 Comic Martha
18 Ancient land of Spain
19 Leader of '45
23 Around
24 Eye-cue tests?
25 Ocean flier
26 Ken-L-Ration competitor
27 Queeg's command
28 Fish basket
29 Wear
30 "Oklahoma!" aunt
31 Singer Reese
33 Vista
35 Realizes
37 Not hands-on
38 Tied
39 Low-fat desserts
44 Picks
45 Spanish ___
46 Charles's game
48 Mightier than
49 Partly open
50 "___ was you!" (mystery denouement)
51 Nostalgic song ending
52 Middle name in Memphis
53 Mr. Musial
54 Take care of
55 Spends
57 Rainy day rarity
58 Soul, in Soissons
59 Virtuoso

198 *by Richard Silvestri*

ACROSS
1 Symbol of stiffness
7 Brewing ingredient
11 Leave it to beavers
14 Julia, on "Seinfeld"
15 Mayberry moppet
16 Mistress Braun
17 "Wait 'Til My Bobby Gets Home" singer
19 Marshy area
20 Dockworkers' org.
21 Four laps, sometimes
22 A Sesame Streeter
23 X rating?
25 Sticker
27 Come to a halt
28 Patron saint of Norway
30 Co-star of "The Producers"
32 Government health program
34 "Hail, Caesar!"
35 Forge materials
36 Where Naxos is
39 Hard water?
40 Contest entry, perhaps
42 The Babe Ruth of Japan
46 Science writer Gernsback
47 Ease up
48 Hymn accompaniment
50 Record
51 Site of the 1960 Olympics
52 Ad writer's honor
53 Lend a hand
55 Cousin of Fortran
56 Former E Street Band member
60 Baseball throw
61 Working away
62 Bar perches
63 Journal addendum
64 Coolers
65 Lake Huron port

DOWN
1 It's seen in anger
2 According to
3 Tenderizing sauce
4 Brook
5 Hoopster Shaquille
6 Place to relax
7 "The Misanthrope" author
8 Harlem theater
9 As it occurs
10 Driving need
11 Trounce
12 Disinclined
13 Place for trophies
18 Barbecue leftovers
22 Implore
23 Tabby's mate
24 Kind of sch.
26 Rhododendron relative
27 Break the 10th Commandment
29 Impair
31 Warfield of "Night Court"
33 Secret supply
36 10^{100}
37 Witch's vessel
38 Therefore
40 They go by the book
41 Cerberus or Argus, e.g.
42 Ranchero's wrap
43 Homes
44 Vandalize
45 Arrive at last
49 1993 treaty
52 Give as a reference
54 Dr. Frankenstein's assistant
56 Shut-eye
57 C.I.A. forerunner
58 "Boola Boola" singer
59 Hush-hush D.C. grp.

199
by Norman S. Wizer

ACROSS

1 Spring weather forecast
5 Grey and others
10 Docs
13 Personal prefix
14 "Simon Boccanegra," e.g.
15 Defense mechanism
16 Tramp
17 Motherly type
18 Seep
19 Plant holder
21 Quickened pace
23 Coin on the Spanish Main
24 Can
25 1995, 2005 and 2003, in China
30 Vowel sounds in "melee"
31 Wheel part
32 Cry out
34 Released felon
35 Spoon
36 High-minded
37 Adolescent
38 Multitude
39 Dresden's location
40 1996, 2001 and 2002, in China
43 Road to Roma
44 Lee or Teasdale
45 Elastic cord
48 Used a pony
52 Parrier's equipment
53 Its capital is Kinshasa
56 Western necktie
57 Fighter of 1899–1902
58 Dreaded computer word
59 Nation on the Strait of Hormuz
60 Remnant
61 Slumgullion and pepper pot
62 Decimal system

DOWN

1 Spray
2 Lay off
3 Important person
4 1994, 2000 and 1998, in China
5 They have many signs
6 "Rocky" villain __ Creed
7 Bottom line
8 Before, before
9 Unbecoming wit
10 Debatable
11 Stun
12 Road ending
15 2004, 1997 and 1999, in China
20 Encored, in a way
22 "__ du lieber!"
24 Blackout
25 Onetime Chinese rebel
26 __ year (annually)
27 Haunted house sound
28 Saarinen namesakes
29 Nonelectric shaver
30 Court call
33 Layer
35 Seckel or Anjou
36 Austronesian language
38 Blessed events?
39 Philanthropists
41 Geneviève, e.g.: Abbr.
42 Place in trust
45 Actress Daniels of the silents
46 Over
47 Shortfall
49 Endured
50 Panache
51 Grandees
54 High school class
55 Sharp feeling

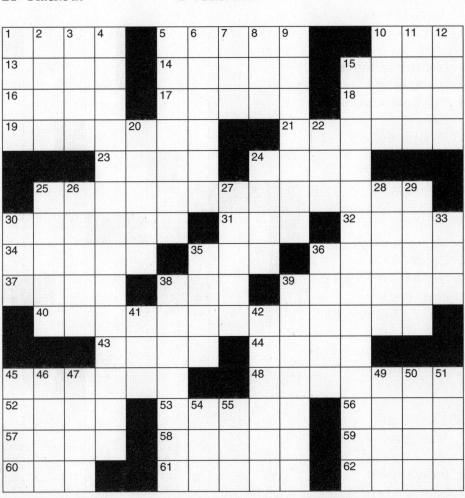

ACROSS

1 Hopeless
6 Where the tiller is
9 Zingers
13 Free
14 Colorado skiing mecca
16 Not right
17 How natives communicate
20 Type of mail
21 Mighty mite
22 __ Rabbit
23 Rebuffs
25 Sort of
29 Droll 1993 best seller
32 "The proof of the pudding __ . . ."
34 Foofaraw
35 Seed
36 Dressing-down
41 Actor Holm
42 Old B'way sign
43 Latch __
44 Not the secretive sort
49 Innumerable
50 Yearbook classmates: Abbr.
51 To live, to Livy
55 Richard Harris movie of 1977
57 Hornless
59 Communicating (with)
63 Mr. Hulot's creator
64 Cabal
65 "__ e Core" (1954 pop song)
66 On __ (freelancer's terms)
67 Mamie Eisenhower, __ Doud
68 Wanderer

DOWN

1 MacLaine's "Out on __"
2 Individualist
3 Soprano Lehmann
4 Heralds
5 Look searchingly
6 Photographer Richard
7 Kind of cry
8 Actress Louise
9 Tribesmen in the film "Simba"
10 Wise one
11 Singing syllable
12 Neighbor of Leb.
15 Hispanic community
18 "I came," to Caesar
19 Reps. and Sens.
24 Lillehammer events
26 "Rome __ built in a day"
27 Part of old discothèque names
28 Hedge shrub
30 H.S. course
31 Palindromic lady
32 Three-time World Cup winner
33 Sub detector
37 It's sold in lots
38 Bungle
39 On a roll
40 Native
41 Computer co.
45 Spike Lee's "Malcolm X," e.g.
46 Uncover
47 Old English royal house
48 New London grp.
52 More bruised
53 Diploma word
54 New Republic piece
56 Related
58 Greek letters
59 Military sch.
60 Rest
61 Geneviève, e.g.
62 Bach's "Partita __ Minor"

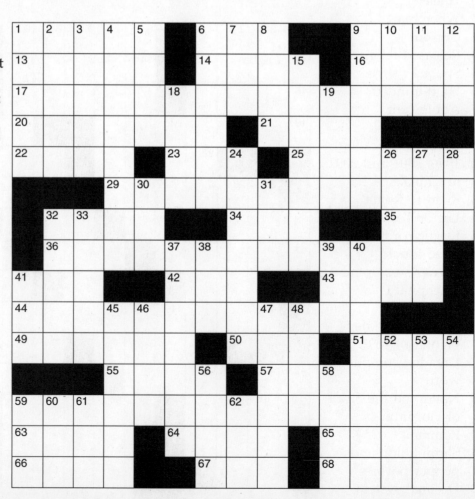

COMING OCTOBER 2002!

THE FIRST BOOK OF ITS KIND!

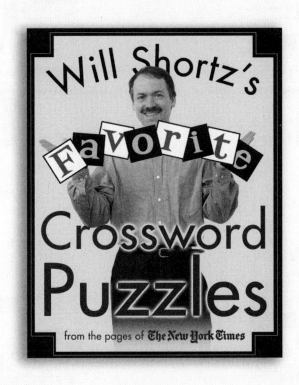

"Will Shortz, crossword editor of *The New York Times*,
is [the crossword book world's] John Grisham."—*Martin Arnold*

"The Riddler's got nothing on Will Shortz"—*Time Out* (New York)

▪ Seventy-five of Will Shortz's favorite crossword puzzles from the pages of *The New York Times* ▪

▪ Special commentary on why each puzzle belongs among his favorites ▪

▪ Two-page introduction ▪

So sharpen your pencil and be prepared for the most interesting,
witty, and fun puzzles from the pages of *The New York Times*!

7

```
A B E L   E G O S   S C A L D
P O L O   M A M A   H A L V A
P L A N   C L A N   O R S O N
T O N G U E A N D G R O O V E
      O R E S   P E E L
C H A S E D   V A N   I R M A
R A L L Y   R O P E   N E A R
E L B A   F E T E S   E A V E
P E E N   U S E R   B I D E N
E Y E D   N P R   R E S E N T
      S E G O   B U R L
O T T O V O N B I S M A R C K
N A H U A   S E T H   N O A H
E L A N D   E T T E   D U M A
S L I D E   S E E D   S E E N
```

8

```
B O O R   S C A M   G A S U P
A L V A   H A N A   O H A R E
W I E N   I R E D   U S A I R
L O R D S N O W D O N   R S T
      R E E L   K O D
R O D   T R I M   A D O R E D
A R O M A   N E A P   N E R O
J O N A T H A N W I N T E R S
A N A T   I S A K   O S S I E
H O T T I P   T W I T   E S S
      E S P   A N I M
L A B   R O B E R T F R O S T
A Q A B A   O R D O   B A L E
P U R E E   D O L T   I H A D
P A N E L   Y O Y O   G U T S
```

9

```
C O A T   E D N A   G O L F S
O K R A   S O A P   A F I R E
P I C K L E D P I G S F E E T
T E H E E   D E E R   C U E S
      I D E E   C I A O
B A I N   F R I E D C L A M S
H U R   S T E P   S H O G U N
A G A P E   D A M   E R A S E
N U T R I A   N A B S   T E A
G R E E N B E A N S   D E S K
      F E D S   D A L E
A S T A   U S E R   E D I T S
C H O C O L A T E M O U S S E
T I G E R   Y U L E   C L A W
S P A D E   S I L T   T E R N
```

10

```
B L A H   C A L E B   F A M E
R U B E   O B E S E   J U I N
A S I A   R E A C T   O T T O
T H E D O G T H A T T R O T S
      I D I   R E E D
T A M E D   P A P   A S C I I
A R E S   D O R M E R   H O D
C E L T   O T T E R   H O N E
I T O   S T E I N S   A S I S
T E N T H   N E T   E R E C T
      R O O T   U T E
A B O U T F I N D S A B O N E
S A L E   M A I R E   E R I C
P I E S   A T T A R   L E N O
S O O T   N E S T S   L O O N
```

11

```
E T A L   P E R S E   P E N N
R A V E   A M O U R   E T T U
I R I S   T E A M S   O C H S
C A V E A T E M P T O R
      D E R   D I A L
C A E S A R   R A R A A V I S
A R G O N   S O M A   I S T
P E R S O N A N O N G R A T A
R O E   E N D S   E N T E R
A L T E R E G O   A S S E R T
   E S N E   E D S
N O L E N S V O L E N S
I N R E   E N A T E   A B E T
N O T A   V I P E R   N A I L
A B E D   I D E S T   A N N O
```

12

```
S A N D   S H U N   L A P E L
O L I O   A U T O   A D E L E
D O N T G O A W A Y F O L K S
S T E E L   C O H E I R E S S
   L O P   A T A
W E L L B E R I G H T B A C K
A Y E   E L E N A   E L S I E
N E A T   F A U S T   E T T E
D O N H O   C S P O T   E E L
A F T E R T H E S E W O R D S
      T A U   S A C
B E L I T T L E S   I A M B S
F R O M O U R S P O N S O R S
A M B E R   O P E N   E M I T
S A S S Y   N Y E T   Y A M S
```

13

```
ALAS  BANDB  GLOB
ROMP  OWNER  LONI
ALAI  LEEIACOCCA
BASKETS   VARIES
    ETS  COSI
BELLE  SPA  TASSO
ERIE  HEARSE  APR
ROBERTEDWARDLEE
ESE  ASTRAY  OSLO
TELLS  HEX  ORALS
   EPEE  FBI
CHAFED  ARISING
LEETREVINO  LOAN
AROO  NIKON  ETNA
PENN  SPENT  EAST
```

14

```
RAYE  DUPE  PLUGS
ELEV  ORAL  ROMEO
STLO  WALLTOWALL
PELLMELL  ITE
  OVALS  SNORING
TOWERS  DESC  LER
HUBS  CAMEO  LEE
UTE  ILLWILL  OSE
MEL  MOONS  AGON
BAL  MVPS  RACINE
STYMIES  LILAC
  ENL  ROLLCALL
VOLLEYBALL  ILIA
ARION  ABLE  ALOT
TRENT  NEST  SYNE
```

15

```
MACE  EMBARK  VON
ALAN  MAIDEN  IRA
RIDDICKBOWE  OAR
IVE  DEES  REALLY
SETTLER  MILLI
  OED  LATEENS
FABER  FOYER  BIN
AMOS  IOTAS  BOZO
BED  ECRUS  BOWER
 SIGNETS  BLY
  DITCH  HEADSET
DODGER  YEAR  AXE
AXL  BEAUXGESTES
TEE  BARREL  HIRT
ANY  EMPIRE  ANTS
```

16

```
HARTE  WELSH  MAB
OLEOS  ALATE  EVA
RAPSCALLION  DEW
AMATEUR  COLLARD
SOYA  GUM  PEEL
  RHESUS  YALTA
NECTAR  LOC  KIEL
ADO  HELLION  ORO
PITA  DEI  TOWNIE
STILT  SONORA
 LARA  NIN  RHEA
WALNUTS  GOOBERS
IFI  SLUMGULLION
NEO  TAMIL  DESDE
OWN  SWORE  ESTER
```

17

```
CHUM  ASSET  ASST
IONA  GEESE  BATH
ARMS  ELATE  ALEE
 SECONDMANASSAS
SER  ADO  SHAKE
CHICKAMAUGA
RITAS  TRAP  MVI
EDEN  AMEND  GEOL
WED  ACES  SELLS
  CHATTANOOGA
ACTOR  ASU  DOS
FREDERICKSBURG
TIRE  AGREE  PARD
OMIT  POEMS  OMAN
NESS  TREES  NADA
```

18

```
PJS  ACH  RECEDE
AAU  MAI  ISOMERS
SPORING  GERMANY
SAME  AHS  NYLON
UNITEDSTATES
 IDA  AURA  LAP
MARNE  GTE  RARE
THEGROUPOFSEVEN
GONE  TVA  AMASS
EYE  BOER  FRO
 GREATBRITAIN
ROLEO  YEA  ESTA
ECONOMY  ENTREAT
STARDOM  RCA  ALE
 ODESSA  SEX  TYS
```

19

```
GAME  SLUMP  EGOS
OMAR  TAHOE  ZOLA
TAKEYOUFORARIDE
ONE RIG    RANT
IDI SCHTICK GIN
TATA   ASA  AMI
   OLYMPICS  PEN
LOOKYOUINTHEEYE
ESP EULOGIES
ACE  REC   CRAW
FUR ASSAULT  USH
 LESS   TAO BLY
WATCHWHATYOUSAY
OTTO ROMEO PINE
NEAT YEARN ANTS
```

20

```
BIER   TAN   TAPS
UNLEAVENED  ERLE
FREDDIETHEGREAT
FEEDER IRANIANS
    YET   UNA
PAP RUGS  SWAMPS
AGRA ALOE  EXALT
SAINTLARRYRIVER
HINDU DESI  SINE
ANTICS STEM  NAP
    STP  LEA
ATSTPRES  DUNNER
QUEENANNIESTYLE
URGE WAITRESSED
ANON  LPS   YEAS
```

21

```
 QTIPS   TAMARA
MARNIE  DETOXES
DEDUCER EXTOLLS
ENDEARING  AGREE
RIA  AARE  SONS
MAFIA LIENS  STS
ALIGNS LETTRES
  OVID  SERA
 SPRITES REPAST
BOS LEFTS  PENNE
AMAS DRIP   OER
SANTA  AREACODES
ALDORAY ANALYZE
LIQUIDS  RELINE
TASTED   SWINE
```

22

```
STALEMATE   CRAB
ASIAMINOR  PHONE
GARGANTUA  LAUDS
ARSONIST  BUNGEE
   AMY  SUGGEST
VISITS  MARIE
ALINE DOMINATED
SLAV PYLON  BOLO
ESMERALDA  PLEAD
   TOGAS  FRESNO
CAVEMEN  HUE
OMORES  DISPOSED
MACAO  PINEAPPLE
THATS  UNDERTAKE
ELLE   POSSESSED
```

23

```
TACOS  GOALPOST
EVENED UNGAINLY
MONACO MERCATOR
PCT SLOSHES  AGA
LARA TAHOE  ARAN
ADAPT FOR  PRINT
ROLLED  ESKIMOS
  EDAM EINE
 HANDBAG  NONCOM
BETTY NUT  NIECE
ONLY MOIRE  AREA
OCA HOLLAND  TAN
TONSURED  DEFINE
HOTPLATE  SNAFUS
SPARKLER   TRYST
```

24

```
MEN  EBOAT    SRI
ARAB TAURI  SPAR
ERMA TRIOSONATA
  RWANDA   REWET
 CEOS SARABANDE
YANQUI    DID
ETTU MINUET  LSD
ATEE PLOTS  GATE
SYR BALLET  ATOM
   PAL  ELVERS
GAILLARDE  YORK
LEVEE  ARMLET
ARIADACAPO  TRUE
DOES PEPTO  EURO
ESS  TREYS   BEN
```

25

```
S O S A D . . . D A N I K E N
A N N I E S . . O P A L I N E
D E A D S E A . U P R O O T S
A L P . C R U M B L Y . W I T
T O B E . A G I L E . R A T E
S A R A I . E N E . L E N Y A
. F I R S T A N D T E N . . .
. . M A T I N E E I D O L .
. C L A S S A C T I O N .
M O S H E . T O L . O R S O N
A N T E . W A T E R . S I V A
S D I . C A B A R E T . N E V
T I N F O I L . S N U G G L E
E N G R A V E . . O N E I L L
R E S A L E S . . . E T T A S
```

26

```
S I N S . H E R D . M A S T S
T M E N . E R I E . E X T R A
R A T E . W I L T . A L A I N
A R T L I N K L E T T E R . .
F E L L S . . S H Y . W I Z
E T E . R O T A T E . C A R E
. . P A L E R . S C A R E D
. F R E D C O U P L E S .
S T E A L S . O R I O N .
A I R Y . T A M E S T . C A M
L E O . Q E D . H E A V E
. C H A R L I E J O I N E R
I D I O T . I D L E . G A N G
M I T L A . B E A R . E D G E
P A Y E R . S A N K . R A E S
```

27

```
L I S P . P A T S . A B C S
O D O R S . A L O T . S L U E
B L U E C O L L A R . T U R N
. E L M E R . D E A R E S T
. . I N I T . S N I P E .
F I B S T E R . A S I D E .
O G L E . N I P S . L E N D S
L O U . T O R S O . C O E
D R E G S . D O E R . S I R E
. B R I B E . T A M A L E S
. B O O Z E . S T A N .
S I N C E R E . O R D E R .
A N N E . B L U E R I B B O N
D E E R . E L S E . A A R O N
A T T Y . R E E L . R O M E
```

28

```
. C R A F T . F A N T A N .
. E A G L E D . A L E R T E D
. S T E E L E . S T E A L E R
S T I R S . P E T E R . A D E
H M O . H A L T E R . A N I S
E O N S . C O E D . A N T E S
W I S E G U Y S . R O T A R Y
. R A T S . L O N I .
A E R A T E . B E D E C K E D
G R A P E . F A T E . S N E E
H A T E . W O N T O N . I R A
A S A . P A R S E . A S T I N
S E T T I N G . R E B A T E .
T R A I N E E . S P O D E S .
. S T E E D S . A B O R T .
```

29

```
B A H S . E N O S . . T H Y
A L E E . A R E N A . W H E E
J O L L Y G R E E N G I A N T
A P P E A R S . . O R R S .
. . N R A . D I N E D .
G R E E N I N J U D G M E N T
R E X . N E A R S . A S I A
E A C H . A S H . N E X T
A C H E . S T O A T . R I A
T H E G R E E N M O N S T E R
. . Q U I N N . L E T .
. F U M E . S E R I A L S
G R E E N B A C K D O L L A R
E A R N . M A R I O . L I S A
D T S . W H I T . S E T S
```

30

```
U S A F . C A S T . A B B A
H A R I . R I P U P . P L O Y
F A T S D O M I N O . R A G E
. R I C O . K I T H . C I A
. C H U B B Y C H E C K E R
. T H E B A Y . S E R A .
C H O R T L E D . R E M O V E
O A K . S O D . R A T
D R E A M T . C A L A B A S H
. . Y U R I . M A L O N E
S K I N N Y D I P P I N G .
H E R . I S A R . B A E R
O N E S . T H E T H I N M A N
C Y S T . S O N A R . Z E R O
K A T E . S E N S . A N E W
```

31

```
P O T A T O   D I A P E R S
E R A S E D   C A P T I V E S
R O C K E D   O B S O L E T E
O N E     S T U   O P E R
T O T A L   E N T     G P A
    S I N A T R A   E R R S
  T A S S O   I O S   R E A P
  B R E A D A N D H O N E Y
P A R T   E R G   E D E N S
E R A S   S P H E R E S
P S I     S O S   S T R A P
  G A M E   U P A   I N A
P E N N A M E S   B E S O T S
E V E N T I D E   C R E D I T
R E D E A L S   S E N E C A
```

32

```
H A R D   P A R C   C L A M
O M O O   A D I O S   A L D A
W I L T   S E O U L T R A I N
  A L E R T   T R E E   N E E
    M O O R   S T E A K O U T
I R O N M A N   P S I
M A D   M E S H   E T H E R
A G E   T I E P I N S   E T E
M U L T I   R Y N E   I T A
    A D S   D E C O R U M
S A L E B O A T   D U M B
A G O   I N S O   L E A R
V A N I T Y F A R E   H U L A
E V E N   S O D A S   A S O N
D E R N   R Y E S   S H E D
```

33

```
  J E O P A R D Y   B R U I T
C O N S T R U E D   O U N C E
P I T T A N C E S   G R E E T
O N E   O H M   P G A
  T R E B L E   R I L L E S
    S Y D   L U X E   B A M
A C U T E   D O M E   S O D A
G A M E S P E O P L E P L A Y
E B B S   R A P S   W R I T S
S A L   B O N Y   C E E
  L E A R N S   R A R E S T
    G I G   K O S   I A N
H E W E D   D E M I T A S S E
A C I N G   I N A N I M A T E
M O N T E   M O N O P O L Y
```

34

```
  D A R T S   C O S T A R
  D E B A S E   O R O I D E S
B A S E M A N   G R A N D A M
E P I C U R E A N   S A U D I
A P R E S   C L O T   S P I T
R E E D   A M M A N   T E E
D R E A M   A E R A T O R
  R O M A N N O S E
R E Y N A R D   A L B A N
S E L   A N T I S   E R D A
U S E R   S I N O   S P O O K
G I V E N   S E M A P H O R E
A D A M A N T   B L O O D E D
R E T I N U E   R E I N E D
S E T O N S   E E L E R
```

35

```
L O O M S   S H A G   K A T
I N G O T   N E G R O   E C O
M E R R Y   O F L A H E R T Y
B I A S E D   E V E N T S
O L D E   R I O T E R S
S L Y S   I R K   S L U D G Y
  O P I E   T I R A N E
A B E A D   S E E   H E M P S
R A N S O M   F R A Y
B R O W N E   F I T   B O O R
  I N S P E C T   I T B E
  T E R E S A   A L G O R E
O S U L L I V A N   A B O I L
F A R   L E E R Y   M E L E E
F R O   R S T U   A N E N D
```

36

```
H O T W I R E D   S H I N E R
A R E A C O D E   P A V A N E
C O N T E N D S   A L E U T S
K I N   T R I E S T E   S E I
I D I S   E E R I E   L E N D
T E S T C A S E S   D I O D E
    A R G   T A C I T U R N
S U R R E A L   L O V E S E T
C L E M E N T E   M E R
A T L A S   C A M P D A V I D
L I O N   M O R A L   L O R E
A M A   D O L L I E S   L A T
W A D S U P   A T T I T U D E
A T E A S E   P R E V O T E S
G E D D E S   S E S A M E S T
```

37

```
I M P A L E . . P E R E . .
S N O O P E R . P L I A N T
I N C L O S E Q U A R T E R S
R A K E S . C U R I E . R A H
E T E . S T E E D . A G I O
N E D . T O I . S E N I L E
. K I L N S . R A Z E S
S T R A I G H T L A C E D
L E H A R . Y E A S T
L A R I A T . E V E . S G T
A C A T . O R A T E . T O R
M O S . S P A C E . P E A C E
A W H I T E C H R I S T M A S
S E C U R E . E L A T E R S
D E N S . D E T E N T
```

38

```
R E B E L . E G B D F . W A G
A R O M A . B R O A D . E E L
M A X I M . B O X C A M E R A
O T I S . V E E . O D I N
A L F . A C H E D . R A Y E D
D U F F . H E L I C E S
M A I L B O X . N A B . S H E
E N C O I L . J O S H U A
N N E . T A J . B O X C A R S
P E R U S A L . I D L E
O P A L S . K H M E R . O Y L
R I C E . O E R . S H A W
S Q U A W K B O X . E M B E R
O U T . I L O V E . A B O V E
N E E . T A X E S . S I X E D
```

39

```
S C A T . L A R D . T H I S
R A S H . A L O E . R O O S T
S T I R . W E A R . E C O L E
O N E E Y E D M O N S T E R
S T E . D E I S T
O N E H O R S E T O W N
P A T E N . L E E R S . R O W
A P A R . A L T . L A M A
L E S . A B N E R . S A V E R
O N E T R A C K M I N D
K O R D A . H I E
O N E A R M E D B A N D I T
G E S T E . G O O F . U V E A
R E T O W . A D Z E . C A R R
E D E R . D O O R . K N I T
```

40

```
S H E D S . B O G Y . O P E N
P I X I E . E G O S . P I L E
A V A N T G A R D E . T E L E
R E M . T R U E . R A I D E D
E L I X I R . M O A N S
F A B L E D . S E C A N T
O B I S . A H W A Z . E R A
A B L A T E S . E Y E B R O W
M E L . R A T E D . A R A L
E D I T E D . S A Y E R S
A N T I C . R U M P U S
D O D G E S . C O A T . D A B
O B O E . P L A T D U J O U R
P L U S . O A T H . M A L T A
T E X T . T Y E S . N Y L O N
```

41

```
C A P P . M A A M . S P A K E
O D O R . O U R S . W A N L Y
M U S E . O N E S . A L G E R
B E T T E R T O . E T A L I I
P E A . L I G H T O N E
A L O N G S . A D O S E
C A N D L E . E L I . S P A N
I L E . E C O . E S S . E L O
D A D E . R U E . T H A N T O
S P E C K . S A V I O R
C U R S E T H E . N E T
U S H E R S . D A R K N E S S
R U I N S . A O K I . U N I T
D A N C E . N U I T . E C T O
S L O E S . E T N A . S E E P
```

42

```
G O D . B U B B A . S N E A K
R A E . Y P R E S . T E R R E
A T M . D E A T H . R U I N G
S H O T I N T H E D A R K
A N D S . A D O
L A S T S . B A L A N C E D
R A T S O . S E L A . A R E
O U T O F T H E P I C T U R E
A R I . R A P S . R U S E S
R A C E W A Y S . R A T E D
R E M . A U N T
S N A P D E C I S I O N S
H O T E L . A G E N T . P I T
A N E S T . M A T E O . E N E
T E N T H . A D O R N . N E W
```

```
J I L T   C A I R D   S O O T
A L O E   O L D I E   P E N A
M E G A   S A I D J U L I E T
  T O R O M E O   E T A L I I
    O N O     I C E S
I F Y O U   W O N T S H A V E
D R U M S   R A T E   L I L
L I C S   P O K E D   D I A L
E T C     O N E R   A R E N A
R O A D S I G N S   L E N D S
    E E N S     C S A
A L B E R T   G O H O M E O
B U R M A S H A V E   S A M S
E R I E   T I L E S   U T A H
T E E D   O P E N S   P A N E
```

```
O R P H A N   B L T   S I C
H O L E D U P   M I R A N D A
S T E A L T H   O L I V I E R
  C A P I T O L C A P I T A L
    B Y T E   C S A
P E L E   O F T   N C A R
A V O W A L   T O M B   A K A
P O P E R Y P O T P O U R R I
E K E   M E R V   H A N G O N
R E D D   E E C   I O N S
  U P A   R O S S
S U M M E R Y S U M M A R Y
P R O P A N E   P A I D O U T
A S S Y R I A   E S T E L L A
R A T   Y E S   H E E L E D
```

```
S A P   S P R I T   G R A M
A L E   E R A S E   P R O M O
L I E   N E I L S   R A T O N
V E R D I S L A S T O P E R A
O N S A L E     A B E
  B E N   S E L L   D E N
A B A B   T A P A   E M I L Y
G A B L E S L A S T M O V I E
E L L E N   T R E E   M E A T
D I E   D A I S   N Y E
  A W L   T E N A C E
W I L L I A M S L A S T H I T
A L I A S   A L E C S   O D A
S K A T E   T I T L E   R E P
H A R E   A P S E S   A R E
```

```
  C R A F T S   E D R E D
T H O R E A U   R E A D E R
H A N D S U P   M E R I N O S
U P D O S   P R I M E T I M E
D E E R   A L A N   D O Z E N
S A L   S C E N E   R E O S
  U S E L E S S   R I N S E
    N O S T A L G I A
S T A R E   C O U P L E D
P U M A   S K I M S   V E G
I N E P T   P E T S   M E T E
C E N T I P E D E   F A R E S
A U D U B O N   R A I M E N T
  P E R I O D   E N L I S T S
  D E A L S   D E L E T E
```

```
M A N I C   M E S A   A L A S
A L A M O   I R E S   R O V E
N O S P R I N G C H I C K E N
Y E T   A B C S   T S H I R T
    F L E E   P R A Y
M E R E S T   C R A Y   J O B
A L O N E   A H O Y   S A V E
D O G D A Y S O F S U M M E R
A P E S   O T I S   R E I N E
M E T   S U E R   A B L E S T
    H E R R   G N A T
S T R U M S   S E E N   S A O
T H E L I O N I N W I N T E R
O O N A   N O M E   Z A I R E
P U T S   G R I T   E N R O L
```

```
R E B E L   O P E C   B A T S
E X I L E   S O D A J E R K S
M A S T S   O P E R A T I O N
E C H O E R   S N O W S
E T O N   H A T   L E Y D E N
T A P   R I G H T   D R O V E
  V E N E E R S   O N E A
L O V E C O N Q U E R S A L L
A K I N   S T U D I E S
R I V E T   S E G N O   D E C
D E A R E R   S E E   D E L E
  A S H O T   S Q U A L L
H U M B L E P I E   U N T I E
I S O L A T I O N   I C H O R
D E W Y   T E N D   Z E S T Y
```

49

```
S L I T · T Z A R A · C E O S
P O O H · A S N E R · O Z M A
A S N E A T A S A P I N I O N
S T A B S · Z A P · C R O O K
· · · A I M S · · · B E A · ·
· H O N D A A C C O R D I O N
L A N D E D · R A N · S T L O
E T S · S E D A T E D · A S I
A L E S · F O B · S E L L E R
H O T C R O S S B U N I O N ·
· · · H U R · · O P I E · · ·
P R O O F · W H O · A S T R O
R U N O F T H E M I L L I O N
A B U L · V I X E N · O G L E
M E S S · A P A R T · W E L L
```

50

```
Q U E E N · B A M B I · Z P G
U T E R O · A L A I N · I A L
M A K E R · C A N O N · N Y E
· · S M O K I N G O R N O N ·
O L A · A V E · · · C O I F S
R E G U L A R O R D E C A F ·
B A R A · · N O U N · · · · ·
· F O R H E R E O R T O G O ·
· · · · O R E O · · P U P A ·
· P A P E R O R P L A S T I C
A H E A D · · I A N · S E T ·
C A S H O R C R E D I T · · ·
E S O · W O O E R · M A J O R
R E P · N A D E R · A X I O M
B S S · S N A K E · L I M P S
```

51

```
S E L F · G A G S · · P E L E
O V A L · A C R E S · L A O S
F I R E E S C A P E · U R G E
A L D E N · N I C E S T · · ·
· · · S I R · D A T E · H O R
O A S · D E S I · · L I M B O
C L U B · C O L O R · T O L D
U L N A · A L O N E · E V A N
L U G S · P I Q U E · M E T E
A R L E S · U S S R · R E Y ·
R E A · A S H E · E O S · · ·
· · S A T E E N · O P E R A
G A S P · W A T E R M E L O N
A G E S · S P L I T · L I S T
P O S E · S Y N E · L E S S
```

52

```
O V E R · M A C E D · D U S T
P E L E · E N L A I · O T O E
T R A F A L G A R S Q U A R E
S O L E N O I D · A U G H T S
· · · R O D E · B L A H · · ·
R E M E D Y · C O L D · A G A
I V A N A · S O L O · I L E S
C I R C L E T H E W A G O N S
E T R E · N A N S · S N O R E
R A Y · E G I S · S T O K E S
· · · Y S E R · F E H R · · ·
A N D E A N · A I R M A I L S
B E R M U D A T R I A N G L E
E R N E · E R O S E · C O D A
L O O N · R E N T S · E R S T
```

53

```
C A M P · S W A G · Q U A C K
O L E O · T I L L · U N C L E
W O R K I N G V A C A T I O N
L E V E R · G A I L · A D D S
· · · R E A L · S A W N · · ·
A S P S · N E V E R A G A I N
S T U · A I R Y · A L L U D E
C A P O N · S I C · S E D E R
A R A B I C · N O A H · R A F
P R E T T Y U G L Y · S A S S
· · · R A G S · L E F T · · ·
E S A U · N U D E · O R A T E
N O N D A I R Y C R E A M E R
D A T E D · E N T O · I M A N
S P I R E · R E S T · T O M E
```

54

```
O S L O · P A T E S · S T A G
F L A P · A W A K E · L O L A
F I V E S T A R G E N E R A L
S T A R T E R S · D E P O N E
· · · · A R N E · P I C T · ·
C A S T E S · L E E K · T E T
E T H O S · O A R S · P E R E
S T A R S A N D S T R I P E S
T A N S · I S E E · E L E C T
A R K · B R E D · A S S E T S
· · · M O L T · F L E E · · ·
T I V O L I · S A T A N I S T
S T A R O F B E T H L E H E M
A S I S · T E A S E · R O T E
R A L E · S A M O A · S P A N
```

55

```
A S P E N · D A L I · A M I D
T H E S E · E G A N · V I V A
T A S T E · M O T S · E L A N
· G O O D N I G H T I R E N E
· P L O · · S E C · · ·
P A R · E L K E · P I E C E S
O R A L · A I L S · E R O D E
L O V E A N D M A R R I A G E
E M E N D · S E M I · S T E M
S A N D A L · R E S T · I R S
· · G A L · · E O N · ·
I L L B E S E E I N G Y O U
N E A R · T E R N · G L A R E
K A T E · E R I N · L O R D S
S K E W · D Y E S · E N S U E
```

56

```
F L A B · R I D E · R O O M S
R A G E · E L A L · A I M A T
O M A R · S L U B · F L O R A
· P R E T T Y B O Y F L O Y D
· T A R · · W I L E · ·
O H M · R A S H · P E A P O D
L E E · S I T A R · S O L O
M A C H I N E G U N K E L L Y
O R C A · M A N O N · L I E
S T A I R S · R E N O · Y E N
· R I P E · · S L O · ·
B A B Y F A C E N E L S O N
A U R A L · L I O N · C R I B
T R I P E · A R E S · A N K A
H A T E R · T E L E · R E E D
```

57

```
· L A N E S · B R A S S
W A G E R E D · S A U T E E D
E D A S N E R · H A N O V E R
E D I T S · S P A · S N I D E
D E N S · F E A R S · E L I A
Y R S · M A U R I C E · L E D
· S T R A U S S · A M B E R
· I L L S · P R E Y
· T E M P T · W O R N O U T
C A P · H E C K L E D · N A M
O B I T · D A R E D · H I T E
E B S E N · R P M · L O F T S
D I O X I D E · I V O R I E S
S E D A T E D · C O N N E R Y
· S E N S E · N E E D S
```

58

```
A A R · C A R R E · D P T
S N I T · O L I O S · D O R Y
H I G H · M I S S S A I G O N
· E D A M E S · D O G M A
· H U R L · B R I G A D O O N
P A T O I S · I M E
O N U S · P I U S V I · W O K
M O R E · R I N S E · M A C E
P I N · S U N D A E · A V E R
· I A N · M C L E A N
F U N N Y G I R L · E A R N
A S I A N · R A I D E R
S H E L O V E S M E · K I S S
T E L L · A N T O N · Y A C K
S R S · L E A S T · M I A
```

59

```
C A L A B A S H · A B N E R
O P E R E T T A · O T O O L E
P E E K A B O O · B O O T I E
· R A N · D I M N E S S
S C A M · T E T E · I S E E
C A N A L · D O N A T E
U N W R A P · R E P O S I T S
T I A · B O O M B O X · T O P
S O R B O N N E · C I C A D A
· U R G I N G · N O L A N
I B E G · O T I C · B O Y S
N O N A G O N · G O T
B O O B O O · B O O H O O E D
A B L O O M · A L K A L I N E
D Y S O N · H O S T E L E R
```

60

```
A F T · S M A S H · M A C Y
D I E · C A C A O · I S A A C
A L E · R I N G O · D O N N A
M I N D O N E S P S A N D Q S
· P I E D · L A S · O U T
L I E N · M E D A L · E R I E
I N S · H A L O · I S M
D O T S A L L T H E I S A N D
· E P A · E O N S · N E E
D A V E · I N S E T · R I C E
U F O · I S A · S A S K
C R O S S E S A L L T H E T S
T I D A L · S C O U R · T I N
S C O N E · E M O T E · T E A
· A O K S · R E N E W · E S P
```

61

```
ASHE  BOSSA  MSGT
CHER  AWAIT  OPIE
MARRYINGFORLOVE
EWE  SLEET  OTOES
  CHEER  ASSN
ABOARD  HOWE  FAR
MIMI  BAYOU  UNE
BEERBARRELPOLKA
ERS  ADAMS  NOLI
RST  LEGS  PREFER
  HAZE  NAILS
OMEGA  ASONE  USE
MUSICOFTHENIGHT
STUN  TRAIL  TAUT
KING  TORTS  ARNE
```

62

```
REWED  HUP  TACTS
ABODE  USA  ALOHA
WORDGAMES  XAXES
LADY  SIRS  IMAMS
STS  HAD  WACO
  QTIP  WONA  WAS
AGUAS  WORDBOOKS
LOAM  WORDS  BRIG
FOREWORDS  DIDNT
ADE  ANDY  PIES
  ACTS  COX  WPA
SLINK  AJAR  MOAN
LUNDI  LASTWORDS
ACARE  AVE  ENTRE
PETER  DAY  ETHEL
```

63

```
WARPS  RACE  CELL
IMETA  ELLA  ARLO
REDASABEET  BIAS
ENOS  SAGAS  ACNE
  SATAN  ONTO
COROT  ERS  LAH
ARENAS  ELI  EEL
SEDATES  REVERSE
ASH  IAM  TERETE
  EGO  END  RADAR
  BRAN  LOUTS
WARM  ATOMS  ARKS
ERIE  REDBUTTONS
RENT  ERLE  AMBIT
EDGE  AYER  POETS
```

64

```
COSTA  CASE  VITA
APLUS  AINT  ENOS
REINS  TMAN  RCMP
PREGNANTPAUSE
EARS  RIO  PUNY
  TERP  MISSTEP
ISMENE  GOBI  IMA
STANDANDDELIVER
LON  ORES  RODENT
AMHERST  PINE
  PATS  PEA  NODS
  THEPARENTTRAP
JETE  ERIK  RIATA
OVAL  GAZE  AFTER
YENS  SLED  MYERS
```

65

```
BACH  CHIC  SHAG
ASIA  HASH  SKILL
SHANGRILA  PULSE
  ROGER  ELTON
SALAAM  MEAL
PREMIERE  CRISIS
AMAIN  ETCH  SENT
RUNT  YAHOO  LAVE
TREY  ERIC  PAGAN
AERIAL  CORONADO
  SULU  ADDLES
STILT  MARNI
HAGAR  BRIGADOON
IRONY  RUDE  ORLY
NARD  AGED  CODE
```

66

```
QUAFFS  JAZZ  ABS
UPROOT  OBOE  LAC
ESSENE  CORR  ITO
  DREADNOUGHT
RAPT  ELSE  MANET
INREVOLT  LOW
AGORA  EASES  TIM
LEXICON  ASTAIRE
SLY  UPSET  ELMER
  CUT  QUILTING
EPSOM  PURR  IDEE
SHOOTBLANKS
SAC  URAL  ITALIC
ASK  BAIL  NAMELY
YES  EDDY  GRATED
```

67

```
S A D · R A I S E S · F I T S
A L I · A S S E R T · E A R L
L I D · M I S T E R M A G O O
S E G O · A U S · O O L O N G
A N E M O N E · S L I T · · ·
· · R E D S · B A L L Y H O O
S P I N E · T U B E S · U G H
P O D S · E R R O R · C L E M
A G O · F L I R T · M A L E S
T O O D L E O O · T A R A · ·
· · · R O M S · S H E R B E T
C E S A R E · D O R · Y A L E
R A T K A N G A R O O · L E N
E R L E · T A L E N T · O N E
E N O S · S P I N E T · O A T
```

68

```
K E E L · S H A L T · F R A N
A N N A · E A G E R · A E O N
S C A M · I N A N E · C A K E
B O M B I N G R A N G E S · ·
A R E · D E E · · D O T O A T
H E L G A · D D T · B O N G O
· · O H S · A A S · F E E T
· S H O O T I N G S T A R S ·
B A A S · Y A Z · T A C ·
A G N E S · M A L · S E T U P
R E D B U G · E A T · A P R
· B U R N I N G D E S I R E
A D A M · A D E A D · A L O E
C U L P · S L A T E · L O A N
E E L S · H E R O D · E R R S
```

69

```
C A V E · R A M P S · B U S T
A G E E · I D E A L · O N T O
H U S K Y V O I C E · X M E N
N E T · E A R N · D R E A M Y
· · T A L E · A D O R N S ·
C H A R T S · C R I B S · ·
L O V E S · G L E N · H A L F
O P E N · S L I N G · O L I O
G I R D · T A C T · P R O M O
· S W A N K · R A T T E D
· T H E E N D · B E N S ·
T O O T E D · M I D I · B O O
H O O T · P H Y S I C S L A B
O L D E · A A R O N · P A T E
U S S R · T H A N K · A S H Y
```

70

```
M I F F · M A M E · S T O L E
A C E R · A L E X · K I L O S
M E N U · L I L I · Y E A R S
A D D I C T E D T O L O V E ·
· · T H E N · R O A N · ·
S P A C E D · L A M B · A L L
A L T A R · C A M P · O L A Y
H O O K E D O N P H O N I C S
L Y N E · W A G S · F E M T O
S S E · H A T E · S Y M B O L
· K E R R · A T O U · ·
· J U N K F O O D J U N K I E
M A N I A · O M O O · U R S A
O D I S T · M I S H · T I N S
B A T H E · S T E N · E S T E
```

71

```
S I P S · M A T C H · A P T
A R I A · E N U R E · A R L O
G E T T I N G B I R D S E E D
A S H · S T E S · A H E A D
· P E A R · U P H O L D S
D A N I E L · B R U L E ·
E C O L · M A G N I · P O E
W H O L E S A L E G A V E U S
Y E N · T E R M S · E A R P
· S H A K Y · C L A S S Y
S A V A N T S · G A E L ·
A M A T I · H A T E · B A A
M A N Y C H E E P T R I L L S
B I E R · A R I E L · M U S K
A D S · T E R S E · P R O S
```

72

```
T R A C T · B R A D · M A R S
H O V E R · O U Z O · A W O L
E N O L A · O T T O · M A L A
· A W L I N T H E F A M I L Y
· A L A · C U R A T E ·
S T A R · I T S · S T L
O A F · F L O O R · H I T M E
P L A N E S O F A B R A H A M
S C R A M · K A Z O O · O C T
· G U S · R E D · M U S S
· S P A R T A · E P A ·
C L A S S I F I E D A D Z E
L I R A · F O N D · E M I T S
A M O K · F O N G · S A N T A
D E L I · S L O E · E N G E L
```

73

```
LIZ  OKS  SPA  ENC
ARI  SOO  LUV  LAI
MAT  CORSAGE  MUD
ANITASBAKER  ESE
     ART  LETTERER
NATS  ALLS  ESSAY
ALOT  ROY   DOR
GAME  KASEM  TICK
  SBA   FLO  ECHO
OCCUR  DION  REAP
HARDALEE  KAI
GNU  BILLYSOCEAN
IDI  LEADIER  VIA
RLS  EON  PAT  IDY
LEE  SNO  SLA  LES
```

74

```
TRAFFIC   BICEPS
REPLICA  GROUPIE
INHABIT  RATRACE
PEERS STA  ABUTS
OGLE  IPASS  SLUR
DEI  CRABPOT  ERE
 DARROW  SLOTTED
   BIN   AUK
CARIBOU  ACROSS
ARA  SUBDUES  PPD
PAPA  TONGS  LORE
SLITS  AAU  WINES
TSELIOT  STOPGAP
AERATES  TORPEDO
NASSER   ATFIRST
```

75

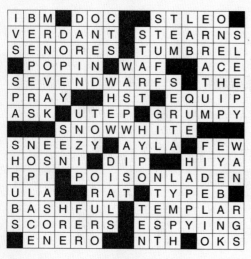

```
IBM  DOC   STLEO
VERDANT  STEARNS
SENORES  TUMBREL
 POPIN  WAF  ACE
SEVENDWARFS  THE
PRAY  HST  EQUIP
ASK  UTEP  GRUMPY
  SNOWWHITE
SNEEZY  AYLA  FEW
HOSNI  DIP  HIYA
RPI  POISONLADEN
ULA  RAT  TYPEB
BASHFUL  TEMPLAR
SCORERS  ESPYING
 ENERO  NTH  OKS
```

76

```
HAVE  USES  SAGA
IMAGE  POGO  AMOS
SINGLESBAR  TERN
 RESALE  DERANGE
   LIT   ENDER
URSA  ESCARP
NIOBE  AROUSES
DOUBLEORNOTHING
 TREMBLE  EERIE
 OBEYED  DEPT
AARON   LOA
GRUNTED  ALLOUT
LUMS  TRIPLEPLAY
OBOE  NODS  CANOE
WART  APSE  LAST
```

77

```
AWED  INCUR  GLEN
CALI  GOOSE  LEVI
THESOUNDOFMUSIC
 LEADA    AISLE
  BIND  AMIN
BELLSARERINGING
ADIET  EARL  MIR
SINS  DATED  RENI
ICE  IMUS  SETON
STRIKEUPTHEBAND
 LISP   SORE
BRAIN    OILED
LACAGEAUXFOLLES
OVID  GENII  EMMY
WEDS  GRIST  DOIN
```

78

```
ALUM  PENS  BAGEL
MENU  OVAL  IVORY
ANDS  TATA  LOLLS
 DOESADOGSLIFE
  ATE   LOD
PRESTO  WHEW  BAT
RENTA  FOOD  MULE
OFTENTIMESBEGIN
VERT  IDES  ALLEE
ORE  UPON  ABSENT
  OSU   UNE
 WITHPUPPYLOVE
DANTE  ROTO  PELT
ALGER  GOON  ERMA
BEERS  ERNE  NOON
```

79

M	A	R	I	A	█	C	A	R	A	T	█	C	A	Y
A	L	O	N	G	█	O	S	A	G	E	█	A	D	O
T	O	M	T	E	R	R	I	F	I	C	█	T	R	U
C	H	A	R	█	Y	E	S	█	T	H	E	B	A	R
H	A	N	O	V	E	R	█	R	A	I	L	A	G	E
█	█	█	A	S	S	█	S	T	E	A	L	█	█	█
T	I	K	I	S	█	A	V	E	█	I	L	I	E	█
O	V	I	N	E	█	L	I	P	█	A	N	O	D	E
W	E	T	S	█	M	A	R	█	R	E	U	S	E	█
█	█	T	O	T	E	D	█	S	A	M	█	█	█	█
P	A	Y	L	O	A	D	█	A	N	S	W	E	R	S
O	C	H	E	R	S	█	A	W	E	█	A	L	O	E
P	T	A	█	P	U	S	S	Y	W	I	L	L	O	W
P	O	W	█	O	R	A	T	E	█	A	L	E	N	E
A	R	K	█	R	E	T	A	R	█	M	A	N	E	D

80

M	A	G	U	S	█	H	E	M	P	█	B	A	S	S
O	C	A	L	A	█	A	L	A	I	█	A	R	I	A
T	H	E	N	U	D	I	S	T	C	O	L	O	N	Y
█	E	L	A	T	E	D	█	T	A	R	█	L	A	S
█	█	█	S	E	T	█	S	E	R	A	G	L	I	O
E	L	F	█	D	O	O	M	█	D	N	A	█	█	█
R	A	R	E	█	U	R	I	S	█	G	L	O	B	█
G	R	O	V	E	R	C	L	E	V	E	L	A	N	D
█	A	M	E	N	█	H	I	T	E	█	O	K	A	Y
█	█	█	R	A	F	█	N	E	R	O	█	S	I	E
I	M	C	O	M	I	N	G	█	I	D	A	█	█	█
O	A	R	█	E	G	O	█	S	T	E	L	L	A	█
T	H	E	B	L	A	R	N	E	Y	S	T	O	N	E
A	R	E	A	█	R	A	C	E	█	S	O	L	T	I
S	E	P	T	█	O	D	O	R	█	A	N	A	I	S

81

T	H	E	F	A	R	S	I	D	E	█	E	R	I	K
H	A	I	R	R	A	I	S	E	R	█	V	E	N	I
E	N	L	I	S	T	M	E	N	T	█	I	S	T	S
C	D	E	█	O	H	O	█	T	E	A	C	H	E	S
A	L	E	█	N	E	N	E	█	S	T	A	G	E	█
S	E	N	D	█	R	E	A	R	U	P	█	P	E	R
E	S	S	E	S	█	█	R	E	N	E	W	E	R	S
█	█	█	L	I	B	E	R	T	I	N	E	█	█	█
R	I	G	A	T	O	N	I	█	█	S	L	I	P	S
E	N	L	█	U	R	A	N	U	S	█	K	N	O	T
S	T	A	M	P	█	G	N	A	T	█	T	R	E	█
P	A	R	A	S	O	L	█	D	U	O	█	E	T	E
I	K	E	S	█	R	E	T	U	R	N	T	R	I	P
T	E	A	K	█	I	N	E	L	E	G	A	N	C	E
E	S	T	S	█	G	A	R	Y	L	A	R	S	O	N

82

S	H	A	W	█	M	U	I	R	█	M	I	D	A	S
E	A	C	H	█	I	P	S	O	█	A	N	I	C	E
T	I	M	E	█	S	T	A	B	█	S	H	O	R	E
█	G	E	T	M	E	O	W	O	F	H	E	R	E	█
█	█	H	O	R	N	█	█	O	E	R	█	█	█	█
G	R	E	E	D	Y	█	M	O	O	R	I	V	E	R
L	O	R	R	E	█	C	O	W	L	█	T	I	R	E
E	U	R	█	M	A	L	T	E	S	E	█	N	I	N
A	S	O	F	█	R	E	I	N	█	Y	U	C	C	A
N	E	R	O	W	O	O	F	█	D	E	N	I	A	L
█	█	█	R	I	M	█	█	M	O	O	D	█	█	█
█	C	A	W	S	A	N	D	E	F	F	E	C	T	█
S	A	R	A	H	█	O	E	U	F	█	R	O	O	T
A	F	I	R	E	█	E	L	S	E	█	G	O	R	E
L	E	A	D	S	█	L	I	E	D	█	O	K	I	E

83

V	A	L	S	E	█	M	A	T	S	█	S	A	D	O
A	R	I	E	L	█	O	L	A	V	█	I	C	E	T
D	O	N	Q	U	I	X	O	T	E	█	M	I	L	O
E	S	E	█	S	O	I	T	█	N	O	O	D	L	E
R	E	D	W	I	N	E	█	A	G	U	N	█	█	█
█	█	█	A	V	A	█	S	T	A	R	L	E	T	█
G	A	B	L	E	█	█	S	A	U	L	█	E	R	I	N
E	T	A	T	█	P	A	T	R	I	█	G	I	G	I
M	O	L	E	█	E	V	E	N	█	P	R	E	E	N
█	P	I	R	A	T	E	S	█	C	U	E	█	█	█
█	█	M	R	E	D	█	C	U	R	E	A	L	L	█
R	A	P	I	E	R	█	J	A	R	S	█	R	I	O
E	M	I	T	█	P	A	U	L	B	U	N	Y	A	N
F	O	N	T	█	A	R	A	L	█	I	R	A	N	I
T	R	E	Y	█	N	I	N	A	█	T	A	N	G	S

84

A	R	E	N	A	█	A	A	B	B	█	S	C	A	T
G	O	B	E	L	█	B	U	R	R	█	U	H	U	H
A	U	R	A	L	█	A	R	E	A	█	B	I	D	E
S	T	O	L	E	N	C	A	R	S	█	P	L	E	A
█	█	█	A	O	K	█	█	S	W	A	I	N	█	█
A	L	H	I	R	T	█	A	B	H	O	R	S	█	█
L	A	I	R	S	█	S	N	E	A	K	█	A	E	C
O	N	T	V	█	C	U	G	A	T	█	S	U	L	U
T	A	R	█	B	A	R	E	D	█	W	I	C	K	S
█	█	E	R	A	S	E	R	█	B	O	P	E	E	P
█	S	C	E	N	E	█	█	S	E	Z	█	█	█	█
B	L	O	C	█	M	O	L	T	E	N	L	A	V	A
L	I	R	A	█	E	L	I	E	█	I	O	W	A	N
A	D	D	S	█	N	I	N	A	█	A	V	A	N	T
B	E	S	T	█	T	O	D	D	█	K	E	Y	E	S

```
A M E B A   D E A F   E V A
S O R E L   I N T O   S N A P
C R I S P   S T A R   C L U E
I N S T A N C E   S P H I N X
    S C O U R   A L I S T
  C L E A N S E   K A N T
P H I L   O E D   E N D M A N
T E S L A   S T A   E L E V E
A Z T E C S   H B O   E N I D
  L R O N   E S C O R T S
  B E L I E   L E A P S
U R S I N E   I N S U L A T E
S A S S   Z E S T   S I L O S
M I L T   E R T E   E S T O P
A N Y   S A S E   S T O N Y
```

```
T O M B   S A D A T   T W O S
A B E L   A G A P E   H A R K
D I C E   L E N I N   E R I E
  T H E Y A S K E D M E H O W
  A P E D   C S A   O L E
M E N   T B O N E   R U L E R
G A I T   O D O   T D S
M U C H I W E I G H I S A I D
  A F L   S U R   R I C E
F R O W N   G E T O N   R E B
R O T   O R E   W O R M
A B O U T O N C E A W E E K
P R O S   A T L A W   A D A M
P O L E   C L A R A   D A L E
E Y E D   H E N N Y   S L E D
```

```
A C A T   C A T E R   A S S
R A G E S   O R A T E   M I T
C R U N C H B E R R Y   O N E
O P E N A I R   P E N A N C E
    L E A   A N G E L
H A R P E R S F E R R Y
A L I A S   I R E D   P O M
R E N D   P A L E D   J A V A
P E G   T I N T   S O R E R
  M A T T H E W P E R R Y
I B E A M   C H E
N I A G A R A   H E N R E I D
L O S   L O N D O N D E R R Y
A T E   E S T E E   S A G A N
W A D   S E E M S   L O N E
```

```
F L E X   S W A P   M A A M
R O R Y   A C A S E   A L D O
E L I Z A B E T H T A Y L O R
T A N   L I N T Y   R E I G N
  C E D E   S I R
A P L A C E I N T H E S U N
T R I P   U R A L   N O V
T Y N E   O P R A H   S I N E
N O D   A C E S   H O E R
  R A I N T R E E C O U N T Y
  B I O   A H O T
O B J E T   M A R I N   I L L
C O U R A G E O F L A S S I E
H A D I   A N N U L   A L F A
S T O A   D U E L   W E E K
```

```
G L U M   A T L A S   E L A L
L I S A   R H E T T   R I T A
A M E R I C A S F R E E D O M
D E D I C A T E   I N C O M E
    N E D S   S C O T
P A L A C E   S A K S   N A B
R I A T A   S E V E   D U M A
I N D E P E N D E N C E D A Y
A G E S   T E E S   O P I N E
M E N   C H A R   S P R E A D
    S H E D   P A T E
E S T H E R   P A L I S A D E
P Y R O T E C H N I C S H O W
O N E R   A R D E N   O O Z E
S E E N   L I S L E   R Y E S
```

```
W A R P A T H   U P S C A L E
E L E C T E E   G E O R G I A
S A N T A N A   L A W Y E R S
T N T   E D D Y   E S S A Y
  B Y T H E   A R T
M E L E E   U M P S   A B E L
E X A L T   N O A H   L O L A
C E L L I S T   G E T B U S Y
C R A B   P E T E   R A T I O
A T W O   A R A T   O L S E N
  T I M   P U P I L
S C O T S   V E R A   I R A
H E R O I N E   N I C E G U Y
A D A M A N T   E N C L O S E
W E L S H E S   R E C I T E S
```

91

```
A B C S   C A R U S O   J A R
R I L L   O P E N E D   U M A
C L A U D E R A I N S   D A M
S K Y G O D   P T A   A D Z E
      L I S   S T E P H E N
U N J I L T E D   E L O I
R O A N   O W E N   O G R E S
S E C T   R E M I T   E S S O
A S K E W   R O N A   E C T O
    L A I C   B A N K S H O T
E M E R G E S   S K A
L A M S   T O E   A S I A N S
I S M   J E F F B R I D G E S
Z O O   O R A T E D   O U S T
A N N   B A S S E S   L E S S
```

92

```
    C A S T A N E T   L I F T
D A L A I L A M A   E G R E T
A N T I P A S T O   A G I L E
U T E   S P A   P R I C E R
B O R S T A L   P E N N A M E
    L E S   C A R E S S E S
  S A A R   P O L E D   S T A
M A R Y   C A R E S   T E E S
I N T   P O P E S   P I E R
S T I M U L U S   D I N
L A C O N I A   P R E S I D E
E C H O I C   H O R   G O V
A R O S E   P R O V O L O N E
D U K E S   A B N E G A T E S
  Z E S T   D I E S I R A E
```

93

```
P A U P E R   A S F A R A S
E N T I R E   S T O R A G E
E Y E L I D   P O L E M I C S
L O R E S   B I L K   P L U M
E N I D   H E R E S   S I R E
D E N   D I G I N   T E L
    E L E V E N   T R Y S T
    A B E T   K I W I
S T A Y S   E U L O G Y
W A R   T A L K S   E D T
I R I S   A R R A S   S L O E
S T E M   L A N K   P U L S E
S E T A S I D E   L A R I A T
  S T R I K E R   A V E N G E
  T A T T E R S   M E R G E R
```

94

```
  C A R O L   M A D A M S
  A R E N A S   A D A G I O S
  P O E T I C   R U B E L L A
S T U K A   H A L L S   L O I
H I S   P R E S E T   L A I N
U V E A   A R T Y   W A I S T
T E R R A Z Z O   G H O S T S
    C L E O   Z O O T
C A L A I S   P A L A Z Z O S
A V A N T   Z O N E   E A S T
D O T E   D E N I M S   M M I
G I T   S E N S E   T A B O R
E D I T I N G   S I E V E S
D E C E A S E   T W E E Z E
  R E A M E R   O R R I S
```

95

```
  S P A D E   S T O N E S
D I A G R A M   C O U R A G E
O N T A R I O   O R A T I O N
D N A   S T A M E N   V I A
G A N T   Y E S E S   T E S T
E M I R S   S O T   E T T E
R E C A L L   F O R T R E S S
    I I I   E E R
S T A N D P A T   F R A P P E
T O M E   C A R   M I L A N
A L A R   T R I A L   N A R C
R U S   A E O L I A   T E A
R E S I G N S   S I G N E R S
E N E M I E S   I N C E N S E
D E S P O T   N E O N S
```

96

```
E M P I R E   D O N O R S
L O U R E E D   E V E R E T T
A N T E N N A   M O L I E R E
S T U N T   I T A   L O N E R
T A P E   C L I N G   N A T E
I N A   D R I P D R Y   C C S
C A T S E Y E S   E A R T H A
    H I S S   L E N O
R E T E S T   M I L K Y W A Y
O D E   M A R I N E S   R U E
M A S S   L I M E Y   L I R A
E S T E S   F E M   N I G E R
O N A R O L L   A G A K H A N
S E T F R E E   N A N E T T E
  R E S T E D   B O S S E D
```

```
COFFEE   MOROCCO
UNROLLS  OVERLAY
STERILE  TIDBITS
HACKS VEINS  MAT
IRKS  PEKOE  ABLE
NIL  GOREN  FLOOR
GOESAPE  STRONG
   TRI   RAH
 ACORNS  CANASTA
IVORY PLUCK  TOT
NORM  PIETY WORF
ECO DODGE  LIPPI
VANDYKE  SPONGER
EDASNER  THREADS
ROSTERS  DESPOT
```

```
NASH  SHOE  DESTE
ASTO  HUNT  EXPEL
CHER  ESTH  STACY
READERHAYWORTH
ENDEAR  PLATE
     SYN   TOMTOM
OSSIE  OPEC  IONA
CHARLATANHESTON
TOGO  BONO  AMORY
OPENTO   WAR
   BUDGE  BLAZER
 LIONELBURYMORE
BEGUN  OONA  IRAN
ATONE  SLID  ERSE
HARDY  SITE  LOEW
```

```
 TOWELS  AMBER
CABARET  MARLEY
AMERICA  NEEDLES
SAL  NOTTE  WEEST
CLIP  QUASI  RAMP
AESOP  EXITS  SEA
 SKIRT  EASEMENT
   SIOUCXITY
FOREGONE  NORTH
ICE  STEMS  NOWOR
LUCE  HAPPY  NOSE
CLOVE  STREP  SIN
HAVARTI  ENACTED
 REDIAL  ETCHERS
 REEDY  SLEEPY
```

```
JUDITH  BASILICA
ETALIA  ARTLOVER
STRICT  SERENADE
TENET  SENAT  NEA
SRS  ALABAMA
   COMAS   SILO
ONPATROL  BAOBAB
NATIONALPASTIME
TRALEE  DAYTODAY
OCHS   PINER
   ORLANDO  ESE
IDA  SHAME  NAXOS
FEDERICO  LOMANS
SAARINEN  AMALIE
ONRECORD  SYNTAX
```

```
BALD  COED  PENN
ALIE  ORLE  LEVEE
ROBS  LAIT  INERT
BUREAU  HARVARD
 DARTMOUTH
  TABU  ORNERY
DEM  ITLL  IONIA
IVYLEAGUESCHOOL
VIRAL  OVAL  SSE
ALASKA  RIBS
  PRINCETON
 CORNELL  KEEPUP
SAMOA  ELLE  PEKE
BROWN  SUER  PREP
ADOS  SSTS  EASE
```

```
EARTH  ANTI  CAR
AROOM  LEAN  AREA
STARSEARCH  LARD
TENT  SMOKE  ASIA
   GPO  RASHER
ELATE  STAIN
SABENA  OUTDOES
THESUNALSORISES
 RETITLE  RESTED
  NIFTY  WEEPS
ARISEN  EDS
MIRE  OPINE  BRAS
PLEA  MOONSTRUCK
LENT  ISLE  BELIE
EYE  CHAD  SWEDE
```

103

```
T H A D _ B A T S _ S O C K O
A A R E _ O L I N _ A S H E N
I L K S _ R I C O _ Y E A R S
L O S E O N E S W A Y _ I R E
_ _ T E N _ G I E _ R S T
I N T O T O _ M O R S E L _
H O R N E _ T A O S _ B I N D
A D A I R _ O H S _ A S F O R
D E V O _ L U R E _ B E T T E
_ E N T I C E _ S E N S E D
G A R _ O O H _ A W L _
O P S _ U N D E V E L O P E D
T R I P P _ O B O E _ S P R Y
T I N G E _ W R I T _ S P E E
A L G A E _ N O D S _ A S I S
```

104

```
A S T A _ T E R N _ O P A R T
M E A L _ K N E E _ V I R E O
P A P A D O C D U V A L I E R
S T E R E _ H O R A _ S A F E
_ _ M Y R A _ A L A N _ _
S O B S _ U N C L E R E M U S
A T E _ M E T H _ T I R A N A
M A G D A _ S I P _ E S S A Y
O R I E N T _ N A G S _ O P S
A U N T I E M A M E _ U N T O
_ _ H A L O _ P L A T _ _
A G A R _ I D E E _ R A N T O
D R J O Y C E B R O T H E R S
D I A N A _ M R E D _ A N I L
S T R E P _ S O R E _ N E M O
```

105

```
C O R M _ I N C A _ S C R A P
O L I O _ M E L D _ A H O M E
M E N U _ P A I L _ S I M O N
M I S S M A R M E L S T E I N
A C E T I C _ B R A E _ _ _
_ _ A T T U _ T R E B L E
E V I C T _ N A P E _ T R O Y
W I S H Y O U W E R E H E R E
E L I E _ L M N O _ L O W E R
S E N S E D _ N O E L _ _
_ _ L I S P _ S N O R E S
W H E N W E M E E T A G A I N
R O M E O _ E T T E _ I N D O
A M I N O _ W A R N _ S T E R
P O L E D _ S L E D _ T O R T
```

106

```
P L U G _ T H I N S _ S T A Y
O O N A _ A E S O P _ P O R E
T U T U _ S I E V E _ I R I S
_ D O N T T R E A D O N M E _
_ _ T O E S _ _ F E E L
M A D L Y _ H U L A S _ _
O G R E _ P R O P E L _ P T A
M E E T M E I N S T L O U I S
S E W _ A L L E Y S _ P R E Y
_ F U E L S _ T E R R E
T H O R _ _ S O O N _ _
B E M Y V A L E N T I N E _
C O M E _ A B O V E _ N E W T
O N A N _ T E N E T _ G R E W
W E N T _ S T E N O _ S O S O
```

107

```
D O L T _ H A F T S _ G L I B
O N E A _ A L L A H _ R E M O
C A N T E R B U R Y _ O O P S
_ _ A X L E _ D U N E S
T E A _ T E E S _ J U S T L Y
A R T E R Y _ P R O P E R _
T E T R A _ P R O L E _ O P T
A C H E _ H E I S T _ S T A R
R T E _ C O R N Y _ T A S S O
_ _ G E H R I G _ T A L K T O
S P A R E S _ S O O N _ Y A P
A L L O W _ M A Y A _ _
B A L D _ T A K E S A W A L K
O T O E _ A N E N T _ O H I O
T O P S _ P A N S Y _ L A P P
```

108

```
A S P _ C A T T Y _ F L E A
S T E P _ A P H I D _ O A R S
S E A L _ T E A M S _ U C L A
E E L Y _ E R N O _ C R E E P
T R E M O R _ K R A I T _ _
_ O P E L S _ D A H L I A
D E M U R R A G E S _ T E R N
A M I T Y _ R I D _ A H E A D
R I C H _ A D V E N T U R E S
T R A C E R _ I N A I R _ _
_ O N E I N _ P E S T E R
S H A L E _ O G L E _ D I V E
L I M O _ E N D O R _ A M O S
A L A N _ L I A N E _ Y O K E
T O N Y _ L A Y E R _ N E W
```

109

```
P E C S   L O A D   B R A I D
L I O N   A N T I   L A U D E
U N S E T T L E S   U N D E R
M E T A R O Y A L I N D I A N
      K E Y   M O N D O
G A L E N A   D E E M I N G
A W A R D   N I G E R   N O R
P A N S   M O V E D   P E T E
E K E   F I V E S   M A R T Y
D E S P I S E   P A S T E S
      A D E L E   L O T
B R A V E R E D M A R I N E R
M O D A L   T W O T I M E R S
O M A N I   T I N E   E L E V
C A M E O   E N O S   S L I P
```

110

```
W O N G   A N Z A C   A C T S
A P A R   M O I R A   L O R I
R E T I R I N G L Y   G R I G
E R A S E   S O U R E D O N
  A L T E R S   G O B I
    L L A M A   A B R A D E
D U D E   C U S S   B A L E D
I R A   P E R K I L Y   L A G
V I S T A   F E T A   D Y N E
A S H A R P   W A L D O
  I N K A   R A I L A T
H A N G A R E D   S P L A T
U R G E   S C R A T C H I L Y
C E L L   O H A R A   I C O N
K A Y O   N O W I N   N E N E
```

111

```
I M A N   A B B E Y   A S T A
N O G O   W R I T E   Z A H N
G R O W   N O N E W T A X E S
A T N O T I M E   I L E N E
    N O N O   D A T E
S E A D O G   N O T H A N K S
A R R E T   C A N O E   A R Y
B A R R   F O G U P   I C O N
I T O   T R E A T   E T H N O
N O W A Y O U T   L A S T E D
    U S E R   B A R N
O T E R O   E A T N O F A T
N O N O N S E N S E   U R S A
E M I R   A D O S E   S A I L
S A D A   N O W I N   E S T E
```

112

```
S A M B A   A C N E   S W A G
A R I E L   S H U N   O H I O
V A N N A W H I T E   N I L E
E L I S   H E N S   D A T E S
    R E N E   M E T E D
N E W T O N   S E E S A W
E T H E L   B E A S T   A D A
S T I L L E R   C A R O T I D
T A T   T R A S H   U P E N D
  E L O I S E   S C A R E S
  S H A P E   A B E T
S L O P S   A W O L   S L I T
P I U S   P E A R L W H I T E
E L S E   E R L E   R O L E X
D Y E D   G O L D   Y E A S T
```

113

```
A L A M O   N A P S   S C A N
L A V I N   A R I A   T A R O
S W E L L   S A L T   I N D O
O N C E I N A B L U E M O O N
    N I L   R O P E R S
W I N D E X   B A D L Y
A R E S   A L A I   S E A
L I T T L E G R E Y C E L L S
E S S   A M E N   R O S S
    S C A M S   S T R E E T
S T A T E N   F A R
W A V E S A W H I T E F L A G
O B O E   T O A D   A L I B I
R O I L   E R I E   T O M E S
N O D E   S E L L   Y E A S T
```

114

```
A P S I S   N A Z I   S L A W
G R A N T   O M A N   P I N A
T E N C O M M A N D M E N T S
S P E A K E A S Y   A L D E N
      E N D S   A T L A S T
A B O A R D   O R T S
S O O N   E E R I E   S S T
H U N D R E D Y E A R S W A R
E T A   O R I E L   A U T O
    S C A T   Z O O M E D
C A M P O S   S T U N
O L E I C   S C H L E M I E L
C A S T O F T H O U S A N D S
A C H E   R A M S   E I G H T
S K Y S   O B O E   C L A S S
```

115

```
A W E D . . . M A O . O S I P
L O V E L Y . A S P . D E M I
B R O C A S . T H E B E A R S
S N E A K E R . E R I T R E A
. . P E R I L . A G T S . . .
B O S O M . G I G . S A T I E
A C A D I A . N O A H . O L D
R A U . C H I C A G O . W I N
E L L . H A L O . E U R E K A
R A B B I . K L M . L U R E S
. E E G S . N E E D S . . . .
V U L G A T E . D R E S S E R
I L L I N O I S . G R I E V E
A N O N . O R A . O S A G E S
L A W S . L E X . . . N A S T
```

116

```
A J A R . C O S T . P R E G O
L U X E . A B I E . R I C E D
A N I M A L E N C L O S U R E
N O S . D I S K . E G E S T S
. . L O B E . A G E R . . . .
A S S U R E . C L A N S M A N
D A N C E R S A L L Y . A W E
A L E E . E T A . A G A S . .
N E V . P I T C H E R C U R T
A M A R A N T H . M A N S E S
. E R N O . S A D E . . . . .
L A S S I E . A N N A . S U E
I N T E N S E Y E A R N I N G
S T U N G . F L A T . E Z I O
P I N T S . T A K E . W E T S
```

117

```
S I Z E . S L E W . S E M I S
E R I K . T O N O . P L E A T
C A P E V E R D E . R I D G E
. . . O N E S . I X I O N . .
. A C T I O N . C O N I C . .
S N A I L S . C H A G R I N .
A G R E E . L A I R S . N O R
G O D S . W E L D S . M E T E
S R I . E A G L E . C O H A N
. A G E N D A S . T A B A R D
. . A N G E L . C R U S T Y .
H E N R I . W O O S . . . . .
U R B A N . N E W J E R S E Y
S T A G E . A R E A . A P S E
K E Y E S . T E R N . M A S S
```

118

```
H A R T E . P U C K . P A L E
A D I E U . O S L O . O N Y X
I L O N G . L E O S . S Y N E
G I J O E . O L Y M P I A N S
. B A R N O N E . O R T . . .
. S E M I S . S O R R O W . .
T S K . O N U S . V O I L A .
H Y A N N I S . S T I N G E R
U N T I E . D E R N . G O P .
S C E N I C . E P I C S . . .
. E L A . C A P E C O D . . .
S E T T L E F O R . T I M I D
O G E E . S A R A . O P E R A
F A R E . A R U T . W I N G Y
A D I N . R O M E . N O S E S
```

119

```
C H A R T . I N C A . C O D E
A I D E S . N E L L . H A I L
T H E H O U S E O F L A R D S
S O N E . T A D S . O S S I E
. . A L A N . E S O S . . . .
. G E T T H E B U T T E R O F
P R I E D . A P E S . E C U
L A D D . T W I S T . S E T S
O P E . H A R Z . E L V E S
T H R E E P I E C E S U E T
. . M I E N . E Y E R . . . .
S O L I D . G E A R . O B I T
P A Y L I P I D S E R V I C E
A H O Y . I N G E . A E D E S
R U N S . A G E D . W R E S T
```

120

```
B A G S . I D E A . S A S H
E L L E R . N E L L . I S E E
N O O N E . G I B E . T S A R
J U S T T H E F A X M A A M
I D S . A I R Y . I N R I .
. A I D . U S O . L A K . .
D O U B L E L O X . P L A I N
O H N O . S O L O S . I N D O
T I P O F . C A R P E T T A X
S O O . E M O . I R E . . .
. P R A Y . F A C E . A P E
Q U A R T E R B A C K S A X
I T L L . U R E Y . T I T L E
D I A L . R I D S . S T E E R
O P R Y . N E S S . E R S T
```

121

```
A P I A N ■ R C A ■ M E A R A
C O S M O N A U T ■ A S T E R
H E R O W O R S H I P P E R S
E T A S ■ G A P E D ■ L E E ■
D I E ■ ■ ■ N O M ■ I N N ■
■ C L I ■ H O N E ■ A R E T E
■ ■ L A U R A ■ I G O R S ■
■ K I N G O F C L U B S ■
■ H E A T H ■ T A S S O ■ ■
P E N D S ■ P A P A ■ T O W
L A D ■ Y E A ■ ■ N I B
A V A ■ D R Y E R ■ A T E E
Y E L L O W S U B M A R I N E
U H L A N ■ E L A S T O M E R
P O S I T ■ D E N ■ O N E R S
```

122

```
J A W ■ C O D E ■ S O D A
E L K E P I R U S ■ I N E Z
E A R ■ S E C R E T A G E N T
P I P E T T E ■ O R N A T E
■ C H E L A ■ M A L I C ■
M Y S T E R Y N O V E L ■
O S C A R ■ A R I D ■ B E E
M E A D ■ E G G O N ■ F O A L
A R N N E A R ■ Q U A R K
■ J I G S A W P U Z Z L E
S A B O T ■ M A R I E ■
A L E R T S ■ R I L E D U P
G O R D I A N K N O T ■ A R I
A N N A L O W E R S ■ Z A X
S E E N ■ T S A R ■ E L Y
```

123

```
P I K E ■ A L O H A ■ S O A K
O N O R R E R A N ■ A L L I
E X O R B I T A N T F L E A S
T S K ■ R O U N D ■ L E G I T
■ H O S P ■ E D A M ■
B E T A K E ■ G D A Y ■ F H A
A T R I A ■ G O O N ■ P R A N
S H E R W O O D F L O R I S T
S E E S ■ P E L F ■ N O L T E
O L D E A S Y ■ S C A L E D
■ F A L A ■ S H A M ■
S T P A T ■ L O C A L ■ T O E
L O O K S F O R A F L I G H T
O M N I A N A R T ■ C I N E
P E E R ■ O G L E S ■ U F O S
```

124

```
C U R A T E S ■ H G W E L L S
E T A G E R E E L A T I O N
E N T R A N T ■ L O Y A L T Y
S E A ■ R E O ■ I S O L A T E
■ B O S N S ■ S U I ■
A U G U S T ■ K R A T I O N S
S N O R E ■ H A I R ■ L O T
A R A B W I T T Y ■ D I N O
N I L ■ I D E A ■ C O V E N
A G L I T T E R ■ N E G A T E
■ N E H ■ S P I N S ■
A C C O R D S ■ A C T ■ T I M
D O O V E R S ■ U K R A I N E
A M M E T E R L E A S E R S
H E B R E W S ■ A L L U R E S
```

125

```
R A G L A N ■ P R O B A B L E
E R O I C A L E M O N O I L
B R U I T S E V E R Y O N E
E E R ■ S A R D I N E ■ K E A
C A M P ■ L O G E S ■ M E A N
C R E E K ■ M E W ■ T A N G O
A S T R O S ■ D E F E N D E R
■ L A I C ■ R E N T ■
C A D I L L A C ■ W E L D E R
A L E T A ■ N U T ■ T E R S E
R A V E ■ V I S A S ■ S A S E
A B E ■ R E S T I N G ■ P E N
C A L L I S T O ■ A R D E N T
A M O U N T E D P I E R C E
L A P I D A R Y S P R Y E R
```

126

```
L A P S E ■ M C S ■ S A T E
E L I H U ■ A R P ■ M E R R Y
S E L I G ■ G U A R A N T E E
■ G E N E R I C ■ I R I S E S
■ G N U ■ I M A G O ■
S T A L E R V O T A R I E S
T O L E T ■ C E D A R ■ C A N
E N O R M ■ O R E ■ E L A T E
A T O ■ A R A B S ■ T I M E R
M O N A L I S A ■ O F F E N D
■ Y E N T L ■ N A E ■
A S S E S S ■ I N E R T I A
S P E A K E A S Y ■ R I D G E
T A N Y A ■ D T S ■ A M E E R
A N T E ■ E S E ■ R E A D S
```

127

```
A C T I   B L E D   T H R O W
L O R N   R O A D   H O O C H
F O O T L O O S E   W R O T E
A L P H O N S E   G A S T O N
      E T T E   T O R E
G O P   T E N F O O T P O L E
C R A N E   A N D   L U I S
L O R E   M A T E S   A T N O
E N D S   A M S   S Y R U P
F O O T I N M O U T H   E S S
      L M N O   N E A T
T O B I A S   L E A D O F F S
A M O N G   P U S S Y F O O T
L A N G E   P A C E   F A R O
C R A S S   D U O S   S L A P
```

128

```
S E M I   G A L A S   A F A R
I R A Q   A L I C E   L U L U
F I R S T O F T H E M O N T H
T E E   A L I S   I N T E R
      F L E E   P I N E
C A L L E R   S E A N   S F C
A L O E   C O N G O   P E R
M I D D L E O F N O W H E R E
E G G   A R R A Y   Y A M S
O N E   Y I P S   E S P R I T
      S O N S   L U C E
W O O L F   T O G A   P I T
E N D O F T H E C E N T U R Y
S T O P   R O M A N   A M O R
T O R E   A P P L E   M A N E
```

129

```
    P A R S E   P E A R S
C R A N I U M   A E S O P S
R E R A T E S   C R E M A T E
A D E L E   R E O   A R A P
S O S O   P L E D   S I E N A
      G A L E N   R A N
I M A   V A N E   E L E V E N
L A W   A N A G R A M   I W O
K I N D L E   A E R O   M E G
      R O T   D A M N S
C H A I N   D E M S   C R O P
L O P E   S I S   P R A D O
U S E D C A R   S T R I P E D
  T R U D G E   I S O M E R S
  S P E A R   R E A P S
```

130

```
D E B R A   P L A C E   A B E
A R L E S   C O N A N   R E D
F R E N C H T O A S T   E N G
N E S T E A   S T A R G A Z E
E D S   T L C   B A A
      I T A L I A N H E R O
J A M   C E L E B   T A K E R
O P A L   R I V E T   N E A L
G O T U P   P E R I L   D R Y
S P A N I S H R I C E
      A C T   A T E   Q B S
D I S R A E L I   A C T U A L
R O T   S W I S S C H E E S E
A N Y   S E T T O   E L L I E
W A X   O D E O N   R E L E T
```

131

```
O A K S   A S P   H I D E
D R I P S   M E A T   O N E A
A L L A H   P A R A S I T E S
  O N T A P   L I S P   E R E
  I R I S   S T A R R E D
P A R A P E T S   E D A M
O V A L   T A T I   I T E M
P I T   P A R A D O X   Z O E
  S T E R   T M E N   A Z O V
  L E A R   P A R A D I S E
S K E L T E R   L E A D
O U T   E D I E   D R E A M
P A R A D I G M S   O D I U M
P L A N   D O M E   N U R S E
Y A P S   R Y E   P E E L
```

132

```
  N B C   T H U G   D E V O
R E I T E R A T E D   E V A N
T H E R M O M E T E R F I L L
E I N   A I M S   T E T L E Y
    H I K E   M E A L
P O P U L A R C A N D Y B A R
A H E M   H I T S   A D O
L Y R E   C L I M E   S T O W
M O O   A R A L   W I R E
A U T O M O B I L E M A K E R
    N E S S   I L A Y
S C I E N T   O K A Y   W A N
W A L T D I S N E Y P O O C H
A R L O   C A M I N O R E A L
M A Y A   M E T E   E S T
```

133

```
  ASCH   SABU   TWI
  WHOOPITUP    IIN
WHOOPIGOLDBERG
RIO   ANN   OSIERS
ETTA    SIP  ANTAL
NEED   MONET    ATO
   MAKINGWHOOPEE
    NOM     ELF
WHOOPINGCRANE
RES    CREAM   OPUS
ALCAN   ANT    DINE
PEELED   ICC   SHE
 NOTWORTHAWHOOP
 ELO   WHOOPDEDO
 SAN   NORN   SEEK
```

134

```
CASABA   ADAM   CAW
ELIDED   BOUT   ASH
LIBERALARTS    SSE
   ING   OLEO  SPAR
OWL   ATOM   STAIR
REAP   SINISTERLY
ONTIPTOE   PAN
  DEALIN   BENGAL
     SEM   PONDERED
LEFTBEHIND   LANE
AGREE   AVIS   BOW
DOOR   TROT   ASI
LIS   PORTOFSPAIN
EST   OBOE   CHANCE
STY   LEWD   CENSED
```

135

```
ORCH   TALK   DROP
CALES   ARON   EINE
THOMASMORE   LOBE
ORVILLEORWILBUR
PAIN   IRMA   CART
IHS   MPS  IKE  ATA
    TAI   ONE   AVON
WEDDINGCEREMONY
OURS   TAT   OPP
WRY   POR   BSA   TBS
 ONCE   DARE   AURA
EMULATEZANEGREY
CARE   ONTHEMONEY
URSA   TEEM   PRIZE
STET   ORCA   APES
```

136

```
BEFIT   WISP   FROM
ORONO   IDEA   RIPE
NIGHTSTAND   ANAT
NEGATE   STRUGGLE
    LEAK   RELIC
FEWER   HAY   CLIP
RAHS   CAL   JEERED
EVE   MONITOR   CRY
DEEJAY   BUT   MUSE
 SLOT   LIT   GASES
   DETOO   UPON
BARBECUE   HOOPOE
EMIL   EDGEDSWORD
LEVO   ALOT   EASED
ANEW   NYSE   DRYLY
```

137

```
BALD   HARTE   COST
ILAY   ONERS   LUKE
DOWNANDOUT   OTIS
SENATORS   ALSOPS
    MIRE   STEEN
OTOOLE   CHEETAHS
LOU   TERRA   SELAH
MOTS   SEEMS   DINO
ANTIC   LEEKS   MOO
NEONATES   INABIT
  LIGHT   SLID
ABUSER   SHIPMATE
WANT   OUTOFSIGHT
ONCE   BLUET   TREE
LEHR   SENDS   SAYS
```

138

```
TAP   ASSUME   DRAB
AVA   SHUTIN   EAVE
REP   PAPERHANGER
PRESIDES   ATTEST
   RARER   ANTI
EUCLID   BICUSPID
ASHEN   HIDE   TARO
REA   SHYNESS   PEN
LUST   ODDS   OBESE
SPEAKERS   ECARTE
   REDO   MURAT
ADAGIO   LOCALIZE
PAPERWEIGHT   GEL
ERST   NATURE   ERA
SEES   STELES   RON
```

139

```
H A L L     A L M S     S I L O
A R I A S   C O A L     K N A P
J A M U P J E L L Y T I G H T
I B E R I A     L I L I   E R S
        E R M A   G Y P
J E L L Y B E A N   T E V Y E
A N A     S O B     O C E A N
M O T I F   N O N   P O R T O
E L E N I   V I P   D E C
S A X O N   J E L L Y F I S H
        E M U   S A U L
A D E   L A R K   S K O A L S
J E L L Y R O L L M O R T O N
A L I T   T R E E   N A O M I
R E E D   A S E A   S P A T
```

140

```
A M A T I     A M I E   S E T S
R U N I N   B O O S   T R I O
K N O C K A B O U T   R I L L
S I N   B L E D   I C I C L E
      B L A S   A M O K
C E L L O S   T R A D E W A R
E L I O T   H I R T   F A T A
S L O W   H E N I E   O L A V
A I N T   O A T S   F R E R E
R E S O U N D S   T O C S I N
        R T E S   L O R E
P R I C E Y   I O T A   D U E
R I C H   P U N C H B O A R D
A L O E   O R C A   I C I N G
Y E N S   T E A L   T A S S E
```

141

```
L A S H   E D G A R   B R A T
A S K A   S A R T O   R O T H
W H A T S T H A T Y O U S A Y
N O T R E   D I A R I S T
S W E A R A T   C L A S P
      C A R A T   T E E N S
P E C K   O L I O   O R R I N
E T O   I W O N D E R   O K A
S T U D S   N E E D   S T E P
T U N I S   D U N C E
      S M U T S   M A H A L I A
  R E P E A T S   I C O N S
W E L L S H U T M Y M O U T H
O B O E   O R E A D   W I R E
W A R D   E M M Y S   S E A N
```

142

```
G A L A S   F U M   J O K E R
A L E U T   I T O   O V I N E
M E A N Y   F A D   T E T O N
Y E R T L E T H E T U R T L E
        I O N E   M I N H
L U B E   D E R   T H E O N E
A N O   H O N E D   E A S E L
I F I R A N T H E C I R C U S
R E S O W   H A R U M   A R A
S D E A T H   B I T   E R O S
      S H A G   V E A L
H O R T O N H E A R S A W H O
A C T E R   O R B   T I E U P
S T E R N   S I L   A N D R E
P O S S E   T E E   R E S T S
```

143

```
B A N D B   L S U   T O R S O
A L I A R   I N N   A P E A R
N A C I O   N A B   C E L L O
    K N U T E R O C K N E
D E A T H V A L L E Y D A Y S
T A N Y A S   E S E   A S E A
S U D   H E A R T   T E S T
      N A T L   E C C E
C A P E   C O R A L   P R O
U T E S   U H F   P U R E E D
B E D T I M E F O R B O N Z O
    A L L A M E R I C A N
B E L I E   I R A   A D A I R
O N E N D   S E L   R I N G O
W E D G E   T D S   S E T O N
```

144

```
R E T I R E     W A D   C S T
E V E N E R   R O M E   R H O
N E A T E R   E R I K   Y O O
    R O S   P A S S E D O U T
S H S   E R O D E S   A F T S
P O O L S I D E   A N T S Y
O M N I   G U M S   U G H
T O M B A   N A T   F L E C K
    Y E P   K N E W   E B A N
R E P R O   D R E S S A G E
E L I A   P A W N E E   N E E
P I L L B O X E S   N O S
I S L   A L E E   M A C H O S
N E O   K E L P   A T H E N A
S S W   E R S   D E S E E D
```

145

```
S C A T   A L I A   Y P R E S
H U G O   C O A X   E L E C T
A J A X   C O M E   S A M O A
H O S I E R S B L E S S I N G
      C L U E     A I M
I M B I B E   D E T R A C T S
M O L T O   M I C A     L E I
P L A Y W R I G H T S F E A R
E L I   E L I O   E R A S E
L Y R I C I S T   J E E R E D
      R A G   K I D S
A C C O U N T A N T S H O P E
R O A N S   O V E N   M I L K
T O S E E   N I L E   A L O E
S T A R S   I D L Y   N Y P D
```

146

```
A L D A   B M I     W I L E
O V E R S E E R   S T A D I A
K I N D E R G A R T E N E R S
    O R E   Q U A N D A R Y
  M E R I T   G I D E
B A S S E T   O R D E R E R
A L T   S A L S A   R E N E S
U T A H   S U I T S   R A F T
R E T O P   G E S T E   M I A
  D E M U R E R   E X C E L S
    E R E I   A T O L L
R O E B L I N G   L O R
I M G O I N G A M I L K I N G
G O O D E S   N O N S E N S E
S O N Y   G I G   R A C E
```

147

```
R A I S E   P A C A   R F D
E S S E X   B A Y O U   E A U
A I R A P P A R E N T   I C E
    S O I R   F O R G E T
H O H O   A N G L I C A N
O N A N   R E D R Y D E R
S E R A L   T I N E A   A X E
T I T L E   I L O   T O N E S
E N A   T O L L S   S U C R E
L A T I T U D E   T E T E
  T E E T E R E D   S S S S
S T A R R S   L O O M
H I C   M I S S M A N A G E S
I N K   A D I O S   T R E V I
P A S   N E X T   O T O E S
```

148

```
H U T S   L I S A   R I C H
O L E O   M U S H Y   E V I E
P U R L   O I L E R   M A N X
E L M   J O S E   F O N D A
F A I R A S A S T A R W H E N
O T T E R   H R E   O R E
R E E D   A T R A I N   E S S
    O N L Y O N E I S
B M T   A L I C E S   A M A S
O A R   Z E N   A M I S H
S H I N I N G I N T H E S K Y
W A L E S   L I R A   L A S
E L L E   Q U I T O   P A N T
L I E D   U S U R Y   R I C E
L A D Y   A C M E   O D E R
```

149

```
B A S S O   B L A B   P L U G
O R E A D   K I T E   R A K E
A G G I E   L A T E C O M E R
C O U N T R Y M U S I C
  N E T T O N   N U R S E
    S A M   A N A C R E O N
B A R   A S C O T   E G A D
O N U S   N O H O W   S A V E
R E C T   O M A N I   L E D
I N H E A V E N   T I P
S T E E R   S C R I B E
  L A Y O F T H E L A N D
M A K E M E R R Y   N O L T E
A P E R   G A O L   I S E R E
D O G S   G L E E   C E D E D
```

150

```
M A S O N I C   T A L O N S
I N A R U S H   P I G I R O N
A T L A N T A   E R E M I T E
S H O T S   G A T O R B O W L
M E N E   S A L T S   L I L
A R G   D A L A I   A B E T S
  S A T E L L I T E D I S H
    O N O   T U T
  F L Y I N G S A U C E R S
A L O S S   R U B I K   I M P
D O O   S O I R S   S P A R
H O M E P L A T E   S H O R E
E D I T I O N   A R T I S T E
R E N N E T S   S H O R T E N
E D G A R S   T O P T E N S
```

151

```
ECHO  YOGA  HUMID
CLOD  EVEN  UTICA
LARD  METS  DARED
ASS  JERSEYSHORE
THECAN    LEO
  ROPING  ANSWER
OMAHA  ALAR  THRU
POCONOMOUNTAINS
AVER  NEWT  RITES
LESTWE  SOFINE
    RAE  UPSHOT
THEHAMPTONS  OWE
AURIC  CORN  LUND
FLICK  ONCE  USED
TANKS  TEAL  VERY
```

152

```
PATIENT  HAIRDO
ADAGIOS  ORDAINS
DEFENSEATTORNEY
SETTEE  STU  EGAN
    COEUR  ROLE
GOINTOLABOR
INTERNE    ABATE
MEANIES  ALTERED
PALEO    VEERING
  SHIPOFSTATE
BUST  IDONT
ANTI  TIO  TAIWAN
SCALESOFJUSTICE
EARDRUM  ORIENTS
  STEEPS  ENTREES
```

153

```
MOSS  ATRIP  CARP
ATTU  MAUNA  OBOE
STUBBORNASAMULE
CONSORTS  TEETER
    CPAS  DIOR
LAUREL  LIMN  OAS
ARTIE  GAVE  INOT
SLIPPERYASANEEL
SECT  DAIS  RAISE
ONA  REIN  STUNTS
    PENN  MAID
ASSENT  CALLISTO
NAKEDASAJAYBIRD
OBIT  TUTOR  LAIR
NUDE  EMORY  EMMA
```

154

```
HARPS  ABEE  MEAD
ADDIE  CELT  ISLE
HOTONTHEHEELSOF
AGENDA  BIRDDOG
    ADE  NEE
HERHEARTWASWARM
AROO  ROILS  CIA
VAMPS  ANS  AGENT
OTE  TOTIE  ERSE
COOLASACUCUMBER
    ATH  PUN
  STRIKES  BIAFRA
POURCOLDWATERON
AINU  SLAY  ERECT
SLAP  HAKE  SODAS
```

155

```
DORM  SEDER  SAMP
ASTI  HAUTE  TRIO
THESPORTOFKINGS
EASTERLY  ARREST
    RATS  ASIS
NADIRS  PETS  STA
IDEAL  PARE  ONER
DAILYRACINGFORM
EGGS  EPEE  AFORE
SEN  SCAR  MISTED
    AIRS  RITE
STAPLE  RELEASES
WINPLACEANDSHOW
ALTA  TRADE  OONA
PEEL  EIDER  NOSY
```

156

```
TIMID  ALPS  AMTS
OCALA  DALE  BOUT
JOLLYROGER  ARNO
ONESTOP  ABSTAIN
    OPEC  TENSE
OCTANE  HARE
RORY  EULER  OFA
GREENEGGSANDHAM
YES  IMAGO  EMMA
    NUDE  PHYSED
HESSE    RHEO
ARTISAN  ARIETTA
TREX  GIANTSQUID
LOVE  ENDS  TURCO
OLES  DOZE  SINKS
```

157

```
S A L T S   R O N S   J I L L
A B O U T   A L O E   E L I E
B E T T E   D I V A   R E N T
E D S U L L I V A N   R U D I
      L U X E   C A Y M A N
J O R D A N     N E I L
O K I E   G L U E   R E H A B
S A D A T   A P O   S W A G E
H Y E N A   D I N G   I V E S
    M R E D     A S S E R T
C A N A A N   R U B E
O M A R   T H E B E A T L E S
R I F T   R E P O   L O O S E
A N T I   A R E A   E R A S E
L O A N   P E L T   D E M O N
```

158

```
D A T E D   H I S S   A B L E
E L I T E   A N T E   C L E M
E L E C T   S T A R   R U N T
M A S H E D P O T A T O E S
    E R E     E P O S
S C A R   B R A   E N T I R E
A R S   P A U L A   K I N E R
B A T T E R E D C H I C K E N
E N E R O   S E T I N   E V E
R E W A R D   R A T   O D E S
    V I A L     U A R
    C R E A M E D S P I N A C H
G O A L   A T O P   M A C H O
O O Z E   S O M E   E T H O S
B L E D   K N E W   D E E P S
```

159

```
    S L E E V E   B A D D I E
    S H O P P I N G A R O U N D
B A R G A I N B A S E M E N T
O L E O     A B A S E
O L D   H A N S E L   D U P E
T E S S E R A     P A Y
    O R O N O   M A L O N E
    T E L E M A R K E T I N G
T E R E S A   B A L E S
U L M     R E S T A R T
B L A H   G I M L E T   L O U
    A R E G O     S C A N
M I N D I N G T H E S T O R E
F A C T O R Y O U T L E T S
A N O O S E   R E S O R T
```

160

```
B A D E   W A D I   D A M E
E A R L   V A S E S   A G O G
T H E S M I T H Y M A K I N G
A S I   E S T E S   L O O K S
    D O T     L E T
H A R D W A R E F O R A N E W
B O A T S   U N A P T   A D A
O R B S   K N O B S   A D I N
M T A   E N T R E   O N I C E
B A T H R O O M R E P O R T S
    O A T     L E N
S C O T T   A L G E R   T O O
H E S F O R G I N G A H E A D
A R L O   A R R A Y   E L S E
D O O R   G O A T   P E T S
```

161

```
M I M I   F I R S T   O H M S
E R I N   A R E N A   L E I S
L I S T   R A N O N   E L S E
    T H E B O S T O N P O P S
    I A G O   P E I   M I R
S P R O U T S   R E P A V E
    A T R E A R   E T E S
    F A T H E R F I G U R E S
M I R E   P E D A N T
E R O D E D   S I S T I N E
G E M   N A P     I N O N
    D A D D Y L O N G L E G S
L O T I   T A H O E   N O U N
E G I S   O T T E R   C O R A
A S C H   N O O S E   E D E N
```

162

```
D O R I S   A S S T   F A D S
E X I S T   S L U R   E D I T
L E F T A T H O M E   Z E R O
  N E O N S   P O P S   E G O
      D E S   A L F R E D
D E T E S T E D   N I L
A M O N   S T E S   C O B R A
M I D D L E O F T H E R O A D
P R O S E   N E R O   A R N E
    U T E   R I N G L E T S
P O M P O N   P E A
A R E   N E M O   S L A S H
S I T S   R I G H T O F W A Y
H E A P   G L E E   O R A T E
A L L Y   E D E N   T O M E S
```

163

```
HUMAN . BATH . ABAB
ABOLT . AREA . SAGE
HERSHEYBAR . TRUE
ARNO . GOOSE . ABET
. . FOUR . . TRESS
RABBIS . SPARER .
AWARD . . UNI . SSS
PARADES . NYMPHET
SYM . LAC . MAORI
. IBERIA . PEPPER
LATER . ROAD . .
LIZA . SHINS . DORA
ADVT . PASSTHEBAR
MEAT . ALEE . ALIKE
ASHY . RENT . MITES
```

164

```
WHELP . REPS . SASS
PIKER . OXEN . ALOU
ACEVENTURA . VANS
. . ICIER . GLORIA
PICNIC . BOGEYMAN
ADA . SET . TYR .
LINA . SASH . OPALS
LOOKATTHEBIRDIE
STEAL . TYRO . EDEN
. . IDO . SOP . UGO
PARAVION . DRAPER
OLIVER . ISLES . .
PAGE . EAGLESCOUT
EMIR . CLEO . TAUPE
SODS . TART . OPTIC
```

165

```
ISAAC . STAS . RASH
MECCA . HUGO . ALLA
PARES . AGER . ZEUS
. REDBARBER . OUST
. . ALDO . EARTHY
SANCHO . ADLIB . .
URAL . NATO . LAHTI
RESOLED . RESCUES
FATSO . ORAL . KLEE
. . ERASE . INSANE
PASSER . LOSE . .
RUTH . INALATHER
IDEA . SIPS . TIMON
MERV . ELSE . ELITE
ANNE . SEEN . DOTED
```

166

```
YANG . CAPS . CHASM
AMOR . ADUE . HADTO
ROTI . LIRA . ANZAC
DIALMFORMURDER .
. . LASS . ROY .
BEDECK . AWN . MATE
OLA . AISLE . ENOS
MINDONESPSANDQS
BAKE . MOTET . RUE
ESEL . ZIP . DONEES
. . TAO . MULE .
. EFOREXCELLENCE
AVAIL . ROLO . DAUB
VERDE . ALOU . EZRA
GROSS . YENS . DIEN
```

167

```
LECH . GALA . STAMP
ALAI . ADEN . HORAE
BITS . LIST . OSAGE
ESS . GOOSEGOSLIN
LETTERS . ALIE . .
. . ERTE . STANDBYS
ELVIS . APERS . EAT
DIES . FRERE . LALA
ANN . TIMES . LOREN
MESSINAS . SERB .
. . AMAD . ATHIRST
WOLFBLITZER . YOU
ANEAR . LOUR . WALL
SCARE . LORE . ENOS
PERIL . OLEO . ETNA
```

168

```
ALONG . REAR . KEPT
ROMEO . EDGE . ALLA
ALEXANDERDARIUS
PANTHEON . CREAMS
. . EAU . TRUE .
MORIARTYHOLMES
UPEND . EASE . WAG
GRAD . RENTS . CEBU
SAD . SHUT . DOLLY
. HECTORACHILLES
. . REDO . RIO .
SHEAVE . MASCARAS
CORTESMONTEZUMA
OPIE . ICON . SOBIG
TIER . AIRY . EVENS
```

169

```
A B E T   B A C O N   I M A S
T A X I   E R O S E   N O L I
E D E N   A G I L E   B U L B
    M A R R Y F O R M O N E Y
A L P   O I L       A R T E L
M Y L I T T L E S O N N Y
E L A T H       P A R E
S E R T   T E S T Y   O G L E
      V I T O       A B O U T
    A R I C H M A N S J O K E
C A N O E     T E A   D E S
I S A L W A Y S F U N N Y
V I D E   G E T I T   E E R O
I D E O   E L E V E   S A I L
L E M S   E L M E R   T R O D
```

170

```
M A L L   Z A N E S   A H A S
A L O E   W I N E S   M A S T
D E B A S E M E N T   B I T E
E S E   H I E       L I T R E
    D E G E N E R A T I O N
D E G U M   S O D O M
A G O G     D E T E S T S
N A N U   P A D R E   E R A S
  D E P L A N E     V I N E
    U L T R A   D E B A R
D E C O M M I S S I O N
A T R I P     T R E   W O E
C H A N   D E P R E S S I N G
H E C K   O R G A N   I D E A
A R K S   N E A L E   T E R N
```

171

```
U S S R   A D A   S C E N E
M E N U   P E G S   A P N E A
A R A B E S Q U E   T U T U S
  P I R O U E T T E   R E Y
  C A S A   T A S S E
T O R O   T A O S   A C N E
O P E N B A R S   T O P H A T
P I P   A B E T T E R   A B U
O N E E A R   R E R O O T E D
L E T T   A R A M   E S S E
  I H A D A   P E R U
S A T   T E M P S L E V E
K N E E S   B A L L E R I N A
I N U R E   O D I E   E R O S
T E R R A   S E N   S E T H
```

172

```
R A J A H   S A L A   P A C
A B O V E   I P S O F A C T O
W A T E R   T E S T T U B E S
    S E W E D   O E D
A C E   T E M   A F R I C A N
L A N A I S   S R T A   O N E
I T A S C A   I C H   C O D A
B A C H   Y A Z O O   U L A R
A L T E   G R E   U R B A N E
B O O   B O A S   G I A N T S
A G R E E O N   P H D   T E T
    R F D   A R T E L
B A T M O B I L E   S I E G E
S A L A R Y C A P   U N D E R
A R C   E E K S   P O S E R
```

173

```
E A V E   D R I P   W A S P
A D O G   I O N I A   I L K A
T O L O V E O N E S E L F I S
U R U   A T M   S E D A N S
P E N A L   S Q U A R E
  S T R I P   U P S Y   S O S
  E A S Y   E O S   A T O P
T H E B E G I N N I N G O F A
E A R S   M O T   N E U N
E L S   T A T I   S W E E P
  P O L A N D   U S H E S
O C E L L I   E L L   E N T
L I F E L O N G R O M A N C E
A T T A   N A O M I   E G A N
F E S S   B O A S   R E P O
```

174

```
D A D A   C L I F F   C A M P
A L O P   A U R A L   U R A L
N O T H I N G I S O F T E N A
S T E R N   S T R A I T E N
    O S S   E R N E S T
G O O D T H I N G T O
A M B I   E M I R   U S U R P
B I O T A   E N E   T H R O E
S T E E D   T O E S   O S S A
    D O A N D A L W A Y S
P L A N E R     P E R
R E S O N A T E   N O I S E
A G O O D T H I N G T O S A Y
T A U S   E A R E D   M E T E
E L L E   D I E T S   S E E D
```

175

```
WATTS   RETICENT
LARRUP  EDUCATOR
ORIANA  DOMINATE
SYLVANUS  MET
   ASSN  LYRICAL
 VIA  FIE  NADA
 WILLIAMFDRAPER
EAR ATIPTOE  ILK
THEODOREHWHITE
COOP  LIA  EVA
HOSIERY  NCAA
   AWE ADORNING
UPSTAGED  ASHLEY
TOLERATE  TAOISM
APOSTLES  SLEET
```

176

```
 CARET  STRATA
SAVALAS  TEABALL
TRINKET  ENTEBBE
ADAGE  ALA  ATBAT
RITE  HBOMB  SINO
TAO  MALAYAN  EIN
SCREAMED  BALSA
   STIR  BYTE
 TVSET  NESTEGGS
FHA  DUNAWAY  ART
RIND  PUTIT  AGAR
UNION  GOT  PURSE
MALTOSE  CHINUPS
PILESIN  HUSTLES
 RAREST  BASED
```

177

```
AROMA  FLEW  APED
MESAS  IONA  LIME
PASTPERFORMANCE
SPAS  METS  AMEER
   SID  SHORE
BALLET  IOTA
ALIEN  INKER  EMS
ISNOTAGUARANTEE
LOT  IVORY  NORMA
   MORE  METEOR
 SINEW  FOE
CANON  ALAD  LIEU
OFFUTURERESULTS
TEEN  SIAM  IRENE
ERRS  OARS  TEXAS
```

178

```
ALGA  IDEA  TARP
SEED  SEWUP  ELIA
CAROLINEKENNEDY
AGA  USE  GOOSES
PULLS  BOLGER
 EDITH  RAYS  LEE
 FORA  INC  FEEL
LEONARDODAVINCI
ERRS  PAL  SINN
XED  AONE  SLAYS
 ENMESH  ELBOW
MTETNA  ESL  RUE
RICHARDDREYFUSS
ETRE  XEROX  ICET
DOUR  BUSY  TEDS
```

179

```
CLOBBER  SAL  FLO
DESERVE  CRATION
SALLIED  IMPASSE
 POLAROPPOSITES
   ENS  EIRE
MAGS  EGO  MONA
APR  EARL  MADDOG
CHILLYRECEPTION
HIPPIE  GALE  UNE
ODES  MGM  AMES
   WHEE  IAN
COOLHEADEDNESS
ONGOING  REDMEAT
KIRSTIE  LARIATS
ENE  EER  ELECTEE
```

180

```
 MEHTA  GASLAMP
MAYORS  TALLULAH
ANEMIA  OBLIGATE
RECAP  SNEAD  NEW
 AGEING  YET
RATE  DAUBS  AJAR
UPC  LEPER  RIATA
MPH  CASTOFF  WIN
PLEAD  OWNED  BLT
SERB  ONICE  ARTS
   COG  SOLACE
ASK  FLATS  SCARS
DOESTIME  KOOKIE
DARKENER  INSECT
SPRINGS  METRO
```

181

```
S W A P   S H A M S   S C A M
A I D A   P I X E L   T A T A
P R E S T I D I G I T A T O R
S E N T I N E L   P R I S M S
      O V E R   S K I D
P E T R O L   T U N S   A S P
A X I A L   A R N O   A L T A
P A R L I A M E N T A R I A N
A L E E   T O N Y   S M E L T
L T D   S T U D   O P I N E S
    T I E R   O D E S
S A D I S M   S P E C T R A L
P L E N I P O T E N T I A R Y
O L E G   T R A N S   C U M E
T Y P E   S E N S E   E L Y S
```

182

```
L I S T S   A R E A S   C I T
I D I O M   L E T U P   A R I
E A G L E   O S A G E   R O C
    H E L D U P T H E B A N K
B A T T L E   E S T   E V I E
U S E   P A L   I W A N T
D I D S H O P L I F T I N G
  O I S E   M A C S
  P I C K E D U P T H E C A R
M I L L E   P S T   R I O
O R L E   O A S   E D W A R D
R A I S E D T H E R O O F
E T C   L E R O Y   N O T E S
L E I   S U I T E   N E E D Y
S S T   A M A S S   A D D O N
```

183

```
M A T A H A R I   C H R O M E
O C A R I N A S   H A U L E D
N A K E D A S A J A Y B I R D
A D E   L A B A N   E N V Y
    F O Y   E D G E
Q U A R T Z   L E E G R A N T
U P D A T E   A S S O O N A S
A T O P       S O D A
C O R P O R A L   C H A S E R
K N E E B O N E   L U R E R S
    I O T A   A M Y
O M A N   F I N E S   D N A
B A R E N E C E S S I T I E S
E D I T O R   S T I R R E R S
Y E A S T S   T A C K E D O N
```

184

```
F D A   V E R B   M A C H O
R E T   S O L A R   A T H O L
A P T   H O T D O G S T A N D
N A H   A M O I   A S I D E S
C R E W   R A P P E R
S T R A W V O T E   E T C H
  A L A I   E A S T   H U E
S O C K H O P   S K I J U M P
A W E   S L A B   I T E M
M E S S   B A L L O T B O X
  T A M A L E   S A R A
A C O R N S   O G P U   R E V
T O B O G G A N R U N   I I I
O L I V E   D E E R E   D D E
P A T E R   D Y E R   E A R
```

185

```
C A R O L I N E   E R A S E R
E L E V A T O R   N O N A M E
S O M E T I M E   M A N U A L
S H O R E S   C R E D E N C E
N A T E   S T I R   A D I N
A S E A   F O O T   B L E A T
  T A R T R A T E   R T E
C R I S T O   M A S S E D
L E M   E G G C R A T E
A L A R M   A L A N   S N A P
S A G E   S L A W   T A T A
S T I T C H E S   W A I T O N
D I N E R O   P O I G N A N T
A V E N U E   E N T R A N C E
Y E S T E R   D E S I S T E D
```

186

```
I N D I A N   S C A M   S P A
N E E D L E   P A C E   T A B
C H E R I S   A N T E D A T E
  I D O C T O R   I S I G H T
    P E S T   A V E R
C H O P S   O M N I   E M I L
L O P E   I N S   O D E
O V E R   I E X A M   I D E A
M E R   N Y E   W E A N
P R A M   K E R N   G I L L S
  O R B S   C A R T
I L E V E L   I O P E N E R
F I R E W O O D   R E E L I N
F R O   E T R E   O N S I D E
Y E S   D S C S   N E S S I E
```

187

```
DOMES  MASK   UMP
ALIVE  ALIE  APER
YINANDYANG   GALA
SOT  ADORES  ANEW
     TERM    WIDEN
LADLE  SESTINA
ALOE   DEER   BUN
DAWDLER  ANEMONE
SIN  OMAR    AUTO
  ADAPTED  GETON
PINED    NUDE
RODE  STEREO  CPA
ATOM  NOWANDTHEN
TAUS  IRAN  EVICT
EST    PELT  SACKS
```

188

```
WOVEN  MAPLE  WAD
INANE  ALLAY  AVA
GOLDENGLOBE   YOM
   DEUS     LENIN
MODULES  FEELERS
ERASED  TORSOS
ABIES  REAMS  WAS
NILS  FIRMA  BONA
STY  BOORS  PORGY
  PELOTA  BILLIE
BALLOTS  BROODER
ALAMO  SEEN
KIN  MOTHEREARTH
EVE  ELIOT  ELIAS
SET  RENTS  REACT
```

189

```
  CORKS   RAVAGE
  RAVINE  RELIVES
BENEFIT  EXIGENT
AMARETTOS  TORTE
LAST  EMIL  RALE
LITUP  RADAR  GEM
SNARES  NEGATES
   EATS  DOPE
  LESSENS  SILICA
MEX  EPICS  DEMON
AGED  SPAT  SPAN
RUMOR  PROSECUTE
IMPLODE  DEVOTEE
NETCORD  GRIPED
ASSETS    EELED
```

190

```
STROP  SPA  SMASH
CIANO  AID  LIMPY
OTTER  LED  AXIOM
WHOLEWATERMELON
LENO  AZANA  DENS
   IONA  DING
SPENCER  ADORNED
CULPA    REUSE
INSOLES  ASSENTS
  RANT  STEN
OINK  CASTE  SAPS
CHICKENTARRAGON
TOTHE  DOR  ALINE
APRON  EAT  VANCE
DEEPS  ETE  EDGER
```

191

```
JAIL  ESPOSA  ATL
AIDE  STORAGEFEE
PRODICINGXRATED
EEL  POLE    TONG
   SORT  IMMENSE
ACCENT  SLOAN
LOAM  MAORI  MAS
MOVIESISNODOUBT
STY  MENSA  PLEA
  MINDY  CHEESY
INSERTS  ARAN
PATE   AMUR  HAY
ARISQUEBUSINESS
SCREENTEST  ERIE
SSS  DEALEY  WEAR
```

192

```
BASEL  AMIS  BALS
ADALE  RANT  IMON
TEXAS  ANDA  SODA
ELOPER  AIRSTRIP
DENS  ONTARIO
   ERNIE  DUAL
MVP  ANTE  DERMIS
GEORGIA  NEWYORK
SECEDE  SAFO  SAY
  ROTO  TREYS
  ALABAMA  ASEA
SPOILERS  TENETS
PENN  SASE  IDAHO
RACE  OVER  NOTON
YSER  PONE  EROSE
```

193

```
S P A S M   J O H A N
G L A N C E   O N A P A R
A R I S T A S   Y E W T R E E
D E P   A L S O R A N   R A T
D A P S   D E V I L   R O P E
U S E I T   D A D   S O W E R
P E R S I A   L E F T T U R N
  Y E G G S   S A R A N
T O W N H A L L   O U T D I D
A S H O T   E I S   M E E S E
S T E R   M E M O S   D R A B
K E N   L A P O R T E   P A U
S A W Y E R S   R E E N A C T
  L E A N T O   O R L E S S
  T W A I N   W E S T S
```

194

```
H A R E   L O B E   A B B A
E L A L   S E P A L   R U E S
L A Y E R O F T H E E A R T H
P R E V E N T S   M U R P H Y
      A D O   H E R A
  P I T Y F O R A N O T H E R
R A N E E   H U R T   A V E
O V I D   F E N D S   C U E D
B E G   I N T O   P E T R O
B R O T H E R O F M O S E S
    W A R Y   E P A
A S S I S I   A S S U R I N G
S O U T H E R N C A P I T A L
A L E C   S O D A S   A T T U
P O S H   T E S T   N Y E T
```

195

```
H O T E L   O A T H   P A U L
A M A N A   D R E I   R U B Y
R A N C H   D E C A M E R O N
I N G A   G L A S W E G I A N
    E S S A Y   A N A C T
B E R E T S   T A T U M
A R I S E   C A S H   E M I L
R I N   S E R B I A N   U S E
K E E L   N E O N   E S S E S
    A S T E R   A V O C E T
  H A V E R   A L A M O
M O N E G A S Q U E   E V I L
A S T R O N A U T   M O I R A
L E O N   T R I O   A N T I C
L A N E   S A P S   G E E S E
```

196

```
A M A S S   M P H   C R O O K
V I R T U I   I L E   H O R D E
E L M E R   G A Y   A B B E Y
R O S E M A R Y L A N E
    P I C A B O S T R E E T
P A H   S H N O O K   T A R E
A M I L E   T Y K E   S T O A
B O G A R T   W H O S I S
L E H R   A C N E   O N I C E
U B E R   T R E N T E   N A T
M A R Y K A Y P L A C E
    K I R S T I E A L L E Y
D E B I T   T U V   K E A N U
A G E N T   A N E   E V I T A
D O G G Y   L E N   S E T O N
```

197

```
C A S E   B A S A L   P I E R
A S W E   E R A S E   A N Y A
P H I L L I S W H E A T L E Y
P E T   E R O S   T R A D E
    N O U N   O T T O
A C C E N T   S P E L L E D
L A R A   S P A R E   L E G
P I E R R E C O R N E I L L E
O N E   E V E R T   C E L T
  E L E M E N T   O P E R A S
    L O N E   A M O S
A S S E T   A B E L   S T U
J O Y C E C A R O L O A T E S
A I N T   A M O V E   C A N E
R T E S   B E N E T   E N D S
```

198

```
R A M R O D   M A L T   D A M
E L A I N E   O P I E   E V A
D A R L E N E L O V E   F E N
    I L A   M I L E   B E R T
T E N   L A B E L   C E A S E
O L A V   Z E R O M O S T E L
M E D I C A R E   A V E
  M E T A L S   G R E E C E
    I C E   P O S T C A R D
S A D A H A R U O H   H U G O
A B A T E   O R G A N   L O G
R O M E   C L I O   A I D
A D A   N I L S L O F G R E N
P E G   A T I T   S T O O L S
E S E   P E N S   S A R N I A
```

Grid 199:

```
M I L D   Z A N E S     M D S
I D I O   O P E R A   M O A T
S L O G   D O T E R   O O Z E
T E N D R I L     C A N T E R
      R E A L   S A C K
  B O A R C O C K S H E E P
L O N G A S   R I M   Y E L P
E X C O N   P E T   M O R A L
T E E N   S E A   S A X O N Y
  R A T S N A K E H O R S E
      I T E R   S A R A
B U N G E E     C R I B B E D
E P E E   Z A I R E   B O L O
B O E R   E R R O R   I R A N
E N D     S T E W S   T E N S
```

Grid 200:

```
A L L U P   A F T     M O T S
L O O S E   V A I L   A W R Y
I N T H E V E R N A C U L A R
M E T E R E D   A T O M
B R E R   N O S   I N A W A Y
    S E I N L A N G U A G E
  I S I N   A D O   S O W
  T O N G U E L A S H I N G
I A N   S R O   O N T O
B L A B B E R M O U T H
M Y R I A D   S R S   E S S E
    O R C A   A C E R O U S
O N S P E A K I N G T E R M S
T A T I   R I N G   A N E M A
S P E C   N E E   S T R A Y
```